HUMAN ACTION
Conceptual and Empirical Issues

HUMAN ACTION
Conceptual and Empirical Issues

Edited by **THEODORE MISCHEL**
DEPARTMENT OF PHILOSOPHY
STATE UNIVERSITY OF NEW YORK, BINGHAMTON, NEW YORK

1969

ACADEMIC PRESS   New York and London

ACADEMIC PRESS, INC.
111 Fifth Avenue, New York, New York 10003

United Kingdom Edition published by
ACADEMIC PRESS, INC. (LONDON) LTD.
24/28 Oval Road, London NW1

LIBRARY OF CONGRESS CATALOG CARD NUMBER: 69-13480
Second Printing, 1972

PRINTED IN THE UNITED STATES OF AMERICA

LIST OF CONTRIBUTORS

Numbers in parenthesis indicate the pages on which the author's contributions begin.

MAGDA B. ARNOLD, Department of Psychology, Loyola University, Chicago, Illinois (167)

JOHN W. ATKINSON, Psychology Department and Survey Research Center, University of Michigan, Ann Arbor, Michigan (105)

DONALD T. CAMPBELL, Department of Psychology, Northwestern University, Evanston, Illinois (41)

PETER MADISON, Department of Psychology, University of Arizona, Tuscon, Arizona (223)

A. I. MELDEN, Department of Philosophy, University of California, Irvine, California (199)

THEODORE MISCHEL, Department of Philosophy, State University of New York, Binghamton, New York (1, 261)

R. S. PETERS, University of London, Institute of Education, London, England (135)

STEPHEN TOULMIN, Department of Philosophy, Brandeis University, Waltham, Massachusetts (71)

PREFACE

The papers collected in this volume are the result of a working conference held at the Center for Continuing Education of the University of Chicago, September 27 through October 1, 1967. The general topic for this conference was A Conceptual Framework for the Study of Human Actions. This topic was intended to be sufficiently broad to allow psychologists and philosophers to exhibit the various approaches which they have found useful in their investigations and, at the same time, to establish a line of continuity among the papers. Participants prepared first drafts prior to the conference. An entire morning or afternoon session was devoted to the discussion of each of the papers. In order to maximize the fruitful exchange of ideas, only contributors participated in these closed discussions. It was hoped that this initial, joint exploration of a rather broad topic might also suggest more specific areas in which this sort of cooperative investigation by psychologists and philosophers may be fruitfully continued with mutual benefit.

George Kelly had agreed to participate in this conference and all of us were deeply saddened by his death. Though my personal acquaintance with George Kelly was, unfortunately, brief, it was sufficient to add my admiration of the man to that which I had long felt for his work.

Wilfrid Sellars participated in the conference and made many valuable contributions to our discussions. The pressure of other commitments made it impossible for him to complete his paper so that, regretfully, we have had to go to press without it. The other papers are printed here as revised by their authors after the conference. I have made only minor editorial changes in these papers, mainly to insure uniformity of style. My introductory chapter and the Epilogue were written after the conference; the former attempts to provide a historical context against which these papers can be read, while the latter attempts to convey some of the issues that arose in our discussions.

I am grateful to the National Institutes of Health for grant MH13825-01 which made this conference and the resulting volume possible. Colgate University, my home base at the time this grant was awarded, deserves my gratitude for long providing me with an environment congenial and encouraging to my work. Both Colgate University and the Philosophy Department of the University of Illinois, where I was Visiting Professor in the fall of 1967, have helped in various ways with preparations for the conference and related matters; to them, as well as to my patient typist, Mrs. Patricia Ryan, my thanks.

Binghamton, New York   THEODORE MISCHEL
December, 1968

CONTENTS

Change of Activity: A New Focus for the Theory of Motivation

JOHN W. ATKINSON

Motivation, Emotion, and the Conceptual Schemes of Common Sense

R. S. PETERS

Human Emotion and Action

MAGDA B. ARNOLD

The Conceptual Dimensions of Emotions

ABRAHAM I. MELDEN

Complex Behavior in Natural Settings

PETER MADISON

Epilogue

THEODORE MISCHEL

HUMAN ACTION

Conceptual and Empirical Issues

SCIENTIFIC AND PHILOSOPHICAL PSYCHOLOGY: A HISTORICAL INTRODUCTION

THEODORE MISCHEL

I. Introduction

"The problems of psychology are the problems of other sciences" (Turner, 1967, p. 1). Perhaps. But it is surprising that a psychologist addressing himself to the foundations of his subject begins with this assertion; one would not expect a molecular biologist, or a relativity theorist, to start out that way. Again, the history of psychology is usually presented as parallel to what, on a popular view, has been the history of the physical sciences: prescientific "philosophical" speculations were terminated by the founding of an experimental science, finally emancipated from philosophy, and this was followed by the orderly progressive accumulation of more and more empirical facts and of theories inductively derived from them (e.g., Boring, 1950). Psychology is thus represented as like the physical sciences, not only in its problems, but also in its pedigree.

1

Yet one of the striking features of the development of psychology as a science is that it keeps being founded anew. Wundt, who established the first psychological laboratory in 1879, is usually credited with the founding, but Herbart had claimed to found psychology as a proper science in 1824 and Watson did it again in 1913. It would be easy to extend the list of theorists who have claimed to found the science of psychology anew both backward and forward in time. This should not be surprising since the Baconian view of science as the patient accumulation of one fact on top of another, which follows once the disputes of the schools are set aside in favor of "unprejudiced" experimental observation, is largely mythological even as an account of the history of the physical sciences. Recent studies (Hanson, 1958; Toulmin, 1961; Kuhn, 1962) have called attention to the intimate connection between conceptual and factual issues in the development of physics, and to the implications of the profound conceptual readjustments involved in "scientific revolutions." Kuhn even argues that "scientific fact and theory are not categorically separable" (1962, p. 7), that the acceptance of a new "paradigm" by the scientific community changes the problems it regards as "legitimate," and that "as the problems change, so often does the standard that distinguishes a real scientific solution from a mere metaphysical speculation" (1962, p. 102). Fundamental disagreements about the nature of the problems to be solved and about what counts as a solution can be found, not only in the history of psychology, but in the history of all the sciences.

But the connection between factual and conceptual issues is much closer in the study of human behavior than in other sciences. For men are brought up in a culture and acquire a language that provides them with the psychological concepts that they normally use to describe and explain the behavior of others, to assess character and appraise responsibility, and so on. And such psychological phenomena as human intentions, emotions, expectations, and motives are intimately connected with language, with the concepts people have learned to use. The discriminations we can make about physical objects may be a function of the conceptual networks (paradigms) through which we view them, but at least it makes sense to suppose that such objects exist independent of our conceptual resources, that they are not constituted by the distinctions we make about them. But it makes no sense to suppose that a man who lacks the relevant concepts of social relationship could feel regret or guilt, or that someone could play a game, say of football or chess, though he fails to understand the relevant rules. Since the objects of (human) psychology are subjects who speak a language, the behaviors possible to concept-using beings, whose actions can be affected by the conceptual distinctions they are able to make, are the phenomena that psychologists must try to understand in terms of their conceptual networks—at least, insofar as they are concerned with distinctively human behavior.

Until fairly recently, problems of this sort have been largely ignored by American psychologists. For reasons to which I will return later, behavioristic psychologists found it necessary to adopt prescriptions about the concepts that could be meaningfully used and the methods that could be properly employed in psychology, prescriptions that severely limited the sort of questions they were prepared to tackle. Their strategy was to focus on animal studies and to set aside the investigation of "higher processes," in the hope that once fundamental laws of behavior, based (characteristically) on "learning" in rats, were established, the more complex phenomena of perception, cognition, and so on might be derived from them. But during the last ten or fifteen years there has been a marked and increasing shift in point of view. This is particularly evident in the contributions to the volumes of _Psychology_: _A Study of a Science,_ whose editor remarks that "an outstanding trend of the study is the presence of a widely distributed and strong stress against behavioristic epistemology" (Koch, 1959, p. 755), as well as "an increased recognition of the role of direct experiential analysis in psychological science" (Koch, 1959, p. 766). One can now find psychologists saying that "the effort to speak the language of behavior only is just inefficient and to do so leads . . . to a truncated set of laws of behavior" (Guttman, 1963, p. 19); there is widespread interest in cognitive and perceptual processes, and even Guthrie now denies "that the psychological description of behavior can be made in physical terms" (1959, p. 166). But while "a far more open and liberated conception of the task of psychology" seems to be emerging, "there has been very little direct effort towards the creative emendation" of earlier methodological prescriptions (Koch, 1959, pp. 785–786). In practice, behaviorism may no longer be accepted orthodoxy in psychology, but the methodological rhetoric of behaviorism lingers on because a more adequate conceptual framework for the empirical study of human behavior has, so far, failed to emerge.

During roughly the same period, "philosophical psychology" has become what may well be the most vital and active area of current philosophical investigation. Ryle's _Concept of Mind_ (1949) and Wittgenstein's _Philosophical Investigations_ (1953) not only called attention to crucial problems about mental phenomena, but also developed methods of attacking philosophical problems whose usefulness is witnessed in the extensive literature on philosophical psychology that has developed since then. Starting from varied problems—for example, the ascription of responsibility; the basis for the intersubjective comparison of mental states; the difference between first-person and third-person statements about mental processes; the characterization of actions in a social context; the relation between an emotion and the object to which it is directed; the difference between explanations of behavior in terms of causal properties ascribed to objects and explanations of human actions in terms of character traits, dispositions, or reasons for acting; and so on—philosophers have tried to gain a better understanding of the way in which our ordinary psychological concepts work. This has often been done by examining "ordinary language," that is, by appealing to forms of expression that would be properly used in various circumstances, because an examination of what we say in various situations can enable us to understand better what we do when we use psychological concepts to appraise actions, ascribe motives, or state our feelings. The concern of philosophers with ordinary language signals an interest, not in lexicography, but in the concepts that are operative in our ordinary commerce with each other, as opposed to the concepts of mathematics and formal logic, or of physics and other special sciences. By examining "action," "intention," "desire," "pleasure," and so on, as they are ordinarily used, philosophers have tried to get clearer about the "logical geography" of the psychological concepts all of us use, and about the presuppositions that inform the account of human conduct that we give when engaged in the normal course of human affairs.

These investigations and those of psychologists who have come to see their task in a "far more open and liberated" way have been largely isolated from each other; yet they seem to have important implications for each other. Can philosophical analyses of the way our ordinary mental concepts work, outside of any scientific context, carry very much weight unless this is related to questions about the scientific explanation of mental processes and the behaviors related to them? Are there no empirical issues concerning the way people learn to use concepts and to follow rules that are relevant for understanding the rule-following conduct of mature, concept-using adults? And are these not matters on which one would expect psychologists to have important things to say? On the other hand, though science may not be bound by assumptions implicit in common sense and ordinary language, a scientific theory that is designed to explain some aspects of human behavior must be about human behavior and not about something different. In other words, the relevance of theories developed by psychologists to our ordinary view of human behavior must be made clear, and since human actions are ordinarily regarded as intentional or unintentional, voluntary or not, intelligent or stupid, and so on, these theories must be related to those distinctions that have interested philosophers. Further, if psychology is, as Koch suggests, "ready to think contextually, freely and creatively, about its own refractory subject matter, and to work its way free from a dependence on simplistic theories of correct scientific conduct"

(1959, p. 783), then a clearer understanding of the way our ordinary psychological concepts work would seem essential. For once the restrictions that allow only descriptions in "physical terms" are dropped, and "experiential," or "psychological," concepts are reintroduced into psychology, the retention of uncritical assumptions about the way these concepts work is likely to play havoc with attempts at more adequate conceptualizations.

The time thus seems propitious for establishing communication between these different, but related, lines of inquiry, and the essays in this volume represent an initial attempt in that direction. In this introductory essay I want to examine some of the historical relations between psychology and philosophy. Obviously, nothing like an adequate history can be provided in the space available. But by highlighting certain aspects of the historical background that are directly relevant to the articles that follow, I hope to provide a context in which they can be read.

II. The Impact of the Scientific Revolution

A. The Hobbesian Approach to Human Behavior

Ever since the revolution in the physical sciences, some theorists have hoped to build psychology on foundations similar to those that physics received in the seventeenth century. In 1931 Kurt Lewin held that psychology had not yet succeeded in "homogenizing" its subject matter by adopting "Galilean modes of thought" (1935, Chapter I), but the attempt to do so goes back to Hobbes, a contemporary of Galileo. For Hobbes deliberately set out to apply the "new method" of Galileo and Harvey to psychology. Starting from the premise that human beings are, after all, material systems—for, says Hobbes, "what is the heart, but a spring; and the nerves, but so many strings; and the joints so many wheels, giving motion to the whole body" (1651, p. ix) * —Hobbes attempted to extend the concepts used for explaining the motions of bodies to the explanation of human behavior.

Hobbes's theory was, roughly, that a stimulus from an object is propagated through a medium to the "animal spirits," which flow through the nerves to the brain and heart, and that this generates both a sensory and a

---

* In all historical references the identifying date is the date of first publication; the volume and page references are to the editions indicated in the list of references.

motor reaction in the organism. For the inward movement of the animal
spirits is reversed, when they reach the heart, by the outward pressure of
the "vital motions"—Hobbes's name for autonomic processes like blood
circulation and breathing—and this "resistance, or counter-pressure, or
endeavor . . . this seeming, or fancy, is that which men call sense"
(1651, p. 2). As for the motor reaction, it is due to the effect of the
incoming motion on our vital motions. For when the motion coming from
the stimulus "helpeth, it is called delight . . . [but when it] hindereth the
vital motion then it is called pain . . . this motion, in which consisteth
pleasure or pain, is also . . . the endeavor or internal beginning of animal
motion" (Hobbes, 1640, p. 31). "Animal motions" are those bodily motions that we usually regard as voluntary and explain by reference to what
we want to achieve or avoid, our appetites and aversions, our pleasures and
pains. But, so Hobbes contends, what we experience as pleasure, appetite,
and so on, is really an infinitesimally small motion, or "endeavor," within
the organism. These minute motions are produced when our vital motions
are increased or decreased by motions coming from some stimulus, and the
operation of various bodily mechanisms amplifies this "internal beginning"
into the "animal motion, otherwise called voluntary motion; as to go, to
speak, to move any of our limbs" (Hobbes, 1651, p. 38). Motor behavior
is thus initiated by an external stimulus, which causes a change in the
autonomic vital motions—a change felt as pleasure or pain—and this
change in motion causes animal motions, "called voluntary," toward and
away from objects in such ways as will tend to increase the vital motions.

Hobbes does not deny the existence of psychological phenomena, of
pleasures, appetites, and other conscious states, but he holds that "that
which thinks is something corporeal; for it appears, the subject of all
activities can be conceived only after a corporeal fashion, or as in material
guise" (1641, p. 62). Since we cannot conceive of something immaterial
carrying on activities, mental states can only be epiphenomenal to bodily
processes. So if psychology is to be scientific, it must explain human behavior in terms of the physical processes that are its underlying causes. Hobbes
therefore eliminates all concepts related to conscious agents, who have
intentions and pursue goals, from his theory. In his view, action must be
understood as nothing but the communication of motion, and an agent is
nothing but a body that sets another in motion because it has itself been
moved (Hobbes, 1655, Chapter X). Where Aristotelian philosophers had
thought of men as agents whose conduct is to be explained primarily in
terms of their purposes, intentions, and so forth, and had then extended
such action-related concepts to explanations for the behavior of animals
and things, Hobbes says "a final cause has no place but in such things as

have sense and will; and this also I shall prove hereafter to be an efficient cause" (1655, p. 132). In his view, common sense is mistaken in supposing that when, for example, we have an appetite and reach for a sandwich, the latter is a goal (final cause) toward which we direct out actions. What really happens is that the stimulus object is the (efficient) cause of a change in our vital motions, and this initiates the animal motion of moving toward the sandwich. It seems, says Hobbes, "as if we draw the object to us, whereas the object rather draws us to it by local motion" (1630?, p. 179). Action, like perception, is to be explained purely in terms of various motions produced in the interaction between a physical organism and its environment.

It may be objected that we normally identify actions, not by specifying space and time coordinates for them, but by specifying the goals to which they are directed (e.g., he opened the window, reached for the sandwich, etc.) or by specifying certain criteria to which the person conforms in what he does (e.g., he is walking, or dancing). Moreover, we cannot attribute actions to people without qualification, unless it is the case not only that these ends or criteria are in fact realized, but also that it is their intention to realize them in what they are doing. If someone opens a window inadvertently while stretching, we cannot describe what he did by saying merely "He opened the window," much as we cannot describe someone who goes through the motions of a modern dance while suffering a nervous seizure as "dancing." Psychological concepts involving consciousness (e.g., intentions, aims, etc.) thus seem essential to the characterization of actions. And just as the way we identify actions differs from that in which we identify movements, so the explanations we normally give for actions differ from those appropriate to movements. Ordinarily, talk about the efficient causes of bodily movement is wildly inappropriate as an answer to "Why did he do this?"; what we want to know is what he intended, what he was trying to achieve or avoid in what he was doing.

Hobbes could, no doubt, reply that this only shows that the way we ordinarily identify and explain actions is prescientific. There are surface differences between, for example, kicking someone intentionally and a reflex kick that lead common sense to distinguish actions from movements and to account for the former in terms of the agent's intention, for the latter in terms of a bodily push. The commonsense question "Why did he do this?" already presupposes that we are dealing with an act, so that the answer must involve the agent's ends or intentions. Of course, talk about the efficient causes of his movements will not answer that question. But the real issue is not what questions we ordinarily ask, but what questions the scientist should ask. Common sense may distinguish actions from movements, but where there are actions there are movements. And if we interpret all human behavior as the movements of an organism, thus "homogenizing" psychology, much as Galileo homogenized physics by disregarding, for example, the surface differences between celestial and terrestrial motions, then we can hope to develop a theory that, instead of accepting surface differences between actions and movements as basic, in the manner of Aristotle and common sense, explains both, in Galilean fashion, as due to the operation of underlying mechanisms.

But how are we to identify an act, say opening the window, in terms of movements? An indefinitely large range of movements can, in normal circumstances, be identified as the act of opening the window. But while "opening the window" describes an act, there is no identifiable pattern of movements to which that expression refers. If we remove the conceptual organization that we get by identifying the act in terms of concepts involving consciousness (i.e., the agent's aim or intention, seen in relation to a pattern of meaningful activities), then what will be left? There will still be an organism emitting and undergoing all sorts of movements, but there will no longer be anything that can be identified as "opening the window." Opening the window is not equivalent to an identifiable range of movements, nor could we specify it as movements that have the effect that the window gets opened. For someone might open the window unintentionally while stretching, or the window might get opened by his arm when a neurosurgeon stimulates his brain, and so on—and these behaviors differ psychologically from opening the window intentionally, though the window gets opened in all cases and the movements involved may be identical.

The phenomena that interest psychology thus seem to be identified at a different level, and in terms of different criteria, from those involved in the identification of movements. (See the articles by Campbell, Peters, and Madison in this volume.) E. C. Tolman called attention to this when he insisted that psychology must distingush between "molar" and "molecular" behavior; between the level at which we identify and explain molar acts, which are "purposive" and "cognitive," and the level at which we identify and explain muscle twitches and other molecular bodily movements (1932, Chapter I). For only in this way can we be clear as to just *what phenomena* our theories are designed to explain. There is, of course, no reason why one cannot attempt to identify and explain human behavior at the molar level as a series of movements. But since this is the province of physiology, psychology, so conceived, dissolves into physiology. The Hobbesian attempt to make psychology scientific by "homogenizing" its subject matter seems to succeed only in changing the subject.

B. DESCARTES ON THE LIMITS OF MECHANISM

An influential alternative to Hobbes's approach was provided during the same period by Descartes. For Descartes held not only that introspection and the *cogito* arguments establish the existence of mind, a substance different from body, in one's own case, but also that minds must be attributed to other human beings in order to explain some of their bodily behaviors. Not that Descartes was averse to mechanical explanations of apparently purposive behavior; he gave purely physiological explanations for all animal and much human behavior, and did this so successfully that T. H. Huxley credits him with formulating the "propositions which constitute the foundations and essence of the modern physiology of the nervous system" (1898, p. 203). But there are two related kinds of human behavior that, so Descartes thought, could never be explained in this way: namely, what people do when they "arrange different words together, forming of them a statement by which they make known their thoughts" and what they do when they "act from knowledge" (1637, pp. 116–117). For in such cases the behavior, instead of being tied to any determinate stimulus, varies in ways that are *appropriate* to changing circumstances and conditions. Intelligent speech seems to be elicited, not by a specific stimulus, but by the requirements of the situation as understood by the speaker. If a man were always to respond with a certain phrase to a certain stimulus (e.g., he emits this phrase whenever a blue light appears), we would soon conclude that he is not *saying* anything at all, that he has no reason whatever for uttering this phrase, and would look for what it is that makes him emit these sounds. His behavior would be like that of a parrot, and Descartes recognizes that there is no difficulty in explaining what the parrot "says" mechanically (1637, p. 117). But this is not what normally happens when people speak. Similarly, when a man acts from knowledge, his movements are not "blind," but vary intelligently with changing circumstances in ways appropriate for achieving what he is after. If he goes wrong, he can correct his mistakes, he can advise others on how to go about doing this, he can respond to advice that others may give him, and so on.

Since behaviors of this sort seem to depend on norms and considerations, rather than mechanisms and pushes, Descartes held that

. . . two different principles of our movements are to be distinguished—the one entirely mechanical or corporeal, which depends solely on the force of the animal spirits and the configuration of our bodily parts . . . the other, incorporeal, that is to say mind or soul which you may define as a substance which thinks (1649a, p. 358).

Thinking substance is the active principle that explains those human behaviors that cannot be explained as passively caused by bodily pushes. In his treatise on *The Passions of the Soul* (1649) Descartes distinguished between "actions" of the soul, which are initiated or produced by it, and "passions," which come over the soul, being caused to occur in it (1649b, p. 331). "Volitions" are actions of the soul that can move the body, while the passions are "perceptions" produced in the soul by the body; the latter include not only perceptions of external objects and of our own bodily states, but also "perceptions which we relate solely to the soul" like joy and anger (Descartes, 1649b, pp. 342–343). Descartes' explanation for behaviors connected with the passions is largely physiological. What happens when, for example, a man runs off in fear, is that a stimulus operates on the animal spirits, nerves, and so on, in such a way that a feeling of fear is produced in the soul while at the same time there are physiological changes, the legs are caused to move in flight, and the soul is caused to perceive their motion—and all this, says Descartes, may happen "without the soul's contributing thereto" (1649b, pp. 348–349). Seeing the object, feeling fear, and perceiving that one is running are, of course, mental phenomena, but they are all caused by a continuous chain of physical processes, so that the mind is passive throughout and contributes nothing to their production. Such behaviors are not really our actions—they are not initiated by us through our volitions, but come over us, being caused mechanically by bodily processes. In contrast, the appropriate rational behaviors that occur when we express our thoughts in language, or act from knowledge, can only be explained as initiated and directed by our mind.

Our ability to speak and act intelligently was thus interpreted by Descartes as due to the presence in us, but not in animals or machines, of an incorporeal thinking substance. Since the mind that thinks is unextended, only the extended body and its movements can be publicly observed, and the relation of thought to observable behavior is a purely external, causal one. That is, language and rational conduct are, for Descartes, only outer manifestations of the presence of mind within; they are caused by mind but are not in any way constitutive of it. Language is only a means for communicating to others thoughts that the mind has in complete independence of language, or other symbols, and acting from knowledge involves a purely mental inner performance that causes outer bodily movements. The mind becomes, as it were, an immaterial bit of machinery that is needed to explain the bodily movements that occur when people speak and act intelligently. So if it were discovered that, for example, the way men arrange words, "forming of them a statement," depends on the presence in them, but not in animals or machines, of certain neurological structures or processes, this would be evidence against Descartes' claim that other men have minds.

For Descartes was, after all, very much a product of the scientific revolution that sought to "homogenize" qualitative surface differences between phenomena and to explain them in terms of their underlying causes. Like Hobbes, Descartes thinks that when we observe people we can only see the movements of their bodies; like him, he thinks that the job of psychology is to provide a causal explanation for these movements. They differ only about the identification of the causes: where Hobbes thinks that all our bodily movements are caused by the motion of other bodies, Descartes thinks that those bodily movements that are connected with our actions —in contrast to those connected with the passions—can only be explained on the assumption that they are caused by immaterial thoughts. If actions are effects produced in the body by the mind, sensations, emotions, and so on are effects produced in the mind by the body. That mind and body interact in these ways is, for Descartes, an inescapable fact of our experience, a fact for which no further explanation can be given (1643, p. 256). All one can do is describe one's mental states introspectively on the one side, and examine the physiological mechanisms involved on the other. If Hobbes reduces psychology to physiology, Descartes splits psychology into phenomenology and physiology.

III. The Empiricist "Science of Man"

These profoundly unsatisfactory views are the heritage psychology received from the Galilean revolution. They constitute the general framework within which philosophers, during the eighteenth and nineteenth centuries, attempted to develop a "science of man" in which psychological and philosophical questions were rarely distinguished from each other. Hume echoes Hobbes's Galilean ambitions when he attempts, as the subtitle of his *Treatise of Human Nature* (1739) informs us, to "introduce the experimental Method of Reasoning" into philosophy. This is, of course, the method of Newton and through its use philosophy can, according to Hume, "discover, at least in some degree, the secret springs and principles by which the human mind is actuated in its operation" (1748, p. 24). These turn out to be the principles of association between ideas and, says Hume, again thinking of Newton, "here is a kind of *attraction* which in the mental world will be found to have as extraordinary effects as in the natural" (1739, pp. 12–13).

Hume, like most other "empiricists," follows Descartes in holding that only mental states can be directly present to the mind. "External objects become known to us only by those perceptions they occasion" (1739, p. 67), and Hume divides the perceptions of the mind into "impressions" and "ideas"; impressions include "all our sensations, passions and emotions," while ideas are "faint images of these in thinking and reasoning" (1739, p. 1). Ideas are thus construed as mental images and thinking as the occurrence of mental imagery. As for language, though Hume devotes little explicit attention to it, he implicitly adopts Locke's view of words as "signs of internal conceptions . . . marks for the ideas within his own mind" (1690, Vol. II, p. 3); since thought is "invisible and hidden from others" man had to develop words as "external sensible signs; whereof these invisible ideas, which his thoughts are made up of, might be made known to others" (Locke, 1690, Vol. II, p. 8).

Since Hume regards words as signs for ideas, and ideas as mental images, his Newtonian approach leads him to present the philosophical claim that the meaning of concepts must be specified empirically as the psychological thesis that we cannot have mental images without having had corresponding sensations (1748, Section II); philosophical questions about the meaning of terms are thus conflated with psychological questions about the genesis of mental imagery, that is, about the derivation of ideas from impressions. Similarly, logical questions concerning the validity of our beliefs, and genetic questions concerning the operations of the mind that produce these beliefs, constantly flow into each other in Hume's writing. For example, after developing philosophical arguments to the effect that we have no rational justification for taking the past as a guide to the future, Hume turns to the very different question of why, in fact, we regularly do this. And he answers that all such reasonings from experience are a matter of habits of association resulting from repetition (Hume, 1748, Sections IV and V). Again, the question what justification we can have for claiming that "A causes B" is put into psychogenetic terms and becomes an inquiry into where our idea of necessary connection comes from, Hume's answer being that, though we never observe any connection between events, the observation of repeated conjunction between two events leads to the habit of expecting one when we see the other, and our idea of a connection between them is the projection into the events of this mental association (1748, Section VII). But while Hume thus brings psychological generalizations into the discussion of philosophical issues, these generalizations are not really empirical. If the philosophical points that interest Hume could be supported by psychological generalizations, these would have to be established empirically by investigating what the origins of our causal notions in fact are (e.g., Piaget, 1930), under what conditions different people in fact report having mental imagery of various sorts, and so on. Of course, Hume did not actually undertake such investigations. These allegedly empirical generalizations are brought in as if they were perfectly obvious—in part, at least, because what really interests Hume is philosophy rather than empirical psychology.

Hume's attempt to adopt Newton's "method" not only led him to conflate psychological and philosophical problems, it also led him to give a mechanical account of the mind. Ideas become like material particles, and the principles of association are like forces that explain changes in the occurrence of ideas—these principles are the "gentle force . . . by which the mind is . . . conveyed from one idea to another" (Hume, 1739, pp. 10–11). We thus get an account of mental life purely from the point of view of a spectator of mental phenomena, an account from which all notions of agency have been eliminated. Hume deliberately modeled his account on Newton and wanted to exclude such obscure "powers" from it, much as "occult causes" had been eliminated from physics in the scientific revolution (1739, pp. xx–xxii). Thinking becomes, not something we do, but the occurrence of mental images whose appearance and disappearance is explained by the "forces" of association. Since habitual associations between ideas are established by the repeated imprinting of external stimuli, Hume notes that we get here "a kind of pre-established harmony between the course of nature and the succession of our ideas" (1748, p. 67); in other words, the order of our thoughts mirrors the order of events in the external world. Our thoughts are thus determined by external events that have been impressed on our mind in a certain order in the course of our past.

An application of this sort of analysis to motor behavior was provided by Hartley's *Observations on Man* (1749). By extending the laws of association so as to include not only associations between ideas, but also associations between ideas and bodily motions, Hartley tried to give a mechanical explanation for those "voluntary motions . . . which arise from ideas and affections and which are, therefore, referred to the mind" (1749, Vol. I, pp. iii–iv). Hartley's strategy was to show that such motions develop out of involuntary ones by a process of association. The child's grasp, for example, is at first automatic, that is, set off by a sensation in the palm. But association makes it possible for this *movement* to be excited by the *idea of that sensation* which originally excited the act; and the idea of that sensation can itself be excited by the *idea of the movement,* since the former persists during the act and so becomes associated with the latter. So what happens when the child grasps voluntarily is this: the idea of an end has become associated with the idea of the muscular act that procured it in the past; this idea is associated with the idea of the sensation involved in the movement, and that idea can, as a result of association, call up the muscular movement in the way the sensation itself would have done. This chain of association is formed gradually, by repetition, but when the behavior has become "perfectly voluntary" there is no awareness of the links in the chain (Hartley, 1749, Vol. I, pp. 103–109). Human actions thus are, for Hartley, "voluntary motions" that can be analyzed into simple ideas (i.e., copies of sense impressions) and automatic motions, and that can be shown to be built up from these by means of association.

This theory was adopted by James Mill in his *Analysis of the Phenomena of the Human Mind* (1829). There is, so argues Mill, no difference between voluntary and involuntary behavior "except that in the voluntary there exists a desire"; thus "shedding tears at the hearing of a tragic story we do not desire to weep," while we desire to lift the arm when we do so to ward off a blow (1829, Vol. II, pp. 350–351). The will is the "cause" of (voluntary) action only in the sense of being the "state of mind which immediately precedes the action" (Mill, 1829, Vol. II, pp. 328–329); and an "ample induction" based on introspection shows, according to Mill, that this state of mind is always a desire to do the act. This desire can be analyzed into an association of pleasure with the idea of this act. So what moves to action is always pleasure: the motive for an act is, Mill holds, always an association between pleasure and the idea of this act of ours as producing it (1829, Vol. II, p. 258). But the occurrence of the motive does not suffice for the occurrence of the corresponding act. Whether or not the motive will, in fact, be followed by the act depends, so argues Mill following Hartley, on whether or not, as a result of previously established associations, the idea of moving the arm calls up the idea "of those internal sensations which originally called the muscles into action" (1829, Vol. II, p. 353). Will, motives, desires, and so on are thus conceived by Mill as introspectible mental states whose relation to bodily behavior is as external and contingent as is the relation of grief to the (involuntary) lachrymal stimulation it produces. "Whatever power we may possess over the action of our muscles," says Mill, "must be derived from our power over our associations," but he immediately points out that this "means nothing more than the power of certain interesting ideas . . . formed into strength by association" (1829, Vol. II, p. 379).

On this theory, voluntary acts are no more "in my power" than are the involuntary movements of my body. For whether, for example, my arm goes up when I desire to move it depends not on me, but on whether the necessary associations have been established in the course of my history. For Mill, as for Hartley, voluntary actions are complex bodily movements, each of which was originally set off automatically by sensations, but which, once the requisite associations have been established, can be triggered by an idea. Learning to perform various acts, where this includes speaking a language or playing an instrument, is seen, to put the point anachronistically, as a process of conditioning, that is, of establishing associations as a result of which an idea acquires the power to trigger behavior in the automatic way in which sensations originally triggered (involuntary) movements (see Mill, 1829, Vol. II, pp. 343–354). The "power" of an idea to produce behavior—the fact that the desire to move the arm is followed by the movement—is not my power, but is the power of conditioning. No wonder Coleridge complained that on such theories we "only fancy that we act" since the very writing of these words is the "mere motion of my muscles and nerves; and these again are set in motion from external causes equally passive" so that I myself "have nothing to do with it" (1817, p. 232).

Mill also systematized the theory of association developed by his predecessors. Hume's three principles of association—contiguity, causation, and resemblance—are reduced to contiguity (Mill, 1829, Vol. I, pp. 106–114). Since "ideas spring up, or exist, in the order in which the sensations existed of which they are the copies," and since the occurrence of sensations can only be "synchronous" or "successive," the order of our ideas can be reduced to contiguity in space or time (Mill, 1829, Vol. I, pp. 71–78). Moreover, there are "degrees in association"; that is, one association can be stronger than another if "it is more permanent . . . performed with more certainty . . . [and] more facility." According to Mill, this "strength of association" is determined primarily by "frequency" and secondarily by "the vividness of the associated feelings" (1829, Vol. I, p. 82 ff). So the order in which external inputs are imprinted determines the order of our thoughts, while the frequency with which they are stamped in determines the strength of these externally forged connections between thoughts.

Association psychology thus construed man as essentially passive, a tabula rasa on which external contingencies imprint themselves through the senses. Descartes had introduced the mind as an active principle that would explain intelligent behaviors connected with language and knowledge. But by the time we get to Mill, it is clear that the mind cannot act in Descartes' sense of initiating either thoughts or bodily behavior. What ideas and what movements occur depends on what associations have been stamped in from outside and there is no room for any kind of internal ordering or initiation of behavior. All the responses the individual "learns" to make, be they bodily or mental, are explained in terms of the order and frequency of the inputs that have been impressed in the course of his history. Since the way a person construes the situation confronting him is simply a reflection of inputs imprinted from outside in the past, reference to thought, that is, to the way he construes the situation, has ceased to be essential. In other words, behavior is really determined by events that occur external to the mind and the mind has ceased to do any work in the explanation of behavior. Yet it is still retained as an inner echo, a private film of these outer inputs that, in principle, cannot be viewed by anyone else. And these shadow processes are regarded as the essence of thought and language— thoughts are, for Mill, mental images, while words are external signs for these private images (see 1829, Vol. II, Chapter XIV).

Since the occurrence of ideas, like that of bodily movements, is in Mill's view completely determined by the associations that have been established in the past, he sees nothing strange in arguing that the difference between the man who is, and the man who is not, able to do arithmetic is that in the former, but not in the latter, the idea of seven added to five is "strongly associated" with the idea of twelve (1829, Vol. I, p. 90). Again, belief, including belief in the truth of propositions, is treated by Mill as nothing but a strong association between ideas. Locke had recognized the need for some sort of normative distinction between correct beliefs, which correspond to the connections between things, and error; but Mill criticizes this on the ground that "wrong belief is belief no less than right belief" and argues that ideas "which are connected in conformity with the connections among things, are connected by custom, as much as those which are connected not in conformity with those connections" (1829, Vol. I, Chapter XI, especially pp. 380–381). The distinction between logical questions concerning validity and norms, on the one hand, and psychological questions of fact, on the other, is completely evaporated as the account of mental processes is completely mechanized.

IV. The Kantian Approach

If we turn to Kant, we find a very different account of thought and action. When, in the *Critique of Pure Reason* (1781), Kant undertook to reexamine the presuppositions of our knowledge in order to discover the ground that makes it possible for us to have scientific knowledge, he found that perception and thought had to be construed as activities we perform. To describe experience as the passive reception of inputs is, for Kant, to misdescribe it, because seeing something is constructing a spatiotemporal object from these inputs on the basis of rules; to describe thought as the passive occurrence of ideas is to misdescribe it, because thinking is the performance of unifying some diversity on the basis of rules. Concepts are, in Kant's view, rules that we follow in thinking, so that to have a concept is to have an intellectual skill that is evidenced by the ability to use the concept correctly. Neither experience nor thought can be understood as things that happen to us, but only as things we do, because they are, so Kant held, synthetic activities that involve construction according to a rule and recognition of the unity of this process. Hume had argued that we go beyond the evidence whenever we take the past as a guide to the future, and that habits, established by past experience, are the psychological explanation of why we in fact do this. Kant countered by arguing that valid knowledge of, for example, the way bodies will move in the future is possible because these phenomena must conform to rules in accordance with which our "intuitions" (roughly Hume's "impressions") are organized into the objects we perceive and know—rules that are not derived from, but prescribed to, experience.

Kant's concern was to justify our scientific knowledge in the face of Hume's "skepticism"; he was interested in the validity of the concepts we use, not in their *de facto* genesis. He regarded these rules as unchanging principles of the human understanding, a move that seemed plausible in his day since they were (allegedly) presupposed by Newtonian physics, and that science was then regarded as objectively and universally valid for all time. The analysis of these rules involved in the synthetic activity of the knowing mind is, for Kant, the a priori task of philosophy; it cannot be the province of psychology, since the very attempt to do psychology presupposes these rules. Psychology, unlike philosophy, is an empirical study but, in contrast to physics, "empirical psychology," so argued Kant, "must always remain outside the rank of a natural science properly so called" (1786, p. 471).

The considerations that led Kant to this view are complex and cannot be discussed here in any detail. I have argued elsewhere (Mischel, 1967) that Kant moved away from a Cartesian psychology, which spoke of desires, volitions, and so forth in quasi-causal terms, toward a different view of the relation between the mental and the physical, a view on which mental states are not in a category that makes them proper candidates for the causes of bodily motions. Kant's recognition that one cannot really assimilate the explanation of actions in terms of "ideas" (desires, etc.) to the causal model of mechanics is, I think, one reason why he held that psychology can never be a "proper" (i.e., Newtonian) science. Further, Kant not only held that, since experience is not "given" but is constructed by us according to rules that we prescribe to it, what we know is always things as they appear to us, never things in themselves; he also insisted that we must distinguish between the different "standpoints" from which agents and spectators view behavior. He was thus developing something like the distinction that psychologists have subsequently drawn between the psychological and the geographical environment. Since the psychological environment is the situation as it appears to the agent, it must be described in terms of concepts involving consciousness; and the response the agent makes to the situation must be identified in the same terms, that is, in terms of the agent's intention, what he takes himself to be doing in this situation. So if we study behavior from the point of view of agents, if we try to explain what people do in terms of the psychological environment that defines the alternative courses of action open to them, then concepts involving consciousness will be essential to our study. But such concepts have no place in Newtonian physics, which Kant identified with science "properly so called."

Kant's view of actions and agents is closely connected with his account of the will as the capacity for acting on a rule or maxim. Kant identified the will with practical reason and held that rational beings "have the faculty of acting according *to the conception* of laws" and therefore have a will (1785, p. 29). Desires, affects, passions—the so-called "driving springs" of action—are linked to behavior not as blind mechanical pushes, but through the will, which is "the faculty of taking a rule of reason for the motive of an action" (Kant, 1788, p. 151). Kant's point is that human beings have "interests," which they can state in rules, and they can follow these rules: they thus act from the "mere conception" of a rule instead of being blindly pushed. Their actions are mediated by meanings, by considerations arising from an understanding of the connections that acts have with each other and with consequences in complex patterns of social life. Reason is practical when it decides what *should* be done in light of the situation confronting the agent and the nature of all his inclinations, desires, and so forth; and willing, which is practical reason, is not a mental push that sets us in motion but is acting on a rule of reason—that is, an action is willed when it is done intentionally, with some end in view and some knowledge of what one is doing and why. Since such actions are guided by the agent's conception of rules, they can be explained in terms of those rules and the agent's construal of the situation confronting him (see Peters, 1958; Melden, 1961; Mischel, 1963, 1964).

Of course, bodily acts involve movements that can be explained in terms of the causal theories of physics and physiology. But Kant's suggestion, as I understand him, is that if we take the point of view of agents rather than spectators, then we connect the behavior with a network of concepts relating to agents who have interests and who follow rules, or maxims, in their dealings with other agents. So what we see is not, for example, an arm moving upward, but a man who is raising his arm in order to attract attention, or to greet a friend, or whatever. When we see an action of a certain sort we thus connect what we see with a conceptual context utterly different from that involved in seeing movements, and this context determines the form of explanation that is appropriate. If we see someone attracting attention, or greeting a friend, we are committed to a different type of explanation from that to which we are committed when we see bodily movements. Still, psychology can be an empirical study that discovers a systematic order operative in human actions at its own level, and from its own point of view. But this account will be of a very different sort from that provided by physics and physiology.

Seen in this way, the study of thought-related human actions becomes a science that must use concepts and explanations different from those appropriate to the study of bodily movements (see Peters, 1958; Melden, 1961; and their papers, as well as that by Toulmin, in this volume). Kant developed his specifically psychological views in a work entitled *Anthropology from a Pragmatic Point of View* (1798) and held that history, biography, novels, and so on are important sources for the development of this study (1798, pp. 120–121). Introspection of inner states, far from being stressed, is repeatedly held to be misleading as well as dangerous because it leads to confusion and even insanity (Kant, 1798, pp. 132–134, *passim*). Not private inner states, but the public social arena in which men, as practical beings, cope with their fellows in the affairs of the world is seen by Kant as important for understanding human conduct. The attempt to construct Newtonian explanations for human behavior, in which ideas have the job of masses and associations the job of forces, thus gives way to "pragmatic" explanations of conduct constructed from the "standpoint" of agents. But Kant's *Anthropology* is not an empirical anthropology; it raises neither genetic questions about the way we become social and moral beings, nor questions about individual and cultural differences, and so on, and so rarely departs from the conventional wisdom of the day, the insights of moralists and novelists. Considering its date, this is hardly surprising.

V. The Experimental Study of the Mind

A. THE WÜRZBURG EXPERIMENTS

The first attempts at an experimental study of thinking and the behaviors connected with it were undertaken by Külpe and his associates at Würzburg early in this century. The Würzburgers shared most of the assumptions of the associationist tradition, failed to distinguish between logical and psychological issues, and set out to discover what judgment, thought, and so forth are, by asking subjects to compare, judge, or perform other thoughtful tasks under controlled laboratory conditions, and to report what went through their minds in performing these tasks. The first things these investigators discovered were what came to be called "imageless thoughts" —subjects reported being "conscious of . . . ," "aware that . . . ," and so on, but their thoughts did not consist of "ideas" in the traditional sense; they were not copies of sense impressions. Mental images, if they occurred at all, were accidental, and the warp and woof of thought contained no trace of sensory or imaginal content. In trying to classify these imageless thoughts, Karl Bühler (1907), whose investigations dealt with relatively complex tasks, distinguished such awarenesses as "consciousness of a rule," "consciousness of relation," and "intention," none of which were ideas in the traditional sense. Where the associationist tradition had assumed that concepts are mental images, that thought operates in terms of such images, and that language only serves to communicate one's thoughts to others, it now seemed that thought had to be linked to language rather than to mental images. The awareness of a rule, or of a relation, or of an intention, could be expressed in words, but it could not be identified with mental images ("ideas").

Further, when Ach (1905) set out to investigate "the activity of will," he found that this was tied up with the more general problem of thinking, and that the directed character of thought could not be explained in terms of the external stimulus. It seemed to depend on the subject's *understanding* of the task that he is to perform, an understanding that, once again, was not mediated by any mental content of which he is aware. In other words, what the subject thinks when he is confronted with, for example, two numbers, depends on whether he has been asked to add or multiply: thought is goal directed, it depends on the motive, on what the person is trying to do; but this motive, or "set," is not an identifiable item in the subject's consciousness. Thinking, it became clear, follows rules or norms, but introspection could disclose nothing interesting about how these rules direct thought. Given the traditional assumption that one finds out about mental phenomena by turning inward and inspecting the contents of one's own mind, one can understand Binet's disillusioned cry: "Thought is an unconscious activity of the mind."

The Würzburg results indicated that the material of thought could not be reduced to mental images, and that the directed rule-following character of thought, and of behaviors connected with it (e.g., the voluntary acts that interested Ach), could not be explained in terms of associations called up by an external stimulus. In trying to account for these results, the Würtzburgers tended to shore up the association theory with which they had started by complicating it with additional hypotheses, for example, a *Bewustseinslage* without sensory content, "determining tendencies" that work on associations, and so on (see Humphrey, 1951). But in the period that followed, some psychologists sought to develop theoretical approaches to the study of intelligent human behavior that departed radically from the simple external control of behavior assumed in association theory. Bühler (1930, 1934) turned to genetic developmental studies and to language, while Selz (1913, 1922) focused on problem solving and productive thinking. Piaget (1926) started his developmental studies of cognitive structure, while Gestalt psychologists (Koffka, 1924; Köhler, 1925) called attention to "insightful learning," which involved not trial and error, but a task or goal and an understanding of what is being done in relation to the perceived situation. Kurt Lewin's (1926) paper on will and intentional actions explicitly took the work of Ach for its point of departure, and formed the basis for his later field theory. But these efforts to account for intelligent molar behavior in terms of "cognitive theories" that start from the psychological environment (Kant's "standpoint" of agents), were outside the mainstream of psychology—at least, until recently. (The work on achievement motivation that has developed since the 1950's, and the related "expectancy × value" theories of motivation, though influenced by S-R theory, clearly owe something to this tradition. See the paper by Atkinson in this volume.) During most of this century, psychology has been dominated, at least in America, by the behavioristic reaction provoked by Wundt's attempt to make psychology into the experimental study of the mind.

B. Wundt's "Physiological Psychology"

Wundt called the science that he hoped to found "physiological psychology," but he was very far from thinking that psychological phenomena could be reduced to, or explained in terms of, physiological processes.

Though the latter view was adopted by many psychologists around the turn of the century—including Titchener (1910, pp. 38–41), who is generally, but misleadingly, regarded as a "Wundtian"—Wundt himself directed his sharpest polemics against this "psycho-physical materialism" (1894, pp. 47–75, 1896, p. 11 ff). According to Wundt, psychological phenomena are always "paralleled" by physical processes, which are studied by physiology, a natural science (*Naturwissenschaft*); but psychology is related to the cultural sciences (*Geisteswissenschaften*), and "the point of view adopted in psychology, or that of immediate subjective experience, is different from the point of view taken in the natural sciences, or that of mediate, objective experience due to abstraction" (1897, p. 320). The physiologist, according to Wundt, abstracts all subjective elements from experience so that, for example, a human action is, from his point of view, "a coordinated sum of muscle contractions, of skeletal movements produced by it" and so on—a succession of objective occurrences that must be explained in terms of theories in which there is no room for volitions or other mental phenomena (1874, Vol. III, p. 782 ff). But when the physiologist's story is all told, we still have not fully understood the behavior, not because the physiologist has omitted something that ought to appear in his story, but because there is another "point of view" from which it must be investigated. For the agent himself can describe the contents of his consciousness as they appear to him as perceiving and acting subject. Now the psychologist, so Wundt held, takes the point of view of "immediate subjective experience" and so sees a human action as "a succession of representations of movements, together with feelings, sensations, and representations of ends which precede the action as motives—elements all of which are immediate contents of consciousness" (1874, Vol. III, p. 731). Psychology must explain the subject's "immediate experience," while physiology deals with "mediate" experience, that is, with objects that are generated by abstracting everything subjective from experience; they both deal with experience, but from entirely different, though supplementary, points of view. (For a more detailed discussion of Wundt's views, see Mischel, 1969.)

This "two points of view" formula made it possible for Wundt to hold that, while there are no limits to what physiology can explain, psychology is an independent science, related to the cultural sciences and not reducible to physiology. But this formula identifies the mental with the private; it echoes the Cartesian view of the mental as an "inner" realm that is epistemologically and psychologically prior to the "outer" (mediate) physical world. And if immediate experience is private, how can it be the subject matter of a (public) science of psychology?

Wundt's answer is "experiments." He spoke of his investigations as "physiological psychology" because he was convinced that psychology must study mental phenomena by means of experimental methods, like those developed by Helmholtz and others in studying the physiology of the senses (Wundt, 1874, Vol. I, pp. 2–3). Indeed, the use of experimental methods is, according to Wundt, what first makes possible for psychology "observation in a scientific sense." For the "natural scientist can return to his object whenever he likes" and so can make observations without doing experiments. But this is impossible in psychology because mental phenomena are fleeting and change when we deliberately set out to observe them. So the "psychologist can return to an inner process observed under certain conditions, only when he artificially introduces the same conditions, that is with the aid of the experimental method" (Wundt, 1883, pp. 167–169, 1894, pp. 97–98).

Wundt's point comes to this: mental phenomena are necessarily private; they are always accessible to me, but you can never tell by observing me what is in my mind. But insofar as mental and physical processes "parallel" each other, one can experimentally manipulate outer physical conditions in order to recall inner mental processes; and this makes it possible to observe and describe them, in much the same way in which external objects are observed and described. As Titchener, whose views on introspection agree with Wundt's, puts it:

> While a newly discovered insect or a rare mineral can be packed in a box, and sent by one investigator to another in a distant country, the psychologist can never put his consciousness in any similar way at the disposal of his fellow psychologists. But the difference is a minor difference: it does not extend to the nature and function of the experiment itself (Titchener, 1896, pp. 42–43).

The inability of others to witness my mental phenomena is regarded as a contingent fact due to the special nature of the phenomena under investigation, and the function of experiments is to make it possible for others, and for myself on subsequent occasions, to correct, add to, or confirm my descriptions of mental phenomena, in just the way in which we corroborate each other's descriptions of physical phenomena. Though introspection can only be applied to one's own consciousness, the use of experiments makes it possible to "arrange matters so that other individuals may be brought forward as witnesses to the facts which we ourselves have observed" (Titchener, 1896, pp. 41–42).

But just what "facts" are being observed and described? Not, of course, the surrounding external conditions, for example, the object at which the observer is looking. No doubt this is what we ordinarily observe and describe, but introspectionists held that such objects are "conceptual" constructions derived from an experience that is "immediate" in the sense of being both genetically and epistemologically prior. As a result of learning and association, one is not normally aware of one's immediate experience but attends instead to objects. In order to become a psychological observer, one therefore had to undergo special training; and the novice, who would naturally describe the objects he sees, instead of his immediate subjective experiences, was thought to make a mistake called "the stimulus error."

C. THE WUNDTIAN IMPASSE

Evidently, the descriptions given by psychological observers in experiments such as Wundt's are not descriptions of, and cannot be checked against, external circumstances. But then what are we to do if two observers describe their subjective experiences differently under the same experimental circumstances? How can we tell which of the two descriptions is correct? What good can it do to tell them to look again, if we cannot tell them specifically what to look at; that is, if there is no way of pointing to features one or the other might have overlooked? Because an insect or a mineral can be "packed in a box," it can be publicly produced and pointed out apart from the descriptions observers give; different descriptions can then be checked against it. But there is no way of producing a mental state for public scrutiny; the most that can be produced is a description of it. This is not, as Titchener held, a "minor difference," but a fundamental one. For it means that these "descriptions" are such that there is nothing against which they can be checked. When I describe an insect, or a mineral, I can check my description by consulting others, or by looking at it again; I can try to remember what it looked like, and I can check my memory by renewed observation, or by looking at a photograph, and so on. But none of this is possible when what I am "describing" is my immediate subjective experience.

There simply is no way of identifying what is supposed to be observed and described in these experiments. Reference to external objective features is ruled out, and what the observer says about his inner processes is regarded as a "description" that may or may not be correct, so that it cannot be used to identify them. But what else could there possibly be? There is no conceivable way of identifying inner processes except by reference to associated external circumstances, or what the person himself tells us about them, or both. Since these are ruled out, there is no way of identifying what is supposed to be described. Experiments have not helped at all, because there are still no criteria for deciding whether such "descriptions" are correct or incorrect.

Wundt, like most writers of his day, was misled by the analogy with physical observation into supposing that when I tell you about my mental processes I am describing something that I, unlike you, can observe. He then tried to open this elusive inner domain to public study by experiments that aimed "in a certain sense, to objectify the psychological processes to be observed, to make them objects of independent observations" (Wundt, 1907, p. 307). But this program was radically misconceived, because there is no way of making mental phenomena into "objects of independent observation." There can be no way of doing this because when I tell you what is in my mind, I am not "describing" something I discover by observation. Normally, I can tell you what I think, feel, imagine, and so forth, without having to "find out," and if you question what I say, you are suggesting, not that I have made an observational error, but that I am lying—possibly to myself. The reason you cannot, ordinarily, correct what I say about my mental processes, as you can correct what I say about physical objects, is not that they happen to be inaccessible to you, but that they are not "objects of independent observation": they cannot be identified apart from external circumstances and what I say about them. This is what Wittgenstein and others have enabled us to understand (Wittgenstein, 1953; Malcolm, 1963).

But Wundt was brought up in the philosophical tradition that identified the mind with a stream of mental states that are necessarily private, but that, so it was thought, can be communicated to others through language, which is an "external sensible sign" for these inner "invisible ideas." The meaning of words was thus tied to mental images, which were, allegedly, observed in the special way called "introspection." But (and this is the force of Wittgensteinian arguments against a private language) if our words gained their meaning by reference to private experience, then it would be impossible to communicate with others; we could never know that we mean the same thing by the words we use. If language can be used intelligibly, as it clearly can be, then its meaning must be explicable, in one way or another, by reference to what is publicly observable and not by reference to mental imagery, which can never be made public. Once a public language has been learned, it might be applied to private mental images—but even then, understanding the meaning of the word used does not depend on the way it is applied to private images (a procedure on which there is no check), but on the way it is applied to things in the public world, something that can be checked by others. There must be standards for the correct use of an intelligible language, and these can only be public standards. These considerations apply to the psychological terms we use (e.g., intention, motive, desire, idea, sensation). If we can use this psychological language intelligibly, as we clearly can, then its meaning must be established in relation to circumstances and behaviors that are publicly observable—what we mean when we speak of various mental states and processes must be connected, in some way, with the public world and not with what must, in principle, be private.

Wundt, however, inherited a very different philosophical account of language and thought, and that account informed his attempt to show that psychology is independent of, yet compatible with, physiology because they study experience from different points of view. Since the point of view of psychology is that of "immediate subjective experience," physical objects, bodily behavior, anything publicly accessible falls under the point of view of the natural sciences rather than psychology. This Cartesian starting point breaks the connection between inner processes and outer circumstances and behavior. We are then asked to use experimentally controlled introspection in order to study these mental processes. But since neither outer circumstances nor verbal reports are to be used as the criterion for identifying them, there is no way of identifying them and, consequently, no way of studying them. (Compare Campbell's discussion of phenomenology in this volume.)

It is not surprising that introspective experiments led to acrimonious disputes that no one knew how to settle because there were no criteria for settling them. Boring reports on a meeting of the Society of Experimental Psychologists at which "Titchener, after a hot debate with Holt, exclaimed: 'You can see that green is neither yellowish nor bluish!' and Holt replied: 'On the contrary, it is obvious that a green is that yellow-blue which is just exactly as blue as it is yellow' " (Boring, 1946, p. 176). One can see why the whole study of mental phenomena was in disrepute by 1910; investigators simply could not agree about the "facts" that our own consciousness presents to us. The reason they could not is that the experimental investigation on which they had embarked was conceptually confused.

VI. Watson, Behaviorism, and the Aftermath

At this point, Watson's "ignoring of consciousness" and his denial that "the realm of psychics is open to experimental investigation" (1913, p. 175) was a liberating move. Though a good deal of debate ensued about whether something is "left out" if one studies only behavior, Tolman was λ

able to show that introspective reports can give us "nothing which, theoretically at least, cannot be conveyed by other more gross forms of behavior" (1932, p. 244). Using arguments that resemble those of the later Wittgenstein, Tolman points out that introspection depends on language: the introspectionist cannot produce, for example, his color sensations ("raw feels") for us, he can only describe them. But the meaning of color words must have been learned by reference to external objects, and consequently anything I can tell others about my color sensations could also be conveyed to them by making appropriate discriminations between objects (Tolman, 1932, Chapters XV and XVI). So introspection cannot be a method that provides psychology with special data not accessible in other ways.

But in rejecting introspection as a method, behaviorists also felt compelled to reject consciousness as a datum and a problem. For they accepted Wundt's notion that psychological concepts refer to conscious states, which are accessible only in one's own case, so that introspection is essential to their use. The rejection of introspection as a method was, therefore, thought to entail the exclusion from psychology of all concepts involving consciousness. "Psychology," says Watson, "must discard all reference to consciousness" (1913, p. 163) and in doing psychology we must "never use the terms consciousness, mental states, mind . . . it can be done in terms of stimulus and response" (Watson, 1913, pp. 166–167). In other words, psychology must never use psychological terms!

The S-R behavior theory that then developed was, as Hull himself has pointed out, a "genuine and perfectly natural evolution of English associationism" (1934, p. 382). Since association psychology specified the control of behavior by events external to the mind (see Section III), it was easy to transpose it into a psychology free of mental terms. William James had already pointed out that, though association is between objects rather than ideas and must be explained in terms of processes in the brain (1890, Vol. I, p. 554), still "the whole body of association psychology remains standing after you have translated 'ideas' into 'objects', on the one hand, and 'brain processes' on the other" (1890, Vol. I, p. 604). Since Pavlov's work seemed to provide a respectable objective basis for what had been called the "association of ideas," behaviorists adopted the stimulus-response idiom and spoke of "conditioned reflexes," or responses, though "associated" responses would, as Hull points out (1934, p. 385), have been more appropriate.

The key problem for behavior theory now became the problem of "learning," that is, of showing how S-R connections are strengthened, or how new ones are established, so that the organism's response to a stimulus can be explained as a function of its history, of the environmental contingencies that have impinged upon it in the past. This, of course, is just the question that had traditionally been investigated by asking how it is that ideas get associated in the way they do. Moreover, just as Hartley and Mill sought to explain all complex behavior by showing that it results from the infant's involuntary movements through the gradual formation of long chains of associations, until finally the "idea of the end" is enough to trigger the whole behavior pattern, so early behaviorists sought to explain all complex behaviors as long integrated chains of conditioned reflexes that, once established, can rattle off automatically. The initial link in chains of associations, having been transformed from the idea of an object into an object, could become the independent variable; the final link, the resulting movements, could become the dependent variable, which is specified in terms of response measures; and the intermediary links could be decked out with physiological trappings, for example, Hull's "pure stimulus acts," which, he says, are "the physical substance of ideas" and the like (Hull, 1931, pp. 505–506). But even the idea that association has a physiological basis goes back at least to Hartley (1749), who held that the association of ideas is explained by a physical law of association between "vibrations" and "vibratiuncles" in the brain, these being the physical equivalents of sensations and ideas (see Mischel, 1966).

The relation between behaviorism and association psychology is, perhaps, deeper than Hull realized, since the very form of S-R theory, the nature of the variables and the way they are thought to control behavior, can be traced to this tradition. Both regarded man as passive and sought to explain the responses he "learns" to make in terms of external inputs that have been imprinted in the course of his history. Since there is no room for any internal ordering of behavior—man never acts, he only reacts—such order as emerges in his behavior must mirror the order of the external inputs. So Mill, as we have seen, reduces association to contiguity and points out that the strength of associations, as indicated by their permanence, certainty, and facility, depends primarily on the frequency with which external contingencies have been imprinted, and secondarily on the vividness of associated feelings. But in addition to associations, some motivational factor was needed to start the organism moving, and so Mill spoke of "pleasure" as the "motive," the factor that moves to action. Mill treated pleasure simply as a mental state, but Alexander Bain, who recognized that "there is, in company with our mental processes, an unbroken material succession" (1875, p. 132), identified pleasure, on its "physical side," with energy. In Bain's view (1855, 1859), the spontaneous overflow of energy from the nervous system leads to random movements of the organism, and according to his "law of self conservation" pleasure, or pain avoidance, is connected with an increase of such random movements. Association, so Bain held, can explain how these random movements become directed, but the connection between pleasure and activity is needed to explain both why associations are "stamped in" and why behavior is initiated (see Mischel, 1966).

Compare this now with Hull's *Principles of Behavior* (1943). Surely "pleasure," or "avoidance of pain," in Bain's sense, looks like a not very remote ancestor of the directionless "drive," rooted in physiological need, that Hull uses to explain both the reinforcement of S-R connections and the activation of behavior. For Hull, "learning" [i.e., an increment in the tendency of a stimulus (S) to evoke a reaction (R)] takes place whenever R takes place "in temporal contiguity" with S, and this is followed closely by a diminution in the (painful) need and the associated drive (D) (Hull, 1943a, p. 71). Hull called this an increment in "habit strength" and it corresponds to what Mill called "strength of association" between ideas. Indeed, for each of the measures of habit strength ($_sH_R$) specified by Hull, there is a clear analogue specified by Mill: probability of correct response (i.e., Mill's "certainty"), speed or latency of the response (i.e., "facility"), and resistance of the response to extinction (i.e., "permanence"). In Hull's theory, as in Mill's, what determines the strength of habits (i.e., associations) is, primarily, frequency (i.e., number of reinforcements), though Mill's vague notion of "vividness of associated feelings" is replaced in Hull's theory by magnitude of need reduction, delay of reinforcement, and degree of contiguity between S and R (1943a, Postulate 4).

The big difference is, of course, the precision with which Hull seeks to tie his variables to a large body of experimental work done, for the most part, with animals. Since association psychology held that what happens "in the mind" is determined by the frequency, and so on, with which contiguous events are imprinted from outside, behaviorists could treat these external events as the independent variables, which are manipulated in the laboratory in order to see what effect this will have on the response. In other words, the conception of behavior as determined in a straightforward way by external conditions lent itself to the development of experimental programs and a great deal of effort and ingenuity were expended in this direction. But it is important to recognize that, terminology apart, the transition from the "science of mind" to the "science of behavior" did not involve a significant change of basic theoretical ideas in psychology. For if the assumptions of associationism could, in the hands of behaviorists, generate experimental research, they also limited that research by circumscribing the variables to be investigated, the questions to be asked in the laboratory. Apart from the history we have been tracing, it would be very hard to understand why "drive" and the associational factors summarized in habit strength ($_sH_R$) should be regarded as the fundamental determinants of *all* human behavior. But, though one can think of a good many other factors that look prima facie more plausible, these variables are the ones on which the experimental program of behaviorism concentrated.

These limitations on psychological research were reinforced by the belief that a science of behavior must "begin with colorless movements and mere receptor impulses as such" and proceed to explain purposive human behavior in terms of "postulates involving mere stimuli and mere movement" (Hull, 1943a, pp. 25–26). This belief about what "a satisfactory natural-science theory of behavior" must look like led behaviorists to criticize the use of cognitive concepts involving consciousness, like Lewin's "expectancy," "life space," and so on, on the ground that they are "subjective" and "introspective," "sheer anthropomorphism" rather than science (Hull, 1943b, p. 287). And these epistemological prescriptions were justified by an appeal to the philosophy of "logical positivism," "physicalism," and "operationism" (Hull, 1943b, p. 273). Here again there is a striking parallel between S-R theory and association psychology: they rely on similar epistemological assumptions. For "physicalism" and related doctrines transpose into logical terms the thesis Hume expressed in psychological terms when he held that ideas must be derived from impressions; this now becomes the thesis that meaningful terms must be explicable in terms of (objective) experience, either directly, by pointing to something that can be observed, or indirectly, by using other words that can be explicated in this way.

But just what can be experienced or observed? If one assumes, as most associationists and behaviorists did, that experience consists of the passive reception of inputs through the sense receptors, inputs that somehow register in the mind as conscious states accessible only to the person concerned, then it follows that the meaning of psychological concepts involving consciousness can never be explicated in the requisite way. For only physical inputs can affect our receptors, and consequently only physical changes can be observed. So while we ordinarily say that we can *see* that Jones is angry, or that he opened the window, or stole the groceries, acceptance of this Humean epistemology tempts us to say that we cannot really see this. What we really see is that Jones's face gets red, his voice grows louder, his fists clench, and so on, and from this we infer that he is angry. Of course, Jones may be angry without behaving angrily, but in that case, so it is suggested, he would act in these ways if certain conditions were satisfied. Psychological statements like "Jones is angry" are, on this view, to be analyzed into statements about the responses Jones would make if he were stimulated in certain ways, responses all of which are explicable in "physical terms" (i.e., his face gets red, etc.). Similarly, we can see Jones's body move in certain ways under certain conditions, and we infer from this that he is opening the window, stealing the groceries, or expecting the mailman. But his expectations, intentions, and so on, like his emotions, can never be seen, and therefore his actions, as contrasted with his movements, can never be seen. If the movements of bodies are the only "hard data," because there is no way in which the intentions, beliefs, and so on, used to identify actions can be imprinted on us through our sense receptors, then the way to make psychology really scientific is to insist that the meaning of its concepts must be specified without reference to consciousness—that is, in physical rather than psychological terms.

They are redefined in Behav Terms, as Ryle.

On the other hand, a Kantian epistemology, with its emphasis on the synthetic activity of the mind—the construal of experience as something that is, at least in part, our construction—would make us skeptical of any sharp, clear-cut separation between seeing and inferring. If seeing is not the passive imprinting of sense impressions, but is the ordering of a manifold according to rules, then all seeing involves interpretation and classification. Moreover, in line with Kant's suggestion that agents and spectators see behavior from different standpoints, one can suggest that there may be different points of view from which events can be legitimately viewed, depending on the interest we bring to them. A Kantian approach would thus suggest that there is no need to insist that only one point of view can reveal what we "really" see, that only one class of descriptions can constitute the basic bricks from which all knowledge is built. It would suggest that our world contains actions as well as movements, and that seeing actions involves no more, and no less, interpretation than seeing movements. What we see, whether actions or movements, will then depend on the standpoint from which we view the behavior, the context that is relevant in light of our interest. Here again there is an interplay between epistemological and psychological theory—Hume underwrites associationism and S-R theory, much as Kant underwrites various forms of cognitive theory.

Modeling itself on the physical sciences, association psychology had set out to eliminate all concepts connected with agents, and to develop instead a mechanical account of the workings of the mind from the spectator's point of view. Similarly, S-R theory set out (in principle, if rarely in practice: see Campbell, 1954) to establish precise correlations between (physical) stimuli and movements ("responses") that are free from any entanglement with the "mentalistic" concepts of our ordinary language of actions. Association psychology did, of course, talk the mental language of ideas; but since the workings of the mind were determined by events that impinged on it from outside, the mind did no real work and only served as a private mirror of these inputs. Behaviorism simply bypassed this unobservable inner record, and focused instead on the observable part of the associationist story: the external events, which can be manipulated in the laboratory, and the effect this has on the movements of the organism. We thus get a return to the Hobbesian picture of human behavior as a series of bodily movements caused by other bodily movements. Since there are no meaningful connections between movements, explaining human behavior becomes a matter of relating events, identified without the use of psychological concepts, to other such events on the basis of past regularities in their occurrence.

Of course, one can attempt to identify what happens when people act as a series of molecular movements; but that is not the way we identify human acts. Tolman, as was noted earlier (see Section II), recognized this and insisted that "behavior as behavior, that is, as molar, *is* purposive and *is* cognitive. These purposes and cognitions are of its immediate descriptive warp and woof" (Tolman, 1932, p. 12). In 1922, Tolman already called attention to Watson's inconsistent characterizations of S and R, to his slide between molar-situational and molecular-physiological criteria for the identification of S and R, and advocated a consistently "non-physiological behaviorism" (1922, pp. 45–46). The fact that most behaviorists have tended to ignore the issue raised by Tolman has resulted in what Koch calls the "fluid semantics over time of the word 'behavior' " (1959, p. 754). That is, behaviorists have simply failed to be clear about what they meant by "behavior"; not only has that term been applied indiscriminately to both actions and movements, there is even talk about "perceptual behavior," "cortical behavior," "fantasy behavior," and so on. Perhaps the issue did not seem important to behaviorists because they thought that the difference was merely one in the "coarseness of the ultimate causal segments or units dealt with" (Hull, 1943a, p. 21). But this is not what is at issue. For, as was noted earlier in connection with Hobbes, there is every reason to doubt that molecular movement descriptions can be added up into a molar description like "opening the window"; such molar descriptions do not seem to be equivalent to any specifiable set of molecular movement descriptions (see Peters, 1958; Taylor, 1964). What is involved are different ways of slicing behavior into identifiable elements for investigation from different points of view, and not just slices of different size or "coarseness."

Tolman, having recognized that the interest of psychologists, as contrasted with physiologists, is at the molar level, and that behavior at this level is "purposive and is cognitive," so that it cannot be described without using the psychological concepts ruled out by the behavioristic program, still tried to be a good behaviorist. His strategy was to treat psychological concepts as intervening variables that can be operationally defined in objective (i.e., nonmentalistic) terms. He thus tried to combine cognitive psychology, which identifies actions in terms of the agents' intentions and so on, with the "objective" program of behaviorism. As Tolman himself has put it, "what I really was doing was trying to rewrite a common-sense, mentalistic psychology . . . in operational, behavioristic terms" (1959, p. 94). But this, it seems, cannot be done. The attempt to specify the meaning of, for example, "the rat expects food at L" in this way (Tolman, Richie, & Kalish, 1946, p. 15) turned out to be, not an explication of the meaning of that expression, but a test for its truth that is only applicable under certain conditions. It is usually easy for the experimenter to determine, in light of his background knowledge, whether the conditions are such that the test is applicable; for example, if a cat is astride the rat's path to the food, then the rat's failure to go down the path is not evidence against its expecting food there. But the range of conditions under which the test would not hold is indefinite, so that there is no way of writing all the conditions into the test, and hence no way of specifying the meaning of "expects" operationally in nonpsychological terms.* Even much more serious difficulties, of a similar sort, arise when this procedure is extended to the use of mental concepts in connection with human behavior. [See Tolman's (1923) attempt to specify anger in terms of its "behavior analogue," and cf. Melden, Arnold, and Peters in this volume.]

What led Tolman and other behaviorists to think that psychological concepts need such operational definition was their identification of the mental with the private (Tolman, 1932, p. 3), and the philosophical thesis, prevalent in the 1930s, that the meaning of concepts must be specified in terms of "observables" that can be identified in the "language of physics." ("Logical empiricism," "logical positivism," and "physicalism" were some of the labels for various versions of this view.) The idea behind this doctrine was that the (empirical) meaning of words must be exhausted by the methods that could be used to verify statements in which these words occur, these methods being the ones used in physics. Linguistic philosophy

---

* This point is discussed in detail by Taylor (1964, pp. 79–82). Tolman himself seems to have recognized this point in 1959, when he said that the strategy he had suggested earlier may not work, because the assumption that the specification of an independent variable (i.e., psychological concept) by a "standard defining experiment" will hold in "new, non-standard, non-defining situations" may be "invalid" (Tolman, 1959, pp. 147–148). See also Section VII.

has reacted against this overly simple account of meaning, and focused the attention of philosophers on the way words are actually used, on the function they have in the language and social practices of people. (See Toulmin in this volume.) This new theory of meaning has led to a much more subtle and sophisticated account of what we do when we use psychological concepts. It has led to the recognition that our mental concepts are not used to refer to private inner states, that their ascription is context bound and depends on very complex patterns of action, actual and potential—actions that can be observed in the world when looked at from a certain point of view, that is, against the relevant background of social practices, institutions, and rules. Once this is clear, it is also clear that there is no need for translating our "common sense, mentalistic psychology . . . [into] behavioristic terms." For the translation is already there; it is implicit in our actual use of mental concepts. Indeed, how else could we understand each other and verify what we say in this language, as we constantly do?

VII. Reassessments

By the late 1950s many psychologists, reflecting on the relation of their actual research to the prescriptions of behaviorism, called for a "reexamination of our fundamental commitments with respect to problems of empirical definition" (Koch, 1959, p. 784); it was becoming clear to them that the variables with which they actually deal are not "direct observables" of the requisite sort (Koch, 1959, p. 745), and that the behavior of higher organisms, particularly that of socialized human beings, is a response, not to physical stimuli, but to the "meaning" that situations have for perceivers (Koch, 1959, pp. 747–769; Miller, Galanter, & Pribram, 1960, p. 7 ff). Guthrie now states his principle of learning as "what is being noticed becomes a signal for what is being done" (1959, p. 186), and Tolman expresses "considerable doubt concerning not only the practical feasibility but also the validity" of his earlier proposal for "objectifying" psychological concepts through operational definition in standard situations (1959, p. 148). Watson's promise that psychology can all "be done in terms of stimulus and response" no longer rings true, and while psychologists are not "prepared to retreat one jot from the objectives and disciplines of scientific inquiry . . . most are inclined to re-examine reigning stereotypes about the *character* of such objectives and disciplines" (Koch, 1959, p. 783).

Such reexamination is a philosophical task, but this confluence of epistemological and psychological issues is, of course, far from new. Psychological questions about the character of perception and thought, and epistemological questions about the nature of knowledge and the relation of fact to theory; factual questions about the genesis of our concepts and rules, and logical questions about their validity; empirical questions about what explains the things people do, and conceptual questions about the meaning of "behavior" and the sort of explanation appropriate to it—these, so our historical discussion has shown, have developed hand in hand. The answers that theorists have given to some of these questions have not only influenced the answers they have given to others, but the very questions were, as we have seen, not infrequently confused with each other. A clear recognition of the difference between psychological and logical or epistemological inquiries, the rejection of "psychologism" in logic and of "logicism" in psychology, is thus all to the good. But the same may not be true of the heavy insulation between psychological and philosophical inquiries that built up in this century, as philosophers became preoccupied with formalization and conceptual analysis, which are independent of "mere psychology," while psychologists, having been "emancipated" from philosophy, became preoccupied with their laboratory experiments. If psychological and philosophical inquiries differ, they can still be of great relevance to each other.

To illustrate: one of the indications of the newly "liberated conception of the task of psychology" is the current interest in language and behaviors related to it. But this new area of research is already involved in epistemological disputes. Skinnerians have tried to show that verbal learning can be encompassed within the framework of "descriptive behaviorism" as a form of conditioning; but Spielberger (1965), Dulany (1967), and others have argued convincingly that the "epistemological assumptions" of behaviorism have influenced the data of the Skinnerians, and that when "procedures for assessing awareness are employed, the conditioning curves of aware and unaware subjects are found to be markedly dissimilar, and there is little evidence of learning without awareness" (Spielberger, 1965, p. 161). Considerable sophistication is shown in the analysis of the data, and there is an obvious plausibility to the suggestion that "awareness" and other "mediating cognitive processes" have something to do with verbal learning and related behaviors. What is astonishing in these discussions, at least to a philosopher, is that "cognitive processes" seems to be used merely as a new label for the "ideas" of the old tradition. Spielberger differs from the Skinnerians, not in denying that cognitive processes are adequately conceived as "private stimuli," but in maintaining that, though "not directly observable, they may be inferred, albeit imperfectly, from the subject's verbal responses" (Spielberger, 1965, p. 162). But if a cognitive process is something different from the subject's verbal report, then what is it? Are we again being asked to identify thought with mental imagery? Until questions of this sort are faced, it is hard to see how methodologically sophisticated theories for using verbal reports as indices of cognitive processes (e.g., Dulany, 1962, 1967) can get us very far. For what is needed, first and foremost, is the clarification of the whole range of concepts lumped under "mediating cognitive processes." Unless these notions are clarified, the current "cognitive renaissance" (Spielberger, 1965, p. 196), that is, the new attempt to explain human behavior in terms of cognitive processes, is bound to provoke another behavioristic reaction, much as did the work of Wundt. But the analysis of concepts is the area in which philosophers are specially trained to make their contribution. Such a contribution can, however, be made only by philosophers who are intimately acquainted with the sort of issues and problems that confront the psychologist when he appeals to mediating cognitive processes and the like. Without this, the analysis of mental concepts that philosophers can provide is bound to strike psychologists as irrelevant to their concerns.

Not only may philosophy be relevant to the problems of (cognitive) psychology, the latter may also be relevant to the problems of philosophy. For it is hard to see how philosophical psychology, or the philosophy of mind, can be pursued very far in complete isolation from empirical psychology. Clarification of the logic implicit in our use of key psychological terms may require no psychology, and may be useful for dispelling some philosophical perplexities. But a philosophical psychology that rigidly limits itself to this task is likely to wear rather thin. And if philosophers allow themselves to look deeper and wider, at the rationale that lies behind the distinctions implicit in ordinary language, at the importance that should be attached to them, and the significance they may have for human experience and the understanding of man, then it is hard to see how they can avoid all contact with empirical questions that fall into the domain of psychology. Indeed, it may even be that the analysis of concepts cannot be divorced from a study of their genesis in quite as sharp a way as philosophers frequently suppose (see Toulmin's essay in this volume). Increased communication between philosophers and psychologists about foundational questions may thus turn out to be of value to both. This, at any rate, is the belief that prompted this volume.

References

Ach, N. *Über die Willensthätigkeit und das Denken.* Göttingen: Vandenhoeck & Ruprecht, 1905.

Bain, A. *The senses and the intellect.* London: Parker, 1855.

Bain, A. *The emotions and the will.* London: Parker, 1859.

Bain, A. *Mind and body.* New York: Appleton, 1875.

Boring, E. G. Mind and mechanism. *American Journal of Psychology,* 1946, **59,** 173–192.

Boring, E. G. *History of experimental psychology.* New York: Appleton-Century, 1950.

Bühler, K. Tatsachen und Probleme zu einer Psychologie der Denkvorgänge. *Archiv für Gesamte Psychologie,* 1907, **9,** 297–365.

Bühler, K. *Die geistige Entwicklung des Kindes.* Jena: Fischer, 1930.

Bühler, K. *Sprachtheorie.* Jena: Fischer, 1934.

Campbell, D. T. Operational delineation of "what is learned." *Psychological Review,* 1954, **61,** 167–174.

Coleridge, S. T. Biographia literaria. 1817. In W. G. T. Shedd (Ed.), *Complete works.* Vol. III. New York: Harper, 1854.

Descartes, R. Discourse on method. 1637. In *Philosophical works.* Vol. I. (Transl. by E. S. Haldane and G. R. T. Ross) New York: Dover, 1955.

Descartes, R. Letter to Princess Elizabeth, June 28, 1643. In E. Anscombe and P. T. Geach (Eds.), *Descartes: Philosophical writings.* Edinburgh: Nelson, 1954.

Descartes, R. Letter to Henry More. 1649a. In R. M. Eaton (Ed.), *Descartes selections.* New York: Scribner, 1927.

Descartes, R. The passions of the soul. 1649b. In *Philosophical works.* Vol. I. (Transl. by E. S. Haldane and G. R. T. Ross) New York: Dover, 1955.

Dulany, D. E. The place of hypotheses and intentions: An analysis of verbal control in verbal conditioning. In C. Eriksen (Ed.), *Behavior and awareness.* Durham, N.C.: Duke Univer. Press, 1962.

Dulany, D. E. Awareness, rules and propositional control: A confrontation with S-R behavior theory. In D. Horton & T. Dixon (Eds.), *Verbal behavior and S-R behavior theory.* Englewood Cliffs, N. J.: Prentice-Hall, 1967.

Guthrie, E. R. Association by contiguity. In S. Koch (Ed.), *Psychology: A study of a science.* Vol. II. New York: McGraw-Hill, 1959.

Guttman, N. Laws of behavior and facts of perception. In S. Koch (Ed.), *Psychology: A study of a science.* Vol. V. New York: McGraw-Hill, 1963.

Hanson, N. R. *Patterns of discovery.* London & New York: Cambridge Univer. Press, 1958.

Hartley, D. *Observations on man.* 1749. (2nd ed.) London: Johnson 1791. 3 vols.

Herbart, J. F. Psychologie als Wissenschaft. 1824. In G. Hartenstein (Ed.), *Sämmtliche Werke.* Vols. V & VI. Leipzig: Voss, 1850.

Hobbes. T. A short tract on first principles. 1630? In R. S. Peters (Ed.), *Hobbes: Body, man and citizen.* New York: Collier, 1962.

Hobbes, T. Human nature. 1640. In W. Molesworth (Ed.), *English works.* Vol. IV. London: Bohn, 1839.

Hobbes, T. Third set of objections urged by a celebrated English philosopher [i.e.

Hobbes]. 1641. In *Philosophical works of Descartes*. Vol. II. (Transl. by E. Haldane & G. R. T. Ross) New York: Dover, 1955.

Hobbes, T. Leviathan. 1651. In W. Molesworth (Ed.), *English works*. Vol. III. London: Bohn, 1839.

Hobbes, T. De Corpore. 1655. In W. Molesworth (Ed.), *English works*. Vol. I. London: Bohn, 1839.

Hull, C. L. Goal attraction and directing ideas conceived as habit phenomena. *Psychological Review*, 1931, **38**, 487–506.

Hull, C. L. Learning. In C. Murchinson (Ed.), *Handbook of general experimental psychology*. Worcester, Mass.: Clark Univer. Press, 1934.

Hull, C. L. *Principles of behavior*. New York: Appleton-Century, 1943. (a)

Hull, C. L. The problem of intervening variables in molar behavior theory. *Psychological Review*, 1943, **50**, 273–291. (b)

Hume, D. *Treatise on human nature*. 1739. L. A. Selby-Bigge (Ed.) Oxford: Clarendon Press, 1888.

Hume, D. *Inquiry concerning human understanding*. 1748. C. W. Hendel (Ed.) New York: Liberal Arts Press, 1955.

Humphrey, G. *Thinking*. New York: Wiley, 1951.

Huxley, T. H. *Method and results*. New York: Appleton, 1898.

James, W. *Principles of psychology*. New York: Henry Holt, 1890. 2 vols.

Kant, I. *Critique of pure reason*. 1781. (Transl. by N. Kemp Smith) London: Macmillan, 1929.

Kant, I. Fundamental principles of the metaphysics of morals. 1785. In *Critique of practical reason and other works*. (Transl. by T. K. Abbott) New York: Longmans, 1909.

Kant, I. *Metaphysische Anfangsgründe der Naturwissenschaft*. 1786. (In Akademie edition) Vol. IV. Berlin: Reimer, 1902. [Transl. by T. Mischel]

Kant, I. Critical examination of practical reason. 1788. In *Critique of practical reason and other works*. (Transl. by T. K. Abbott) New York: Longmans, 1909.

Kant, I. *Anthropologie in Pragmatischer Hinsicht*. 1798. (In Akademie Edition) Vol. VII. Berlin: Reimer, 1902. [Transl. by T. Mischel]

Koch, S. Epilogue. In S. Koch (Ed.), *Psychology: A study of a science*. Vol. III. New York: McGraw-Hill, 1959.

Köhler, W. *The mentality of apes*. (Transl. by W. Winter) New York: Harcourt Brace, 1925.

Koffka, K. *The growth of the mind*. (Transl. by R. M. Ogden) London: Kegan Paul, 1924.

Kuhn, T. S. The structure of scientific revolutions. In Otto Neurath, Rudolf Carnap, and Charles W. Morris (Eds.) *International Encyclopedia of Unified Science*. Vol. II, No. 2. Chicago: Univer. of Chicago Press, 1962.

Lewin, K. Vorsatz, Wille und Bedürfnis. *Psychologische Forschung*, 1926, **7**, 330–385.

Lewin, K. *A dynamic theory of personality*. (Transl. by D. K. Adams & K. E. Zener) New York: McGraw-Hill, 1935.

Locke, J. *Essay concerning human understanding*. 1690. A. C. Fraser (Ed.) Oxford: Clarendon Press, 1894.

Malcolm, N. *Knowledge and certainty*. Englewood Cliffs, N. J.: Prentice-Hall, 1963.

Melden, A. I. *Free action*. New York: Humanities Press, 1961.

Mill, J. *Analysis of the phenomena of the human mind*. 1829. J. S. Mill (Ed.) (2nd ed.) London: Longmans, 1869. 2 vols.

Miller, G. A., Galanter, E., & Pribram, K. H. *Plans and the structure of behavior*. New York: Holt, Rinehart, & Winston, 1960.

Mischel, T. Psychology and explanations of human behavior. *Philosophy and Phenomenological Research*, 1963, **23**, 578–594.

Mischel, T. Personal constructs, rules and the logic of clinical activity. *Psychological Review*, 1964, **71**, 180–192.

Mischel, T. "Emotion" and "motivation" in the development of English psychology: Hartley, J. Mill, Bain. *Journal of the History of the Behavioral Sciences*, 1966, **2**, 123–144.

Mischel, T. Kant and the possibility of a science of psychology. *The Monist*, 1967, **51**, 599–622.

Mischel, T. Wundt and the conceptual foundations of psychology. *Philosophy and Phenomenological Research*, 1969, in press.

Peters, R. S. *The concept of motivation*. New York: Humanities Press, 1958.

Piaget, J. *The language and thought of the child*. New York: Harcourt Brace, 1926.

Piaget, J. *The child's concept of physical causality*. London: Kegan Paul, 1930.

Ryle, G. *The concept of mind*. London: Hutchinson, 1949.

Selz, O. *Über die Gesetze des geordneten Denkverlaufs*. Stuttgart: Spemann, 1913.

Selz, O. *Zur Psychologie des produktiven Denkens und des Irrtum*. Bonn: Cohen, 1922.

Spielberger, C. D. Theoretical and epistemological issues in verbal conditioning. In S. Rosenberg (Ed.), *Directions in psycholinguistics*. New York: Macmillan, 1965.

Taylor, C. *The explanation of behavior*. New York: Humanities Press, 1964.

Titchener, E. B. *Outline of psychology*. 1896. (3rd ed.) New York: Macmillan, 1902.

Titchener, E. B. *Textbook of psychology*. New York: Macmillan, 1910.

Tolman, E. C. A new formula for behaviorism. *Psychological Review*, 1922, **29**, 44–53.

Tolman, E. C. A behavioristic account of the emotions. *Psychological Review*, 1923, **30**, 217–227.

Tolman, E. C. *Purposive behavior in animals and men*. New York: Appleton-Century, 1932.

Tolman, E. C. Principles of purposive behavior. In S. Koch (Ed.), *Psychology: A study of a science*. Vol. II. New York: McGraw-Hill, 1959.

Tolman, E. C., Richie, B. F., & Kalish, D. Studies in spatial learning. *Journal of Experimental Psychology*, 1946, **36**, 13–24.

Toulmin, S. *Foresight and understanding*. Bloomington, Ind.: Indiana Univer. Press, 1961.

Turner, M. B. *Philosophy and the science of behavior*. New York: Appleton-Century-Crofts, 1967.

Watson, J. B. Psychology as the behaviorist views it. *Psychological Review*, 1913, **20**, 158–177.

Wittgenstein, L. *Philosophical investigations*. Oxford: Blackwell, 1953.

Wundt, W. *Grundzüge der Physiologischen Psychologie*. 1874. (6th ed.) Leipzig: Engelmann, 1908–1911. 3 vols. [Transl. by T. Mischel]

Wundt, W. *Logik*. 1883. Vol. III. (3rd ed.) Stuttgart: Enke, 1908. [Transl. by T. Mischel]

Wundt, W. Über psychische Causalität und das Princip des psychophysischen Parallelismus. *Philosophische Studien*, 1894, **10.**

Wundt, W. Über die Definition der Psychologie. *Philosophische Studien,* 1896, **12.**

Wundt, W. *Outline of psychology.* (Transl. by C. H. Judd) Leipzig: Engelmann, 1897.

Wundt, W. Über Ausfragenexperimente und Methoden zur Psychologie des Denkens. *Psychologische Studien,* 1907, **3.**

A PHENOMENOLOGY OF THE OTHER ONE: CORRIGIBLE, HYPOTHETICAL, AND CRITICAL

DONALD T. CAMPBELL

I. Introduction

We are easily deceived respecting the operations of sense-perception when we are excited by emotions, and different persons according to their different emotions; for example, the coward when excited by fear and the amorous person by amorous desire; so that with little resemblance to go upon, the former thinks he sees his foes approaching, the latter that he sees the object of his desire; and the more deeply one is under the influence of the emotion, the less similarity is required to give rise to these illusory impressions. (Aristotle, *On Dreams*) *

This quotation illustrates the several themes of this essay. Aristotle deals with the role of motivation in distorting perception. He is focused on *phenomena,* but these are the phenomena of other persons, not himself; he as a scientist is hypothesizing the contents of other minds. Corrigibility of phenomena exists at several levels: the perceptions of the coward and the lover can be wrong, subject to illusion. In addition, Aristotle would prob-

---

* I am indebted to my former colleague Professor Robert I. Watson for calling my attenton to this apt quotation.

ably agree that although he believes the law to be true, in the sense that scientists believe scientific laws, he could be mistaken in particular instances in his inference as to the conscious contents of a lover or a coward —his knowledge of the phenomenal given of these others is not incorrigible or immediate, but is rather indirect, inferential, mediate, and presumptive, like scientific knowledge of material states. He would agree that the coward and lover are unaware of the distortion or its motivational source. He would probably also concede that evidence might eventually prove the law wrong.

Also, in accord with this essay, Aristotle believes that conscious contents can be predicted, and that such prediction requires knowledge both of the external stimulus field and the motivational state of the perceiver. In further accord, he sees laws about what will be perceived inextricably related to laws about responses.

This article will be primarily psychology. Within psychology its focus is on an egalitarian coordination of behaviorism and phenomenology. However, because some advocates of each have claimed an epistemological advantage for their approach, and have used this claim to deny the legitimacy of the other, I have inserted first an argument against such claims in general, an argument to the effect that firm foundations or anchors for knowledge are unavailable. In doing this I endorse a common denominator among a quite diverse set of critics of logical positivism and sense data phenomenalism, including Quine, Popper, Hanson, Toulmin, and Polanyi. There is no nonpresumptive knowledge. All knowledge claims go beyond their evidence, are highly presumptive and corrigible.

II. Anchorless Knowledge

Consider a scientist's theoretical curve superimposed upon a series of observational points, a relationship, that is, between a theory and the crucial data that confirm it. It is characteristic that in advance, no one of the points has been regarded as incorrigible. No one provides in itself an "operational definition" of theoretical parameters. Somehow, the agreement between theory and data has been stated, at the same time allowing each observation to be corrigible. If enough precision of observation is attained, *none* of the points exactly agrees with the theoretical value. Even if some observations seem to coincide exactly with the theoretical value, upon replications of the experiment, departures at this point would be expected, just as in the present data other points diverge.

An analogous point can be made from the history of science: a correction of one assumption is in fact made by tentatively assuming the truth of numerous other assumptions, each of which may in turn be similarly criticized. No single touchstone of certainty exists, the quasi-certainty employed in particular revisions is a collective "knowledge" based upon components *all* of which are corrigible, all of which may in time be replaced. As Neurath said, in science we are like sailors who must repair a rotting ship while it is afloat at sea. We depend on the relative soundness of all of the other planks while we replace a particularly weak one. Each of the planks we now depend on we will in turn have to replace. No one of them is a foundation, nor point of certainty, no one of them is incorrigible. Popper has a similar analogy, of building on piles driven into a bottomless bog. Even in a more analytic activity, such as geometry, it is clear historically that the stability lies in the collective bulk of the theorems, the supposedly "fundamental" axioms being continually subject to revision.

Consider the evidence from the eclipse of 1919, crucial for the acceptance of Einstein's theory of relativity. The evidence for the bending of the light from the stars as their beams passed close to the sun was dependent on a comparison of photographic plates of "the same" set of these and nearby stars prior to, during, and subsequent to the passage of the eclipsed sun near to the apparent position of these stars. Let us not examine in detail the presumptions involved in identifying the stars as the same on these three and other occasions—although this involves the challenged assumption that light travels in a straight line—and focus our inspection on the evidence showing that the rays of light passing near the sun were bent. The evidence is of the form that, on the eclipse-coincident photographs, the stars near the edge of the sun are nearer to the other more remote ones than they are on the prior and subsequent photographs. To interpret this greater proximity as evidence for the bending of the light rays requires that we assume the position of the stars fixed relative to one another: we know actually that this is not so in fine detail; only by assuming on inadequate evidence that we know the fine laws of their movement can we rule out such movement as explanation. We also assume a perfect lens system, or an exact duplication of beam-on-lens positions in subsequent photographs. Neither of these assumptions was true in detail, and a lens anomaly coincident with the tangent stars for the eclipse photograph is a possibility we eliminate only by presumption. The history of criticism on this point actually invokes lens distortion due to the heat of the sun's rays to explain part of the effect. We have to assume the effective absence of other temperature differences that, through expansion, would modify the internal dimensions of the optical system. A distortion such as found could be explained by a wrinkling of the negative, and photographic emulsions are never completely flat. Photochemical change in photographic emulsions can be triggered by stray cosmic rays as well as by starlight, and these might imitate a star. The evidence shown secondary observers (few enough of these there were, in fact) could have been faked. The measurements from the plates could have been biased. Even presuming all of these away, values of displacement of 1.61 seconds of arc and 1.98 seconds of arc were found, "confirming" the predicted value of 1.745 seconds of arc. (Subsequent "confirmations" have included values of 1.72 seconds of arc, 2.2 seconds of arc, and 2.0 seconds of arc.) More detailed examination would but enlarge the number of presumptions, without uncovering any one fulcrum of certainty against which to compare fallible measures. How science achieves practical "knowledge" without points of certainty, how validity is evaluated without "truth" to compare it with, is a puzzle not to be treated here (see Campbell, 1966), but somehow it is managed.

When we come to the knowledge products of vision, the situation is analogous. Vision, insofar as it has referents, insofar as it provides expectations or leads to presumptions about objects and events other than itself, has a comparable particulate corrigibility. As can be demonstrated with a reduction screen, the smaller the segment of the visual field, the more equivocality. The more external events and objects there are that could have generated the experience. From a physiological point of view, the fewer retinal cells involved, the more equivocality (not, however, to identify these with particulate sense data). When the whole visual field is involved (or when large numbers of retinal cells are involved), the equivocality is minimal and goes utterly unnoticed in ordinary visual perception; this practical unequivocality is not, however, due to any part being completely dependable. Unanchored knowledge, corrigible in all particulars, is again the rule. In linguistic epitomes of knowledge, the same principle holds: the smaller the fragment, the more equivocal the meaning. Somehow, with long continuities, relatively precise meanings are recorded and communicated, but this achievement is not to be attributed in any manner to the incorrigibility or unequivocality of its elements, be they words or sentences. As a statement of knowledge or a communicative act, an isolated letter is more equivocal than a syllable, a syllable than a word, a word than a sentence, a sentence than a paragraph, a paragraph than a chapter. Alternatively stated, a word is most equivocal in isolation, less so when imbedded in a paragraph. For a letter or a syllable, the same principle holds. Although the stages are not equal, a word is but an intermediate stage in a hierarchy of equivocalities, and no efforts at clarification nor improvement of definition will make it a firm foundation for knowing.

Words approach unequivocality when they are a part of a coherent context, each fragment of which is highly equivocal alone.

Quine has stated this well, if poetically:

> Taken collectively, science has its double dependence upon language and experience; but this duality is not significantly traceable into statements of science taken one by one. The idea of defining a symbol in use was an advance over the impossible term-by-term empiricism of Locke and Hume. The statement, rather than the term, came with Frege to be recognized as the unit accountable to an empiricist critique. But what I am now urging is that even in taking the statement as a unit we have drawn our grid too finely. The unit of empirical significance is the whole of science.
>
> The totality of our so-called knowledge or beliefs, from the most casual matters of geography and history to the profoundest laws of atomic physics or even of pure mathematics and logic, is a man-made fabric which impinges on experience only along the edges (Quine, 1953, p. 42).

III. Claims for the Incorrigibility of Phenomena

In the heyday of introspective psychology Wundt was able to gloat over the advantage that psychology as a science had over physics: the evidence of physics was mediated (*mittelbar*) and indirect, whereas the data of psychology were immediate, unmediated (*unmittelbar*). One would have thought that in making this claim, he aspired only to a psychology of W. H. Wundt. Not so. Somehow he spread this claim of immediateness to a generalized individual psychology descriptive of other and all persons (Mischel, in press). Wundt went further: when in his second career he became a folk psychologist, he extended this claim to a knowledge of group minds, as known through language.

It was against this set of claims by a futile and quarreling introspectionist psychology that the behaviorist slogan, "a psychology of the other one," appealed as a sensible willingness to share the "disadvantaged" position of physics and the other objective sciences. But the revolt against Wundt's position need not have been (and was not) solely in the direction of behaviorism. A "hypothetical phenomenology," a "phenomenology of the other one" was also possible, remaining a phenomenology in content, but dropping the epistemological claims to directness and incorrigibility. It is a theme of the present article that psychology today needs such a phenomenology and that it can be related via contingent laws to a similarly modest behaviorism. Whether or not we have such in Gestalt psychology and in modern phenomenology, I am not scholar enough to answer definitively, and no doubt an exhaustive survey would find inconsistencies on this point in each.

Gestalt psychology aspired to laws about phenomena holding for man in general. Almost immediately (e.g., Köhler, 1915) these laws were extended to animals, with methodological discussions making clear the mediate nature of such confirmations. That the knowledge of conscious contents was mediate is perhaps made explicit by the fact that for their human studies (as, to be sure, for Wundt too), the data reported in articles were primarily data from persons other than the author.

This corrigibility of the scientist's knowledge of the phenomenal contents of another is but one relevant corrigibility. It is perhaps most similar to the philosopher's problem of "other minds," but, treating the existence of such minds as a working hypothesis, goes further into hypothetical detail as to the phenomenal contents, and laws relating to these.

A second corrigibility issue deals with the validity of the knowledge claims phenomenally present for the perceiver. This is closer to the traditional epistemological issues of British philosophy, as raised in the argument from illusion. While there may be occasional denials of the usefulness of the concept of illusion in Gestalt writings, in the overall the Gestaltists' position seems clearly in favor of this corrigibility. Note their vehement rejection of the "constancy hypothesis" of which they accused the older introspectionists, that is, the assumption that external object and percept were identical. While the Gestaltists' principal activity was establishing laws relating external stimulus conditions and percepts, these laws were not statements of identity or isomorphism, but allowed for lawful qualitative differences. Thus in Wertheimer's (1912) founding study on apparent movement, two discrete environmental events, if similar in form and closely sequential, lawfully gave rise to a singular perceptual event of a moving object. Note also in Köhler's neglected contribution to epistemology, *The Place of Value in a World of Facts* (1938), his insistence on the distinction between thing-percepts and physical objects, his espousal (citing Lovejoy) of an epistemological dualism, and no doubt too of Lovejoy's critical realism. Note that Mandelbaum (1964) espouses a critical realism and acknowledges Köhler's influence, in close, if inexplicit, juxtaposition. The very willingness to posit an isomorphism between brain processes and experience speaks of this general orientation, and keynotes the difference between the Gestaltist phenomenology and that of the Husserl tradition (though of course the Gestaltists acknowledge Husserl's priority and influence on many points, and join him in the criticisms of the earlier contaminated introspectionism).

A third corrigibility issue deals with the agreement between independent scientists. Without making any epistemological claims in this direction, the Gestalt psychologists did criticize their introspectionist predecessors on this issue, deriding the school-determined contents of contaminated indoctrinated phenomenologies. In practice, they limited themselves to a few simple, dramatic phenomena, on which interexperimenter replicability was very high, phenomena striking enough to convince even those schooled to disbelieve them. We can probably treat phenomenological social psychologists such as Asch (1952) and MacLeod (1964, 1968) as essentially a part of the Gestalt tradition on these matters, although much less explicitly so. For current perceptual research, Natsoulas (1967) makes the basic points I am arguing in a thorough and brilliant review.

Is modern phenomenology, or that common denominator shared by, for example, Merleau-Ponty, Thévenaz, and my Northwestern colleagues William Earle and James Edie, also the corrigible phenomenology I seek? In conversations with Edie, I find him quick to deny charges of a solipsistic viewpoint in favor of a phenomenology achieving truths about all men. On the other hand, I find him and Earle dismissing as unnecessary, if not irrelevant, any efforts to relate the phenomenal world to nerves and brains and the physics of objects and light, since these latter are facts of a dependent epistemic character, inappropriate to the criticism of phenomena because known only indirectly by way of phenomena. This epistemic primacy of the phenomena-of-the-moment I can see as justified only for a solipsism-of-the-moment and lost when a phenomenology of persons-in-general is aspired to, or when memory is admitted. Certainly the phenomenal contents of other minds are known no more directly (though perhaps more sympathetically) than are physical objects in the perceptible range of sizes. They are certainly known with less phenomenal certainty.

Again, on the ground that there is no base from which to criticize the phenomenally given other than the phenomenally given, my friends tend to deny the meaningfulness of the concept of illusion. There is no "external" reality more real than the phenomenal reality, which is, after all, all that we can ever experience and the only reality for us. [Köhler's (1938) argument for transcendence, paradoxically based upon phenomenal grounds, seems to me to provide an appropriate reply.] Edie (1962, p.18), while denying that phenomenology is antiscientific, says: "What phenomenology does is to 'situate' science and to go beyond it in the direction of its experiential roots, its foundations which are to be found in a more original noetic contact with the real. Husserl showed that the world of science was not the world it has claimed to be but a derived construction, an abstraction several stages removed from the primary world of lived experience." This seems close to Wundt's epistemological gloating, even if in relation to a far

different, and more accurate, phenomenology. Moreover, Edie and Thévenaz (1962), among other phenomenologists, endorse the Cartesian approach of deriving epistemic certainty from phenomenal indubitability.

The case for Merleau-Ponty is complex. He continually calls for a phenomenology in contact with the rest of science, not a substitute for science.
He clearly aspires to a descriptive phenomenology true of others than
himself, and built in part upon the experiences of others with bodily pa-
thologies that Merleau-Ponty himself has not known. He is willing to talk
of brains as well as minds. He accepts the possibility of illusion, at least
when rejecting the "constancy hypothesis" and for phenomenal contents
referring to objects external to ourselves (Merleau-Ponty, 1962, pp. 7–8,
294–295). He cites the experimental work of the Gestaltists on men and
animals, favorably in the large part, as where he uses their data to criticize
third positions. He cites the same animal research by Lashley and Tolman
as I have used to argue the corrigibility of responses (Campbell, 1954,
1963); again, most of the citations are favorable (Merleau-Ponty, 1963).
But where he criticizes Köhler, Koffka, and Wertheimer, or Tolman and
Lashley, it is for not going far enough, or for their needless effort to tie
their psychology to the natural science explanatory system. As the title of
one essay indicates (Merleau-Ponty, 1964), he gives primacy to perception. And no doubt passages could be found that do claim an epistemological directness for the phenomenally given, parallel to the quotation from
Edie in the preceding paragraph.

As to modern phenomenology more generally, MacLeod (1964, 1968)
emphasizes the tradition of *Fremdverständnis,* going back to Scheler, accepts the legitimacy of hypotheses about the conscious experience of animals, and correspondingly accepts corrigibility. He emphasizes the technique of "bracketing" in the context of a critical phenomenology, critical
of unbracketed phenomenology. He recognizes that the bracketing, the
suspension of biases, is never complete (MacLeod, 1964, p. 52), and in so
doing avoids any claim of immediateness or incorrigibility even for brack-
eted experience.

IV. The Behaviorist Claims to Epistemic Priority

With equal sincerity, some philosophically inclined behaviorists have
from the beginning claimed epistemic priority over the phenomenalists
(e.g., Weiss, 1925). Even with the widening of behaviorist tolerance for
concepts such as perceptions and feelings, hypotheses about responses are

treated as more directly confirmed than are hypotheses about percepts (e.g., Brody & Oppenheim, 1966, 1967). Although I speak knowing that I will be unconvincing to a second generation of psychologists taught this as obvious, I want to deny just this. Behavior samples taken as evidence of habit strength (or other behavioristic constructs) are equivocal and corrigible indicators, which do not usefully function as definitions of theoretical constructs, and which are more equivocal as the behavior samples are shorter.

Note that, unlike Watson and Hull, Skinner (our currently dominant behaviorist) has given up definitions of response in terms of the body musculature of the animal. What his cumulative recorders tally are selective and partial symptoms of a joint organism–machine interaction—they are fully as much reports on the behavior of the machine as of the rat; they are acts and achievements, not movements. Note further that of all possible acts, Skinner has opportunistically selected a few (lever pressing with mechanically instrumented effects for rats; disk pecking for pigeons) that in practical fact are highly replicable and intersubjectively verifiable. These are very unrepresentative samples of behavior, and his practical success in their case no more establishes the epistemic certainty of all responses than does the parallel practical success in intersubjective verifiability of the basic Gestalt demonstrations referred to earlier.

As I have documented in more detail elsewhere (Campbell, 1954, 1963), when stimulus is defined as single sense-receptor activation, and response as muscle contraction, almost no stimulus-response consistencies are in fact found, particularly for higher animals. Just as any one retinal cell activation may be a part of a wide range of differently significant percepts, so too a given muscle contraction (or larger leg movement) can be a part of many different acts. These specifiable particles are inevitably equivocal. Their utility (or the utility of lever-press records) in regard to a learning theory is not as operational definitions of theoretical terms, but as corrigible but nonetheless useful confirmations of hypothesized entities and states, such as habits or meanings or perceptions, that are only indirectly confirmed and that are thus relegated to that limbo of uncertainty shared by the entities and processes of physics, chemistry, and astronomy.

As another illustration of the fundamental equivocality of responses, consider the assignment of diagnosing the habits, the stimulus-response regularities, of a rat trained at another laboratory. Advocates of operational definitions though they have been, in practice the behaviorists have evaded the problem of the operational definition of learning, or habit, by confusing specifications of input (i.e., training conditions) with a specification of product.

For the most part, habits have been studied only by observing their gradual development, and then only in the specific situation in which they have been learned. The learning theorist has rarely faced the problem of specifying what the habit was about, or what habits an animal has. He has been able to limit himself to a study of the degree of habitualization of a certain series of behaviors occurring within the artificial limits imposed by the apparatus and recording procedures. But the problem of the social scientist, the anthropologist, or the clinical psychologist is different; it is to diagnose the residues of experience in persons whose prior life history he has not observed and whose prior mazes he has not seen.

To parallel this problem, let us pose to a hypothetical animal psychologist the problem of diagnosing the habits of an aged and experienced rat shipped to him from another laboratory. What would happen? The process would be a hit-or-miss, random, trial-and-error procedure. The foreign rat under varying degrees of deprivation would be placed in all the likely pieces of apparatus available in the diagnostic laboratory. Knowledge that the rat shared some common culture, i.e., that it was a university-psychology rat, would make the selections of apparatus somewhat less random. The rat would be tried in a lever-pressing Skinner box, while buzzers buzzed and lights flashed, and any combinations that resulted in increased lever pressing would be taken as symptoms of some habit. The rat might be placed on a Lashley jumping stand while various colors and designs were placed in the card slots; and if jumping occurred, an effort would be made to find to which cue cards the jumping was most consistent. Multiple T and Y maze segments would be tried. The process would be one of random search, and the presence of a common culture merely serves to limit the range of things tried or to make certain guesses more probable. And no matter how clever the research, there would still be the possibility that important and highly routinized habits of the rat went unnoticed by the diagnostician.

The diagnostician makes the initial definition of stimuli and the initial classification of response. They represent classes of objects and behaviors which the experimenter can consistently discriminate, and which he guesses the animal might also. Once he finds some evidence of the stimulus-response consistency on the part of the rat, the experimenter would typically start varying stimuli and varying his classification of muscle movements in order to approximate more closely the appropriate *genus proximum* for the habit; that is, he would try and find out whether certain subtleties discriminable by him were also discriminable and being discriminated by the rat. Thus, if he found that the rat jumped to a yellow circle, he would start varying the shape and the color of the stimulus card to find which degree of yellow, if any, maximized the response, which shape maximized it, or whether shape made any difference. At the same time, he would strive to learn the appropriate classification of the consistency of response. Was it a consistency of muscle contraction, or a consistency of locomotor achievement, an object consistency, etc.? Gradually, by trial and error, the diagnostician would obtain a more specific and appropriately labeled stimulus-response correlation. The final classification, however, would still be in the scientist's terms, and would be limited to discriminations that the scientist could make. Occasionally in a search for the sources of consistent behavior in the animal, the scientist may have to add to his own natural senses. This seems to be the case in studies of homing behavior in bees, in which cues from the polarization of sunlight are utilized (von Frisch, 1950). A similar quandary might be observed were a scientist to be given a job of diagnosing the habits or stimulus-response consistencies on the part of Berkeley's (1951) mechanical squirrel,

which responds differently to lights impulsed by alternating and direct current. By mechanically adding to his discriminatory capacities, the scientist might find out toward what the machine is responding consistently via a trial-and-error process, with no solution guaranteed. Improving of the fit of the habit diagnosis is just as much trial-and-error process as was the initial hitting upon evidence of some stimulus-response correlation. By the same token, there is no guarantee that the habit would ever be diagnosed perfectly or even noticed at all.

Although the definition of stimulus and response are in the experimenter's language, there still is a verifiability to his diagnosis. This proof is the simple actuarial matter of a co-occurrence of stimuli and response at a great enough frequency to rise above the general "noise level." The experimenter can legitimately claim that he has located a stimulus-response consistency if certain actuarial standards are reached. What he cannot claim is that his is the optimal classification of the stimulus and response for maximum predictability. If, however, two experimenters differ in their diagnoses or in their classification of stimulus and response, the same actuarial approach can say which experimenter's classification scheme is the most efficient and, in this sense, the more nearly correct or implicitly closer to the "animal's own" definition of stimulus and response (Campbell, 1954).

There are some other technical problems that would be involved, and these potentially have epistemological implications too. Once the experimenter had achieved a definition of stimulus and response that seemed to maximize predictability for the rat, it would be necessary to cross-validate this on a new sample of the rat's behavior in which all stimulus conditions except those deemed relevant were varied; the same procedure would be used for response opportunities. As observed in test-construction work, the degree of fit achieved from repeatedly reanalyzing a limited bit of the animal's behavior would involve considerable capitalization on chance, and cross-validation would be necessary to demonstrate that an effective genus had been designated.

An equally important technical problem is that rats may acquire new habits during the testing for the old ones, or that old habits may be extinguished if learned stimuli are introduced without expected rewards. Thus, if the testing procedure is very long and the habits weak, it would soon become impossible to distinguish between newly acquired habits and the residues of the original experience. Methodologically, the cleanest approach would be to have the training school supply a large number of rats with equivalent experience, so that the habits diagnosed on one rat could be cross-validated on other rats who were uncontaminated by the residues of the experience from the inappropriate diagnostic efforts. While far-fetched, this seems to suggest a legitimate precaution in anthropological studies, i.e., that a group of the best potential informants be set aside, not to be interviewed or observed until the anthropologist has learned the culture in first approximation.

Note a general limitation on this process: the diagnosis of the rat's behavior is only possible in so far as the rat and the scientist to some extent overlap in their classifications of the environment into things. Were the rat indeed to be responding to constellations of molecules or atoms sharing no boundaries with the constellations the scientist was able to discriminate, the diagnosis of the rat's habits would be impossible (Campbell, 1963, pp. 101–104).

In an expanded treatment of the problem, it would probably be possible to parallel for behavioral analysis the three corrigibilities described for phenomena. The diagnostic parable just given parallels the first. The earlier

comments on intersubjective verifiability parallel the third. The second corrigibility would translate to the fit of the rat's running pattern, or cognitive map, to the maze itself. In this setting, of course, no learning theorist has implied incorrigibility; "errors" are freely attributed, even to a well-trained rat.

The behaviorist should not, in fact, feel that he is renouncing a fundamental claim in acknowledging the corrigibility of responses as an epistemic base. The sophisticated behaviorists of the first generation were content to join physics in making do with a mediate, indirect epistemic base. They were not attempting to replace the introspectionist's claim for incorrigibility with another incorrigibility claim, but instead were recognizing that psychology as a generalizing science had to renounce such claims altogether. This is brilliantly expressed even in the title of Max Meyer's (1921) *Psychology of the Other One*. What led to the abandonment of that early sophistication was definitional operationalism, a particularly misguided offshoot of positivism. If there are operations that exhaustively define terms in a theory, then a kind of incorrigibility is claimed. This, on the one hand, denies the practical fact of imperfection (including both systematic and random errors) of every actual measurement process (Campbell & Fiske, 1959; Webb, Campbell, Schwartz, & Secrest, 1966; Campbell, 1966, in press). On the other hand, it reverts to a kind of pure phenomenalism in which every perception and every operation defines a separate construct.

I have not covered here the full details of the debates still raging between behaviorism and phenomenological psychology. I can but refer you to such samples as the collection by Wann (1964) and the recent interchange in the *Psychological Review* among Brody and Oppenheim (1966, 1967), Zaner (1967), and Henle and Baltimore (1967). My position is however, simple and clear. I agree with each side when it is criticizing the claims to epistemic superiority of the other. I agree with each side when claiming psychology's need for its type of data, if these claims are divested of epistemic primacy. For it is our existential predicament to have to depend in both personal action and science upon anchorless knowledge, to have to build without firm foundations. Direct knowing, nonpresumptive knowing, is not to be our lot.

V. Phenomenal Absolutism

Critical phenomenology should go beyond establishing the possible and occasional occurrence of illusion, and should hypothesize general laws re-

garding the misleadingness of the phenomenally given. The term *phenomenal absolutism* has been chosen (Segall, Campbell, & Herskovits, 1966; Campbell, 1967) in an effort to designate one such general principle. Köhler (1938) and others have described the phenomenal objectivity of the phenomenally given. Experience is, in general, not at all phenomenally subjective or personal. Experience instead commits us immediately to a belief in a world accessible to all others, available for them to see exactly as we see it. It is one aspect of this phenomenal objectivity of the phenomenally given that I wish to designate: experience bears no phenomenal testimony (in general) to its own corrigibility, nor to the equivocality of its informational base (e.g., physical and neurological), nor to the implicit decision rules invoked in resolving the equivocality. Experience is naively realistic. Whereas the informational base is inevitably indirect, relativistic, and presumptive, the phenomenally presented appears as absolutely known, as directly known.

Consider a classic experiment by Duncker (1929) on induced movement. In a darkened laboratory are a luminous dot and a large luminous frame. Each are on tracks and can be moved. The experimenter moves the frame to the left, leaving the dot untouched. With phenomenal certainty every observer sees the dot move to the right, with the frame remaining stationary. The essential information used by the visual system has been the relative motion of dot and frame. Some prephenomenal neurological routing, constituting an implicit decision rule, has resolved the equivocality of the relative movement into one absolute fixity, one absolute movement. The decision rule seems to be that, in case of doubt, it is the largest bulk of the visual environment that has remained stationary, the smaller fragment that has moved. Considering a mechanism evolved in predatory fish swimming in currents they had no way of independently estimating, this seems a very reasonable rule: it is the rocks, sand, and coral that have remained still, the little prey that has moved. Or consider ancestral man running after a rabbit: it is the rabbit that has moved, not the ground and the trees. Evolutionarily and ecologically speaking, it is a very good rule on the statistical average, and this goodness might even lead to a kind of pragmatic acceptance of a Cartesian trust in what was phenomenally indubitable (Campbell, in press). But the phenomenal directness, the phenomenal nonmediateness, is misleading. The informational process involves presumptions not in fact verifiable without other presumptions, and presumptions that are occasionally wrong. The presumption and decision rules are nonphenomenal, or prephenomenal in terms of the isomorphism to be discussed below.

A common thread in the skeptical tradition in philosophy can be seen as offering this descriptive contribution to a critical phenomenology. Plato's allegory of the cave asserts that in fact vision is based upon presumptive interpretation of shadows, but that the perceiver does not recognize this, and mistakenly believes he sees directly. Locke and Berkeley tell us that although we phenomenally experience hot and cold as directly known attributes of the water, in fact the experience is contributed to equally by the prior temperature of the hand; that our perceptual system is turning a relative contrast into an absolute objective fact, and occasionally misleadingly so when the presumptive base is in error.

VI. Unifying Phenomenology and Behaviorism

In the final two sections of this paper, I want to present briefly a program for unifying a corrigible hypothetical behaviorism with a similarly modest phenomenology. For the purposes of this exposition I will employ a Hullian behaviorism (Hull, 1952; Spence, 1956), although I regard it as outmoded and to be replaced by a purposive (Tolman, 1932) or cybernetic behaviorism (Miller, Galanter, & Pribram, 1960; Campbell, 1956, 1963) that, however, will undoubtedly retain the specific laws that will be used here. For the phenomenological psychology, I will employ Asch (1952), Sherif (1936; Sherif & Sherif, 1956), or Krech and Crutchfield (1948), choosing social psychologists because they deal more than the classical Gestaltists with the products of past experience. Kurt Lewin (1935, 1936) would also serve, although he did not intend his constructs to be literally phenomenological, in spite of using that vocabulary. The perceptual period of Bruner (1951) and Postman (1951, 1953) would also serve, with the same qualifier. Many others could be cited (Campbell, 1963). My goal is the more complete psychology, indicated in the bottom line of Table I as a wedding of Asch and Hull, or using Asch to fill the phenomenological gap in Hull.

Brain states play a minor role in each, but can be conceptually helpful in the unification. Hull and other learning theorists pay little attention to brain processes, but probably would agree that they provide an always present part of the material base of habits, drives, and so on. For the social phenomenologist, the relation of brain states to conscious experience is not focal, but is accepted from the classic Gestalt point of view. In terms of Euler diagrams, the relation of brain to responses is as in Fig. 1a. Not all brain processes result in behavior, but all coordinated behavior involves "corresponding" brain processes. The relation of brain processes to conscious experience is as shown in Fig. 1b. The Gestalt postulate of iso-

TABLE I
COMMON COMPONENTS OF THEORETICAL SYSTEMS

System	Present physical objects and events, stimuli	Past history of events, actions, and outcomes	Present internal stimulation, drive, drive stimuli	Central nervous system activities, brain processes and states	Phenomena, perception	Actions, responses, locomotion, behavior
A. Skinnerian behaviorism	X	X				X
B. Hullian behaviorism	X	X	X	X		X
C. Classical gestalt psychology	X			X	X	
D. Phenomenological social psychology (Asch)					X	X
E. Combination of Hull and Asch (B and D)	X	X	X	X	X	X

morphism states that for every differentiation and detail in experience, there is a "corresponding" differentiation in brain processes, but not that every brain process has a corresponding experience. The hypothetical descriptive claim of the position here advocated is shown in Fig. 1c; that is, that there are common brain states isomorphic to both experience and behavior. As drawn in Fig. 1c, this is not a complete overlap. Some stimulus-response relationships are executed without conscious concomitants. Some conscious experiences do not have behavioral counterparts. The claim is thus not as strong as that implied in the phrases "isomorphism of experience and action" (Asch, 1952, p. 159), "unity of preception and action" (Murphy, 1947, p. 354), or "unity of experience and behavior" (Sherif & Sherif, 1956, p. 72), but the same point is being made. My way of understanding the nonoverlapping areas would legitimize using an experiential terminology in dealing with behavioral coordinations of which one was unaware, for example, to speak of unconscious perceptions, as a Freudian might.

We are thus looking for the conscious-experience correlates of lawful stimulus-response relationships. While Table I and Fig. 1 may have made this seem reasonable at the programmatic level, there are two very difficult

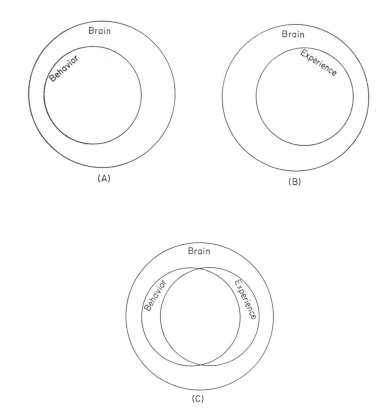

FIG. 1. Overlap between brain process, behavior, and conscious experience.

conceptual hurdles that have prevented the unification from spontaneously emerging. The first hurdle is the "orientation" of conscious experience in the central nervous system; the second is the "location" ("downstream" or "upstream") of conscious experience. Efforts to convey these problems have led me to the monstrosity shown in Fig. 2. (I am indebted to Richard A. Swanson for the artwork of Fig. 2.)

There is a bias in conscious experience toward the sensory or perceptual. George Herbert Mead (1934, p. 42) stated it thus in the course of criticizing Wundt: "The required parallelism is not in fact complete on the psychical side, since only the sensory and not the motor phase of the physiological process of experience has a psychic correlate." Social scientists have for years been trying to diagnose behavioral dispositions by way of the phenomenological interview. Suppose we take students who have just collaborated in a human conditioning study, and ask them afterward, "Well, what

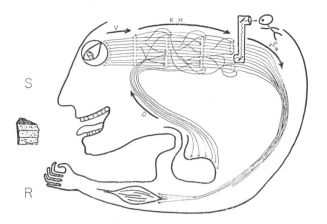

Fig. 2. Conscious experience conceived as a periscope lowered into the central nervous system. V, stimulus intensity; K, incentive; H, habitualization or familiarity; D, drive; $_sE_R$, likelihood of response or response strength.

have you learned?" Were these reports to be in stimulus-response terms, there would be no problem. Were the students to say, "When light A flashes I lift my right finger" there would be an automatic relating of experience to action, for there would be phenomenological contents (verbally reported) explicitly referring to responding. Instead, such contents are generally missing. The answer is predominantly in terms of the perceived nature of the apparatus—reports on which feature shock, which ones reward, which signal which, and so on. The conscious-experience counterparts of approach and avoidance are the phenomenally objective goodness and badness of parts of the apparatus; phenomenally, one has learned about the nature of the world, not about one's own response tendencies.

Cortical stimulation of the brain, as by Penfield and Rasmussen (1950), also documents this bias. Where cortical stimulation elicits conscious experience, it is at least 98% of the time of a sensory or perceptual sort. (The 2% of exceptions were a few experiences of "intent to move.") Stimulation of motor projection areas produces muscle movements without concomitant awareness (although there is a subsequent peripherally referred sensory feedback, e.g., "I felt my toe move"). In focal epileptics Penfield and Rasmussen have been able to elicit coordinated motor movements analogous to the first part of an epileptic seizure. For these, the conscious-experience concomitant has been a hallucinated environmental event (e.g., a hallucination of being attacked), with the motor concomitants being "appropriate" but unselfconscious (e.g., defensive arm movements).

This bias corresponds to the phenomenal objectivity of experience discussed in Section V. One of the most awkward features of Fig. 2 is the result of an effort to represent this. In that diagram, an epiphenomenal point of view is both utilized and ridiculed by way of the little homunculus-self who somehow eavesdrops on the neural information flow. A wiretap analogy would have been less ludicrous: a higher brain center monitors, via induction coils, the messages going on in the operating trunk lines. But a telephone wiretap picks up messages going in either direction, it "faces both ways," whereas the nerves of the brain conduct messages only in one direction. And in spite of many feedback loops, the preponderant direction is from sensory input to motor output. (The strong directional arrows in the diagram are meant to remind one of this.) Thus wherever in the neural flow conscious experience taps in, it gets a message coming from the sensory or perceptual direction. It is to illustrate this point that the periscope faces upstream; any messages it gets come in a perceptual or pseudoperceptual guise.

An equally important issue is the "location" of conscious experience in the central nervous system, in particular, whether or not it lies prior to (upstream of), or subsequent to (downstream of), the association areas and the motivational input. The answer has been anticipated in Table I in placing the column for perception toward the right. It is dramatized by the location of the periscope downstream in Fig. 2. As Gardner Murphy (1947, p. 333) says: "We do not really see with our eyes or hear with our ears. If we all saw with our eyes, we would see pretty much alike; we should differ only so far as retinal structure, eyeball structure, etc., differ. We differ much more widely than this because we see not only with our eyes, but also with our midbrain, our visual and associative centers, and with our systems of incipient behavior, to which almost all visual perceiving leads."

One would think that this would be a matter of indifference to the behavioristic experimental psychologist—that he would be agnostic regarding conscious experience, would have no stake in where the periscope was lowered. Or that if he were to take a stand, he would emphasize the contribution of learning to perception, endorsing the old distinction between sensation and perception, in which the latter involves learned meanings and expectations, and would hence agree with the downstream location. Unfortunately, this is not so, as I have discovered in trying to convince experimentalists that people with different environments and life histories *should* see differently (Segall *et al.,* 1966). Many behaviorist experimental psychologists are crypto-phenomenologists and with the wrong phenomenology. They are direct realists, phenomenal absolutists, phenomenologists of a periscope upstream of the association and motivational areas. Gestaltists such as Asch (1952, pp. 64–65) make an analogous error when they identify the perceived object with the behaviorist's stimulus and then scold behaviorists for not recognizing that the stimulus may be quite different for two persons who are in "the same" laboratory setup. From the point of view here advocated, "perceived object" is closer to the behaviorist's concept of response disposition $_sE_R$ than to his concept of stimulus.

Let us consider a simplified version of Hull's theory, which can be stated as follows.

$_sE_R$	$=$	V	$\times$	D	$\times$	K	$\times$	H
Likelihood of response, response strength (likelihood of perception of the stimulus)		Stimulus intensity		Drive		Incentive, value		Habitualization, familiarity

Intrapsychic determinants (bracket spanning Drive, Incentive value, Habitualization familiarity)

Stimulus and response are not explicit in this formula except as subscripts. To make them explicit, and to organize them analogously to the information flow of Fig. 2, the formula could be written thus:

$$S \rightarrow V \rightarrow D \times K \times H \rightarrow {}_sE_R \rightarrow R.$$

Where in this formula should a (P) for phenomena, conscious experience, or perception be entered? Certainly not as a substitute for V. Since memory, value, expectancy, and momentary drive influence perception, the (P) must come after the $D \times K \times H$, as in this epiphenomenal version:

$$S \rightarrow V \rightarrow D \times K \times H \overset{\nearrow (P)}{\rightarrow} {}_sE_R \rightarrow R.$$

Or this direct-line alternative:

$$S \rightarrow V \rightarrow D \times K \times H \rightarrow (P) \rightarrow {}_sE_R \rightarrow R.$$

(P) is more nearly a concomitant of $_sE_R$ than of S or V.

VII. A Behavioral-Phenomenal Analysis of Aristotle's Lover and Coward

It is my sincere belief that the straightforward application of a standard aspect of Hull's theory predicts the details of Aristotle's examples. This aspect is the effect of increased drive and incentive in elevating the generalization gradient.

Let us take for illustration the study by Thomas and King (1959) in which pigeons learn to peck a translucent disk illuminated by one hue (550 mμ) to release occasional grains of food, and are then offered the opportunity to peck novel hues of differing degrees of dissimilarity (e.g., hues of 490, 500, 510, 520, 530, and 540 mμ). Their rates of pecking show an ogival form, with 540 mμ receiving almost as many pecks as does the correct 550 mμ, and with disk 490 mμ receiving few if any. (In these generalization tests, as in original training, only one disk is present at any one time.) The results can be plotted as a generalization gradient, and this has been done as the lower curved line of the left face of Fig. 3. When the birds are starved longer before the generalization test, the gradient is elevated, keeping the same general ogival shape, but with more responses occurring at each level.

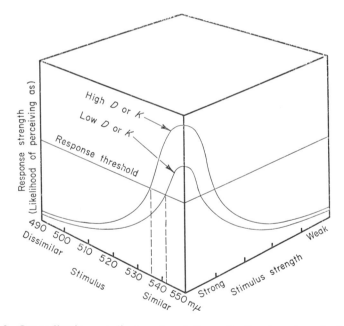

FIG. 3. Generalization gradient and relation of stimulus strength to response strength for two levels of motivation.

This is a plot of the relationship between response strength, drive level, and stimulus *similarity*. A similar function relates response strength, drive level, and stimulus *strength*. This has been shown in many other studies, and could have been introduced in the Thomas and King study by illuminating the disks more strongly or faintly with the 550-mμ hue. This relationship is shown in the right-hand face of the three-dimensional graph of Fig. 3. The stronger the stimulus, the stronger the response; but under high drive conditions, all stimuli produce more responding.

The response measure, number of pecks in a given time period, operates more or less as a continuous variable, as did the salivation of Pavlov's dogs. In other cases the response would be all or none, and the continuous measure would be a probability of occurrence. In some cases, the concept of a response threshold would be appropriate, the response occurring if the underlying response disposition $_sE_R$ got above that threshold. The threshold concept makes graphically clearer the implications present under all conditions, and so will be employed. Parallel to the base line in Fig. 3 has been drawn a response threshold.

While the graph has been designed for responding, I argue that it can be used also for perceiving, reading on the vertical axis "likelihood of perceiving," "likelihood of noticing," and so on. Several lines of argument are available in addition to those we have already used. All perceptions by others must be measured via responses (including the verbal responses employed in reports on perceptions). For these responses, the same response laws hold. But more presumptively, I would like to allege that the law also holds for experience as experienced, that the threshold relation for disposition to perceive is homologous: the stronger the disposition, the more likely the perception. But what is it that is being perceived? The generalization gradient is a gradient of confusing a dissimilar stimulus for the focal and relevant one with regard to which the learned response is "valid," or "appropriate." Making this response to other, different stimuli is to respond to them "as though" they were the other.

Basic to the translation here attempted is this equation of "responds to as though to" with "perceives as." The identity of an equals sign is too strong here, for in both behaviorism and phenomenological psychology similar actions will often be made as a part of dissimilar dispositions, or to dissimilarly perceived objects. The relationship in the other direction is, however, stronger. Every instance of the same "perceives as" will have the same "responds to as though to":

> *"Perceives as"* entails *"Responds to as though to";*
> *"Responds to as though to"* does not entail *"Perceives as."*

This calls attention to a fundamental equivocality in diagnosing perceptions from responses. This equivocality should of course be accepted, but it should also be recognized that it is the same sort of equivocality that is involved in all relationships of theory to data (Popper, 1959, 1963). This is the sort of problem to which behaviorists often point when claiming epistemic priority for responses—but they can only claim such priority for an utterly untheoretical ungeneralizing enumeration of past responses. As has been so ponderously demonstrated earlier (Section IV) in the parable of the rat whose habits must be diagnosed at another laboratory, the relationship between habit and response is also of this nature:

$$Habit \text{ entails } Response \quad \text{but}$$
$$Response \text{ does not entail } Habit$$

and

$$_sE_R \text{ entails } R \quad \text{but}$$
$$R \text{ does not entail } _sE_R$$

So also is the relationship of data and theory:

$$Theory \text{ entails } Data, \quad \text{but}$$
$$Data \text{ do not entail } Theory$$

In spite of this nonentailment, we somehow use data to establish a science of theory. The nonentailment is Hume's scandal of induction. The mode of science, as Popper has perhaps best described, is to use the theory-to-data entailment to corroborate or falsify guesses as to theory. It can never prove or confirm them. A theoretical behaviorism and a theoretical phenomenology are in this same boat with the rest of science.

Returning to Fig. 3, on its left face is reported the gradient of likelihood of responding to a given stimulus hue as though it were 550 mμ. Translated, this is the likelihood of perceiving a given hue as though it were the rewarding 550 mμ. Thus our phenomenological translation is not to a gradient of likelihood of recognizing each hue as itself, but rather to the likelihood of mistaking a given hue for the rewarding 550 mμ. Translated "mistakenly responding to" becomes "mistakenly perceiving as." For the pigeon, we have no phenomenological interviews to augment our analysis. Aristotle's examples will help.

Let us reidentify the parameters of the graph for Aristotle's lover. For 550 mμ substitute the lover's one true beloved. For 540 mμ, 530 mμ, and so on, substitute other persons, quite similar at 540 mμ, decreasingly similar for 530 mμ, 520 mμ, and so forth. Aristotle and the lover are walking together, approaching the crowded agora, where the lover expects to find his beloved. Among the crowd are these somewhat similar persons. Aristotle observes his companion's behavior. The lover starts to run off in a given direction: "I think I see her," he says. Aristotle's evidence is "responded to as though to," which he equates to "perceived as." With regard to Fig. 3, Aristotle would agree that the more similarity, the more likely the lover "will think he sees the object of his desire." But more important and less obvious is the fact that "the more excited by the given emotion, as the amorous person by amorous desire, the less similarity is required to give rise to the illusory impression." This is Aristotle's version of the law: the higher the drive level, the higher the generalization gradient.

The occurrence of the perception "my beloved" is a joint product of stimulus similarity to the beloved *and* drive level. Focusing on the perception threshold (response threshold) feature of the diagram, we can note that, indeed, under the high drive condition less similarity is needed to give rise to the mistaken perception (i.e., the mistaken response). Aristotle has made a subtle contribution to a predictive, hypothetical, critical phenomenology, and I know of no other theory in modern psychology that would represent this insight as elegantly as does Hull's, although the motivational perception school of Bruner (1951) and Postman (1951, 1953) also clearly predict it.

The right-hand face of the graph is added to make especially clear another feature of this principle, found both in Hull and in Bruner and Postman. The influence of greater motivation is not solely in the direction of autistic wishful self-deception. It also adds a veridical selective awareness. Were the amorous person's beloved to be half hidden somewhere off in the crowd, the more excited he were by amorous desire, the more certain he would be to notice her (i.e., to perceive her, to respond to her). This feature is also present in the left face of the graph. At some high degree of similarity, similarity becomes identity, and for that point or narrow band on the stimulus dimension, perceiving (responding to as though to) is "correct." For this point, the higher the drive level, the more probable is this correct response or correct perception. Adding the right face of the curve makes more explicit another law in the basic Hullian formula: the stronger the V (or S), the stronger the response disposition $_sE_R$ (or R). It also corresponds to Bruner and Postman's research technique of comparing perceptual accuracy to weak stimuli (e.g., 1/100th of a second exposure time and stronger stimuli (e.g., 1/20 or 1/10 of a second exposures). Bruner and Postman ended up with separately stated laws, depending on whether relevant or irrelevant (identical or dissimilar) stimuli were being presented. The law of *perceptual sensitization* states that the stronger the motivation, the more accurate the perception of the motive-relevant stimulus when that stimulus is actually present. The law of *value resonant errors* states that the stronger the motivation, the more apt one is to mistakenly believe the motive-relevant stimulus is present when it actually is not. It is the elegance of the Hullian graph to make these two laws simple coaspects of the one principle. This also accords with a contentious research literature, which has finally decided that perceptual sensitization is a matter of increased responsiveness rather than of increased discriminatory refinement (Dinsmoor, 1952; Zeitlin, 1954; Goldiamond, 1958a, b; Campbell, 1963). For Dinsmoor and Goldiamond, this makes the sensitization nonperceptual. With this I strongly disagree, and argue instead that it shows perception to be "downstream," influenced by meaning, lust, and past experience.

In the Hullian tradition, pigeons differing in degree of starvation differ in "Drive." In Aristotle's lover, the emotion is probably a mixture of deprivation period (D), hormone level (D), and memory of the rewardingness of the beloved (K) that generates anticipations of future reward (K). In the monster diagram of Fig. 2, we have represented D by drive stimuli, that is, sense receptors that monitor the state of bodily organs, blood sugar level, and so on. This is not the only physical mechanism by which bodily need states, hormonal conditions, and so forth get represented in brain processes. Some hormones are transmitted by the bloodstream to the brain, where they selectively modify nerve-to-nerve conductivity. One way or the other, drives affect brain processes, and there is no good reason at all to assign such effect to a postphenomenal place in the neural stream. As a memory and expectancy factor, K is represented in the neural association areas, as is H, the habitualization of a given response to a given stimulus.

Many psychological findings fit this diagram. Consider the baby bird, which instinctively pecks at a red spot on a parent's beak to initiate a regurgitation of food from the mother's crop into the baby's gullet. Research has been done on how crude an imitation of the mother's beak will elicit this pecking response. One finding is, appropriately, that the more similar to the real head and beak, the more pecking. It is also found, as Aristotle and Hull would predict, that the hungrier the baby bird, the less similar the imitation can be and still elicit the response. But, the cryptophenomenological behaviorist will ask in this case (and in that of the pigeons), is it not instead the case that the baby bird recognizes that it is probably not his mother, but feels so hungry that he does not want to take a chance on missing food? Is he not behaving just as a rational mathematical decision theorist would advise? This is, of course, an empirical question we are not likely to settle with animals to whom we cannot give a phenomenological interview. It may be that their periscopes are not as far downstream as are those of Aristotle's lover and coward. But the stubborn certainty I find in my experimental psychologist friends on this point bespeaks not only a naive realism, not only a crypto-phenomenology (for they end up being just as certain as I about the baby bird's conscious experience), but also a mentalistic dualism. They forget that thinking, decision making, or rational inference is carried by brain tissue fully as much as are automatic reactions. They tend to think of them instead as purely mental. They argue as though all the decision making took place after an accurate mental image had been projected upon a television screen in the brain, observed, and decided upon by an unmaterialized ego. They forget that if the model of rational decision making is an accurate representation of a survival-relevant relationship to the environment, biological evolution is apt to have hit upon and retained approximations to such decision rules in the very structure of the brain, and from an anatomical point of view there is no reason why these processes should not be located in the pre-phenomenal parts of the brain (as they obviously are in the Duncker movement illusion discussed earlier).

Aristotle's coward represents an avoidant disposition to a noxious stimulus. For both Hull and the motivational-perception tradition, there are parallel equivocalities. High past pain (producing high current acquired drive or negative K) can be associated with response inhibition for a punished response. This is the behavioral equivalent of *perceptual defense,* a tendency to inhibit the perception of a noxious stimulus. But if there is a useful avoidant or escape response, then higher past pain, higher fear, leads to stronger response strength, that is, a greater tendency to perceive the noxious stimulus if it is actually present (*perceptual vigilance*), and a greater tendency to misperceive similar neutral stimuli as the noxious one. Aristotle's coward illustrates the latter case. Aristotle's coward, and Hull's diagram, admirably display the basic emergent principle in a contradictory research literature on anti-Semitism and ability to recognize Jews in photographs. When photographs of Jews and non-Jews are mixed, and persons low and high in anti-Semitism are asked to guess which are which, and when accuracy is scored in terms of the miscalls of both Jewish and non-Jewish photographs, the initial studies (and occasional subsequent ones) find anti-Semites more accurate, while other studies find just the reverse or no difference (Allport & Kramer, 1946; Carter, 1948; Lindzey & Rogolsky, 1950; Scodel & Austrin, 1957; Himmelfarb, 1966). But in all studies, a consistent finding has emerged: anti-Semites judge more pictures to be Jewish, both Jewish pictures and non-Jewish ones. They are thus like the highly fearful version of Aristotle's coward. Also in accordance with the diagram, Jewish photographs are more often judged Jewish by both groups than are non-Jewish ones.

VIII. Summary

Neither behaviorism nor phenomenology have any justified claims to epistemic priority. Both psychologies, like science in general, must do without anchors or firm foundations at any point. All knowing is highly presumptive, involving presumptions not directly or logically justifiable. If we forget this for ordinary visual perception, it is because the well-tested presumptions built into the nervous system are not phenomenally represented.

Psychology needs a "phenomenology of the other one," corrigible, hypothetical, and critical. Such a psychology would have laws predicting the conscious contents of others, including laws of illusions. Such a phenomenology would occupy a status no more indirect, no more presumptive, no more difficult of verification, than a law-giving behaviorism. In addition, it should be unifiable with such a behaviorism once certain stubborn and wrong predilections for the mode of unification are overcome. Overcoming these is abetted by recognizing that by the very nature of the predominant direction of neural information flow from sensory to motor, conscious experience is sensory and perceptual in its contents, even when it is isomorphic to meaningful response. Still more important is recognizing that meaningful conscious experience is isomorphic to the neural brain stream posterior to the areas of memory, association, and motivational input.

As an illustration of such a phenomenology, Aristotle's observations on the perceptual distortions of lover and coward, under high and low states of motivation, are mapped into Hull's behavioristic law of the effect of drive in elevating the generalization gradient.

REFERENCES

Allport, G. W., & Kramer, B. M. Some roots of prejudice. *Journal of Psychology,* 1946, **22,** 9–39.

Aristotle. *On dreams. In The Oxford Translation of Aristotle,* vol. III, pp. 458–462, 1908–52. Edited by W. D. Ross. Reprinted by permission of the Clarendon Press, Oxford.

Asch, S. E. *Social psychology.* Englewood Cliffs, N. J.: Prentice-Hall, 1952.

Berkeley, E. C. Light sensitive electronic beast. *Radio Electronics,* 1951, **23**(3), 46–48.

Brody, N., & Oppenheim, P. Tensions in psychology between the methods of behaviorism and phenomenology. *Psychological Review,* 1966, **73,** 295–305.

Brody, N., & Oppenheim, P. Methodological differences between behaviorism and phenomenology in psychology. *Psychological Review,* 1967, **74,** 330–334.

Bruner, J. S. Personality dynamics and the process of perceiving. In R. R. Blake & G. V. Ramsey (Eds.), *Perception: an approach to personality.* New York: Ronald Press, 1951. Pp. 121–147.

Campbell, D. T. Operational delineation of "what is learned" via the transposition experiment. *Psychological Review,* 1954, **61**(3), 167–174.

Campbell, D. T. Perception as substitute trial and error. *Psychological Review,* 1956, **63**(5), 330–342.

Campbell, D. T. Social attitudes and other acquired behavioral dispositions. In S. Koch (Ed.), *Psychology: a study of a science.* Vol. 6. *Investigations of man as socius.* New York: McGraw-Hill, 1963. Pp. 94–172.

Campbell, D. T. Pattern matching as an essential in distal knowing. In K. R. Hammond (Ed.), *Egon Brunswik's psychology.* New York: Holt, Rinehart & Winston, 1966. Pp. 81–106.

Campbell, D. T. Stereotypes and the perception of group differences. *American Psychologist,* 1967, **22**(10), 812–829.

Campbell, D. T. Evolutionary epistemology. In P. A. Schilpp (Ed.), *The philosophy of Karl R. Popper. The library of living philosophers.* LaSalle, Ill.: Open Court Publ. Co. (Volume in preparation; copies of this chapter available since August, 1966.)

Campbell, D. T., & Fiske, D. W. Convergent and discriminant validation by the multitrait-multimethod matrix. *Psychological Bulletin,* 1959, **56**, 81–105.

Carter, L. F. The identification of "racial" membership. *Journal of Abnormal and Social Psychology,* 1948, **43**, 279–286.

Dinsmoor, J. A. The effect of hunger on discriminated responding. *Journal of Abnormal and Social Psychology,* 1952, **47**, 67–72.

Duncker, K. Über induzierte Bewegung. Ein Beitrag zur Theorie optisch wahrgenommener Bewegung. *Psychologische Forschung,* 1929, **12**(6), 180–259.

Edie, J. M. Introduction, in Thévenaz, P. *What is phenomenology.* Chicago: Quadrangle, 1962. Pp. 13–36.

Goldiamond, I. Indicators of perception: I. Subliminal perception, subception, unconscious perception: an analysis in terms of psycho-physical indicator methodology. *Psychological Bulletin,* 1958, **55**, 373–411. (a)

Goldiamond, I. Vexierversuch: The log relationship between word frequency and recognition obtained in the absence of stimulus words. *Journal of Experimental Psychology,* 1958, **56**, 457–463. (b)

Henle, M., & Baltimore, G. Portraits in straw. *Psychological Review,* 1967, **74**, 325–329.

Himmelfarb, S. Studies in the perception of ethnic group members: I. Accuracy, response bias, and anti-Semitism. *Journal of Personality and Social Psychology,* 1966, **4**, 347–355.

Hull, C. L. *A behavior system: An introduction to behavior theory concerning the individual organism.* New Haven, Conn.: Yale Univer. Press, 1952.

Köhler, W. Optische Untersuchungen am Schimphansen und am Haushuhn. *Berliner Abhandlungen,* 1915.

Köhler, W. *The place of value in a world of facts.* New York: Liveright, 1938.

Krech, D., & Crutchfield, R. S. *Theory and problems of social psychology.* New York: McGraw-Hill, 1948.

Lewin, K. *A dynamic theory of personality.* New York: McGraw-Hill, 1935.

Lewin, K. *Principles of topological psychology.* New York: McGraw-Hill, 1936.

Lindzey, G., & Rogolsky, S. Prejudice and identification of minority group membership. *Journal of Abnormal and Social Psychology,* 1950, **45,** 37–53.

MacLeod, R. B. Phenomenology—a challenge to experimental psychology. In
T. W. Wann (Ed.), *Behaviorism and phenomenology: Contrasting bases for
modern psychology.* Chicago: Univer. of Chicago Press, 1964.

MacLeod, R. B. Phenomenology and cross-cultural research. In M. Sherif and C.
Sherif (Eds.), *Problems of interdisciplinary relationships in the social sciences.*
Chicago: Aldine, 1968.

Mandelbaum, M. *Philosophy, science, and sense perception.* Baltimore, Md.: Johns
Hopkins Press, 1964.

Mead, G. H. *Mind, self and society.* Chicago: Univer. of Chicago Press, 1934.

Merleau-Ponty, M. *Phenomenology of perception.* London: Routledge & Kegan
Paul, 1962.

Merleau-Ponty, M. *The structure of behavior.* Boston: Beacon Press, 1963.

Merleau-Ponty, M. *The primacy of perception.* Evanston, Ill.: Northwestern Univer.
Press, 1964.

Meyer, M. F. *Psychology of the other one.* Columbia, Missouri: Missouri Book,
1921.

Miller, G. A., Galanter, E., & Pribram, K. H. *Plans and the structure of behavior.*
New York: Holt, Rinehart & Winston, 1960.

Mischel, T. Wundt and the conceptual foundations of psychology. *Philosophy and
Phenomenological Research,* in press.

Murphy, G. *Personality.* New York: Harper & Row, 1947.

Natsoulas, T. What are perceptual reports about? *Psychological Bulletin,* 1967, **67,**
249–272.

Penfield, W., & Rasmussen, T. *The cerebral cortex of man.* New York: Macmillan,
1950.

Popper, K. *The logic of scientific discovery.* New York: Basic Books, 1959.

Popper, K. *Conjectures and refutations,* London: Routledge & Kegan Paul, New
York: Basic Books, 1963.

Postman, L. Towards a general theory of cognition. In J. A. Rohrer & M. Sherif
(Eds.), *Social psychology at the crossroads.* New York: Harper & Row, 1951.
Pp. 242–272.

Postman, L. The experimental analysis of motivational factors in perception. In
J. S. Brown *et al.* (Eds.), *Current theory and research in motivation.* Lincoln,
Neb.: Univer. of Nebraska Press, 1953. Pp. 59–108.

Quine, W. V. *From a logical point of view.* Cambridge, Mass.: Harvard Univer.
Press, 1953.

Scodel, A., & Austrin, H. The perception of Jewish photographs by non-Jews and
Jews. *Journal of Abnormal and Social Psychology,* 1957, **54,** 278–280.

Segall, M. H., Campbell, D. T., & Herskovits, M. J. *The influence of culture on visual
perception.* Indianapolis, Ind.: Bobbs-Merrill, 1966.

Sherif, M. *The psychology of social norms.* New York: Harper & Row, 1936.

Sherif, M., & Sherif, C. W. *An outline of social psychology.* (Rev. ed.) New York:
Harper & Row, 1956.

Spence, K. *Behavior theory and conditioning.* New Haven, Conn.: Yale Univer.
Press, 1956.

Thévenaz, P. *What is phenomenology.* Chicago: Quadrangle, 1962.

Thomas, D. R., & King, R. A. Stimulus generalization as a function of level of motivation. *Journal of Experimental Psychology,* 1959, **57,** 323–328.

Tolman, E. C. *Purposive behavior in animals and men.* New York: Appleton-Century-Crofts, 1932.

von Frisch, K. *Bees, their vision, chemical sense, and language.* Ithaca, N. Y.: Cornell Univ. Press, 1950.

Wann, T. W. (Ed.) *Behaviorism and phenomenology: Contrasting bases for modern psychology.* Chicago: Univer. of Chicago Press, 1964.

Webb. E. J., Campbell, D. T., Schwartz, R. D., & Sechrest, L. B. *Unobtrusive measures: Nonreactive research in the social sciences.* Chicago: Rand McNally, 1966.

Weiss, A. P. *A theoretical basis of human behavior.* Columbus, Ohio: Adams, 1925.

Wertheimer, M. Experimentelle Studien über das Sehen von Bewegung. *Zeitschrift für Psychologie,* 1912, **61,** 161–265.

Zaner, R. A. Criticism of "tensions in psychology between the methods of behaviorism and phenomenology." *Psychological Review,* 1967, **74,** 318–324.

Zeitlin, L. R. A response oriented analysis of the concepts of autism and perceptual sensitization. Unpublished doctoral dissertation, Northwestern Univer., 1954.

CONCEPTS AND THE EXPLANATION OF HUMAN BEHAVIOR

STEPHEN TOULMIN

I. Introduction

We think only through the medium of words. Languages are true analytical methods . . . . The art of reasoning is nothing more than a language well arranged.

In the Introduction to his *Traité élémentaire de chimie,* Lavoisier quoted this classic motto from Condillac in order to explain how his initial ambition to revise chemical nomenclature had insensibly led him to a complete reconstruction of chemical theory. Questions of terminology turned out to be inseparable from questions of substance, and vice versa; so the most effective approach to a "reconceptualization" of chemistry began with linguistic analysis. There is thus a good historical precedent for the belief on which the plan of this volume is based, namely, that recent discussions of human action by analytical philosophers have something to gain from criticism by professional psychologists; while, in return, the theoretical obscurities afflicting contemporary psychology may be seen in a clear light if looked at from the standpoint of analytical philosophy.

71

The aim of this particular essay is a broad one: to throw light on three general questions that arise at the boundary between analytical philosophy and psychological theory:

1. How are the ways in which we *talk* related to the ways in which we behave?

2. How are the particular ways in which we talk about *human behavior* related to the broader patterns of that behavior?

3. How are the various *explanatory* ways in which we talk about human behavior related, both to each other, and to our ways of explaining other things?

The hope is that, having analyzed the categories of psychological explanation from a linguistic point of view, we may find—as Lavoisier did—that this analysis throws fresh light on substantive issues also.

Our discussion falls into two main parts. The first ("Concepts and Behavior") sets out to show how recent insights in the philosophy of language dovetail with current work on intellectual psychology, and gain in depth by being put in their psychological setting. The second part ("Explanations of Human Action") starts from the chief conclusion of the first, namely, that the "meaning" of linguistic expressions and the "significance" of human actions derive from a common source, and reconsiders the question what special features are to be expected of psychological explanations, as contrasted with explanations of other types.

II. Concepts and Behavior

A. The Behavioral Context of Language

The first of our three general questions—How are the ways in which we *talk* related to the ways in which we behave?—has played a crucial part in the philosophy of language throughout the last thirty-five years: notably, in the later lectures and writings of Ludwig Wittgenstein (e.g., his *Philosophical Investigations,* 1953), and in the mature papers of Professor J. L. Austin. As our starting point it will be convenient to summarize, compactly and explicitly, the doctrines about the relations of language to the rest of human behavior scattered through the pages of the *Investigations* or implicit in the examples Wittgenstein used so freely, both in the book and in lectures. How then does Wittgenstein encourage us to think about the "meaning" or "significance" of linguistic utterances, and how are linguistic modes of behavior connected with, or dependent on, other modes of behavior?

In one sense, as we shall immediately see, Wittgenstein regarded semantics itself as a behavioral science. In this sense, linguistic analysis leads straight on into psychological explanation: no hard-and-fast line can be drawn separating the (analytical) meaning or significance of *speech-acts*, or other linguistic behavior, from the (explanatory) meaning or significance we place on the associated *nonlinguistic* actions and behavior patterns.

Wittgenstein's central doctrines about language involved three basic elements, which he referred to respectively as "expressions," "language-games," and "forms of life." An expression is (e.g.) a word, a phrase, a sentence: this is the strictly linguistic term in his analysis, such as might be defined in a dictionary, or discussed in a treatise on grammar or usage. Wittgenstein's earlier philosophical associates, such as G. E. Moore and Bertrand Russell, had made it their business to analyze the meanings of problematic expressions ("number," "right," "probable") by finding other equivalent or synonymous expressions—which might be stated either in formal terms (e.g., in the symbolism of *Principia Mathematica*) or else informally, using other everyday words and phrases. To do this alone was, in Wittgenstein's eyes, to remain trapped within the linguistic realm, and did nothing to make the relations of language to other things any less mysterious. The meaning of language could no more be explained by showing how one form of expression can be substituted for another than the meaning of money can be explained by showing how drachmas and pesos can be exchanged for dollars and pounds: it is knowing how money functions in substantive transactions that counts.

As the fundamental step in his later style of philosophy, therefore, Wittgenstein taught that one should analyze terms, rather, by "looking for their use"—and by the term "use" he meant not "usage," but function or *mode d'emploi.* The standard use of an expression was to be shown by describing the place it was given in a "language-game": and by this phrase one was to understand some such linguistic activity as counting out change, or identifying flowers by name, or proposing marriage, or labeling fabrics by color, or expressing approval of a musical performance, or (perhaps) thanking God for an escape. Any expression owes its linguistic meaning (Wittgenstein taught) to having been given a standard rule-governed use or uses, in the context of such activities: in isolation from any activity of this sort, the expression itself would lose all linguistic status and would become a mere mark or noise—an "idle wheel," engaging with nothing.

Language games in turn, however, must be understood in their own broader contexts; and for those contexts Wittgenstein introduced the phrase "forms of life." The pattern of linguistic activities fixing the meaning (i.e., the standard uses) of an expression is simply one element or component in a larger constellation of activities; and a language game derives its effective point from being geared into other nonlinguistic activities. In the last resort, then, we shall understand the meaning of an expression aright—and so be in a position to give an adequate analysis of it—only if we see it in the context, first, of the language games by which the expression is put to use; and then, of the forms of life from which these language games derive their significance.

An illustration will help. When philosophical difficulties arise about (e.g.) the relation of *names* to *things,* we must set about analyzing the concept "name." Now, we might initially be tempted to satisfy ourselves with a purely verbal analysis, such as the formula, "A name is a word that stands for a thing." But this would do no more than shift the obscurities surrounding the word "name" onto the phrase "stands for." Instead—as J. L. Austin showed so clearly—we should ask:

> How are words given a use as 'names', and what is involved in so using them? Suppose, for instance, that the words 'I name this ship *Queen Elizabeth II*' are uttered in earnest, on the appropriate occasion: what is presupposed by this speech-act, what are its effects—legal and other—and what understandings does it create?

The manner in which names signify is, accordingly, understood by seeing how significance comes to be attached to them, in the context of the particular language games (e.g., ship naming) by which they are given specific uses; and, as Wittgenstein went on to suggest, bearing in mind that any general term, like "name," is commonly used within a wide range of somewhat different language games (since ships, babies, breakfast cereals, colors, and electrical units come by their names in rather different ways, having differing consequences and implications), there will be plenty of room for philosophical cross-purposes and mystification as a result.

Yet even a language game as seemingly familiar as ship naming may not be quite as self-explanatory as it appears. For how do we come to give names to ships at all? On second thoughts, the very practice of naming ships current in our particular culture has idiosyncratic features of its own. Indeed, the whole pattern of communal attitudes and behavior involving ships—and the whole subpattern of language games associated with it—might take a different form in another cultural context: where, for instance, all boats were identical in shape and size, were held in common, and never received individual names, or where the act of naming a ship after a god or a saint was held to put it under his sacred protection. The very nature and implications of our actual "naming" language games must therefore be seen in its relation to our broader "forms of life." In treating the words "Queen Elizabeth II" as a ship's name, we are acting in a way whose significance remains unaltered only for so long as the wider situation remains the same in all relevant respects.

To sum up, below the surface of a philosophical question like "What is a *name?*" lie deeper questions, namely: within the context of what linguistic activities (specifically, language games) are names given a use, and subsequently used; and what understandings do these activities conventionally create? And to go deeper again: below that linguistic question lies a broader and only partly linguistic question, namely, what overall constellations of behavior and attitudes (what "forms of life") are presupposed in the performance of these language games? And what changes in these patterns would deprive our current language games of their point, thus destroying the existing meaning of such expressions as "I name this ship *Queen Elizabeth II*"?

What goes for naming goes likewise for other linguistic activities, such as promising, counting out change, or identifying colors by name; and so for the philosophical problems that arise about the binding force of promises, the nature of numbers, and the reliability of sense perception. In each case, questions about meaning lead one on to questions about linguistic routines; and these in turn to questions about how those linguistic routines are related to nonlinguistic attitudes and actions. The unit of significance, according to this account, is not the single expression or utterance. It is, rather, the overall syndrome or constellation of standard behavior that determines the (largely unspoken) conventions for understanding such an expression or utterance. The unit of significance thus becomes a *behavioral* unit.

Clearly, if we accept such an account of "meaning," its effect will be to open, between philosophy and psychology, a communicating door of a kind that cannot easily be closed. The rest of this essay explores, in a preliminary way, some of the consequences that flow from such a step.

B. What Is a Concept?

As a start, we may usefully consider some of the consequences of this step for philosophy itself. Let us begin with the term "concept" and its cognates, "conceptual," "conceptualization," and so on. These terms have been widely used during the last fifty years to indicate the particular object of philosophical analysis. Philosophers raise questions about "the concept

good" or "the concept *number*," or even "the concept *red*"; they embark
on "conceptual analysis," expound "conceptual truths," study "conceptual
systems and/or frameworks," detect "conceptual necessities" and "conceptual impossibilities"; and so on. Yet how precisely such terms as "concept"
and "conceptual" are to be understood is rarely explained and frequently
obscure. By now, in fact, the words have become a kind of catchall, corresponding to the "ideas" and "notions" of eighteenth-century epistemology. The concept "good" (it is implied) has something to do with "the
ways the word *good* is used"; but just how the words, and the speech-acts
in which they figure, actually relate to the nonlinguistic behavior associated with them, remains to be systematically explained. This is one subject (we shall see) that philosophers could expound more satisfactorily,
given a closer study of psychology.

Consider, for instance, P. T. Geach's book *Mental Acts:* this offers a
provisional criterion for recognizing whether a man has a "concept,"
namely, the question whether he knows how to use the relevant words.

> It will be a *sufficient* condition for James's having the concept of *so-and-so* that he
> should have mastered the intelligent use (including the use in made-up sentences) of
> a word for so-and-so in some language. Thus: if somebody knows how to use the
> English word 'red', he has a concept of red; if he knows how to use the first-person
> pronoun, he has a concept of *self:* if he knows how to use the negative construction
> in some language, he has a concept of negation. (Geach, 1957.)

On the face of it, this criterion looks a bit oversimple: if nothing more
needed saying, how did we ever come to draw a distinction between "linguistic skills" and "conceptual grasp" in the first place? And Geach himself
agrees that conceptual grasp cannot be equated with the use of words: the
intelligent use of language may be a *sufficient* condition of "having a concept," but it is not a *necessary* one:

> If a man struck with aphasia can still play bridge or chess, I certainly want to say
> he still has the concepts involved in the game, although he can no longer exercise
> them verbally.

Closer attention to the psychological material confirms the importance of
this qualification, and indicates how we might clarify the relationship between concepts, language, and behavior.

The example of colors can be revealing. In the course of learning about
colors, a child picks up a complex constellation of associated skills. Some
of these involve overt linguistic acts; others (on the surface at least) are
nonlinguistic in character. He learns to *match* blocks, or crayons, or fabrics
by color; to *discriminate* objects of nearly the same color; to *name* the

colors of objects; to *label* them; to *report from memory* the colors of objects he is no longer looking at; to *point out* objects in response to color words; to *arrange* them by hue or shade or intensity, and so forth. All these skills commonly go together, and a child who learns most of them usually catches on to the remainder, with minor qualifications to cover such defects as red/green color blindness. Once the child has learned them all, we do not hesitate to say, "Now he knows about colors (has the concept 'color')"; and we might even agree, though with some reservations, to say, "Now he has the concepts 'red,' 'green,' 'blue,' 'yellow,' and so on." But what if he does not pick up all the relevant skills? The operative question then is: "What proportion (or selection) of these skills must be acquired before we can agree that someone 'has the concept'? And do linguistic skills carry, in practice, the priority that Geach's initial criterion implies?" More specifically, we must ask: "Would a man's losing the relevant linguistic skills, while retaining all the associated nonlinguistic ones, compel us to say that he had—on that account alone—lost his grasp of color concepts?"

Are these questions perversely hypothetical? Not at all: cases in fact occur sufficiently like these to demand a ruling on our part. The classical description is that given by Geschwind and Fusillo (1966) from the Aphasia Research Center at the Boston Veterans Administration Hospital. A patient was referred to them with a suspected neurological damage. He displayed the following pattern of skills and deficiencies.

> The patient failed to name seen colors correctly and could not select a color from a group when given its name; in other words, he showed an isolated difficulty in uttering or comprehending names of seen colors. By contrast, difficulties in color perception were ruled out by the following tests: the patient correctly matched colors by hue, despite great differences in saturation or brightness, correctly matched colored papers and uncolored pictures of objects, and performed without error on two pseudo-isochromatic tests of color vision. Verbal memory for color names was intact since he correctly named objects corresponding to named colors and named colors corresponding to named objects.

In short, the patient retained unimpaired all the nonlinguistic skills associated with the use of color concepts, while losing entirely the very linguistic capacity philosophers are tempted to regard as fundamental for "knowing colors," namely, the capacity to name colors at sight. He did retain certain linguistic skills in the use of color words, but only those involving verbal memory without fresh observation. (Q: "What color are bananas?" A: "Bananas are yellow.") "The best characterization of his syndrome," the authors conclude, is "an inability to match seen colors to their spoken names." The investigators' provisional diagnosis was of a lesion affecting the pathways connecting the "speech-regions" of the brain to the visual cortex: and this was later confirmed by a postmortem examination.

Now: would it be appropriate in this case to pick on "knowing how to use color words" as the preeminent mark of "having color concepts"? In that event, we should be forced to say that this patient had effectively *lost* the concepts, despite all his continued skill at sorting, matching, and so on. However, the indeterminate usage of the term "concept" gives us some leeway at this point; and we may surely prefer to allow the practical skills the patient retained as much weight as the linguistic ones he lost. True, many of these practical skills are of kinds he might never have developed in the first place, unless he had formerly known how to use color words. (This hints at an important point, to which we shall return in Section II, C.) Yet a distinction remains between the practical skills commonly associated with a particular family of words and the ability to use those words themselves; and this distinction is worth insisting on. For in deciding whether someone "has a concept" or not, a good case can be made out for attending to practical skills quite as much as to linguistic ones. With this convention, we need no longer treat a loss of the linguistic skills *alone* as entailing a loss of the corresponding "conceptual grasp."

(At this point, no doubt, a rearguard action could be mounted, in the hope of keeping Geach's initial criterion on its feet. The very fact that the use of color words plays an essential role in the development of the associated practical skills could be cited to show that, in an extended sense, those practical skills are themselves one element in "the use of the words." But we need not pursue that argument here. For the case of Geschwind and Fusillo's patient confirms our impression that, on a narrow interpretation, Geach's initial criterion has paradoxical consequences. And the effect of reinterpreting the criterion in the extended sense is, in its own way, just as paradoxical: we shall then have to say that the patient "knew how to use color words" simply on account of his skill at sorting, matching, and so forth, even though he was in fact unable to use those words to name colors when he saw them.)

So Geach's initial account of "having concepts" needs to be supplemented. Evidently, learning the standard uses of a particular family of words—learning how to play the relevant language games—is an important element in acquiring the concepts carried by those words. But we still need to elucidate the detailed relationship between the linguistic skills characteristic of a given family of language games and forms of life within which those linguistic activities feature. Until this has been done, identifying "a grasp of the concept" with "the use of the words" necessarily involves us in begging questions whose answers we do not yet know.

To go further: the questions that here remain to be answered are not purely philosophical questions. We shall achieve an adequate understanding of what "having concepts" involves only if we pay attention to both the philosophy and the psychology of language. We cannot afford to assume that our present perplexity—namely, exactly what weight should be put on linguistic skills, and what on practical ones, in judging a man's conceptual grasp—can be resolved by an arbitrary philosophical decision, taken on the basis of common knowledge about the behavior of normal adult language users. We cannot assume (in other words) that the solution requires only linguistic analysis. On the contrary, we shall be in a position to take this decision confidently only in the light of better information about the ways in which concepts are acquired, used, and lost; in particular, better information about the developing relationship between linguistic and practical activities involved in the learning, employment, and loss of conceptual skills.

The study of this developing relationship represents an area of common ground where the philosophy of language overlaps into psychological fields, into the neurology of language defects, into what Jerome Bruner calls "the theory of instruction," and into intellectual psychology generally. Indeed, in exploring this particular border area, to continue distinguishing sharply between the philosophy of language and the psychology of language may be as arbitrary as, for example, to insist on labeling Einstein's analysis of "simultaneity" (indebted as it was to Hume and Mach) as "physics" rather than "philosophy," or vice versa. Along the ambiguous frontiers between intellectual disciplines, such insistence becomes merely polemical.

C. The Stratification of Concepts

Can we piece together any tentative picture of conceptual development from a first study of this common ground? And does such a picture have any relevance to philosophical ideas about concepts and about the meanings of linguistic expressions?

Before answering these questions, let me remark on one further point in Wittgenstein's later teachings, which marks his position off from that of many analytical philosophers. Even today, many "linguistic analysts" would declare outright that, in the nature of the case, we can throw no light whatever on the question when a man is or is not to be judged to have a concept, by considering how concepts are acquired. Quite the contrary, they would reply: unless we already have some prior criterion for judging when a man has a concept, we shall be in no position to ask how he acquired it. Even to pose such a question presupposes that we have a criterion. To imagine the contrary—to appeal to facts about the acquisition of concepts as throwing light on the nature of concepts once acquired— would, in their view, be a crude example of the genetic fallacy.

If that were the last word, our present argument would be at an end. But the point can be countered in general terms by replying as follows.

All scientific experience indicates that one cannot analyze the criteria for recognizing when a process is *completed,* in a final and definitive form, until the actual *course* of the process has been studied. Rather, the two investigations must proceed *pari passu.* We start out with a first, rough criterion of 'completion'; but, as our understanding of the process improves we progressively refine that criterion—developing, as a result, more satisfactory conceptions *both* of the actual course of the process *and* of its completion.

So here: though Geach's linguistic criterion may provide a first rough test for recognizing when a man has grasped a particular family of concepts, there is every reason to suppose that we can improve on it (as, indeed, we must do) in the light of a better understanding of concept acquisition.

In contrast with most analytical philosophers, Wittgenstein openly recognized this possibility. His later lectures repeatedly cited examples concerned with the learning of language games, so making explicit aspects of those linguistic practices that we might otherwise have overlooked. These examples were not intended (he emphasized) as psychological hypotheses about how we in fact learn language; rather they served to select out, and focus attention on, situations in which, so to say, we lay the foundations of our conceptual equipment. In this way he underlined the fact that certain of the language games involving (e.g.) the words "red," "good," or "number" are primary or fundamental, while others are secondary or derivative. Our concepts—the totality of skills and activities (linguistic and practical) associated with a particular family of words—are thus not all of a piece: they have inner complexities on which their morphogenesis throws light. Just as the possibility of a theory of personality development, such as Erikson's, was implicit in Freud's ideas about psychoanalysis (though Freud himself denied that genetic hypotheses were his direct concern), so likewise Wittgenstein's analysis of concepts in terms of language games and forms of life had implicit in it (though this was not his direct concern) a possible theory of conceptual development.

Two preliminary points are worth making about the form of such a theory. The first was touched on earlier in passing, and has been discussed at greater length elsewhere, notably by Vygotsky (1934, pp. 56 ff.). It is this: that language plays different roles in relation to behavior at the *learning* stage, and in the subsequent *employment* of concepts. As Vygotsky puts it, at the learning stage, language is a "means" or "instrument," while in the subsequent employment of concepts, it is a "symbol." A child is taught (for instance) to sort out, match, and class together objects falling within the ranges marked off by some standard system of color terms: at this stage, color words are used as instruments for teaching him to classify objects according to that system. He learns to perform the practical tasks (putting things in classes as the system requires) *and* to understand the color words, at one and the same time; and his progress in both groups of tasks is measured by his performance in them *jointly*. (Initially, indeed, there is no clear way of distinguishing the two groups of tasks; we have no criterion of his "understanding" other than his practical performances.) Subsequently, however, the constellation of practical skills inculcated in this way develops an autonomy of its own. Once a child has acquired the skills, he can continue to exercise them in abstraction from the words through whose use he was initially taught them. At this stage the words have become, in Vygotsky's terms, merely "symbols"; and eventual loss of the linguistic skills may leave the associated practical skills unimpaired. (Recall Geschwind and Fusillo's case.)

The second point must be discussed more fully: it has to do with the "inner complexities" within our concepts hinted at by Wittgenstein. These complexities are something that the philosophical techniques of "ordinary language analysis" have, in fact, tended to conceal. For, so long as one concentrates on the minutiae of *adult* speech, remarking (e.g.) that it makes sense to talk of a man's "walking doggedly" but not of his "arriving doggedly," the concepts under scrutiny are being treated as finished products. Using these techniques, we can explain what our concepts are, but not why they are as they are: that is, we can understand the classical morphology and functioning of adult speech and thought, but without acquiring any deeper grasp of how we come to operate with these particular concepts (meanings, language games) rather than with some conceivable alternatives. We can go deeper only by analyzing the development of our concepts into sequences of stages, so as to show (*a*) how experience in the language games learned at one stage may become a prerequisite for learning those of subsequent stages; and (*b*) how traces of the behavior patterns learned in earlier stages may survive recognizably in the adult uses of the expressions concerned.

If we embark on such a morphogenetic analysis, evidence of stratification in our linguistically mediated behavior is not hard to find. For instance, a child must learn to add before we try to teach him to multiply. He must learn to understand categorical sentences before he can grasp hypotheticals, understanding "I shall buy you an ice cream" and "I have some money in my pocket" before he learns to understand (e.g.) "*If* I have some money in my pocket, *in that case* I shall buy you an ice cream." He must learn what it is to choose overtly between possibilities before we teach him to "choose, but do not show which you have chosen." He must learn to express wishes in verbal form openly and straightforwardly before we train him to conceal or dissimulate them when society requires. He must learn to discriminate, match, and name colors at sight, before we start introducing him to such secondary questions as "Is it *really* red, as it appears from here, or is the *apparent* color only a trick of the light?"

In each case, successive stages in the acquisition of a concept are differentiated by characteristic language games; and what "makes sense" in terms of the language games available at one stage may well be nonsense at another. Thus, the young child first learns to choose; that is, to perform an overt speech-act whose effect is to select one of a number of items, using (e.g.) the words "I choose *this* one." At this initial stage the instruction, "Choose, but do not show which you have chosen" (*sc.* "Choose silently," or "Make a mental choice") will be unintelligible to him, since initially the acts of "choosing" and of "showing one's choice" are one and the same. Subsequently, new and more sophisticated language games are superimposed on the earlier and simpler ones: the child learns to defer the overt expression of his choice, or even to suppress it—so creating the distinction, which had no sense for him previously, between the choice itself and its overt expression. (On this point, cf. Toulmin, 1960.) As an integral part of each such transition, the expressions employed in the earlier language games cease to be "instruments" and become "symbols," while those of the new language games become "instruments" in turn.

The conceptual stratification exemplified in this kind of case is very far-reaching in its application. It can be observed at the earliest stages in language learning, yet it has counterparts even at the most highly specialized and technical levels. As in our everyday language and behavior, so in the most complex sciences, each new concept is dependent for its significance on earlier, presupposed concepts. The concept "optical dispersion" presupposes the concept "refractive index," which in turn presupposes the concept "light ray"; and the explanatory techniques involved in the application of one concept—for example, drawing a graph of refractive index against wavelength to record optical dispersion—presupposes the explanatory techniques involved in the presupposed concepts, for example, ray tracing. (Arguably, indeed, the internal structure of scientific theories is best represented as a stratified sequence of secondary dependent concepts and primary presupposed concepts, rather than as a Euclidean system of axioms and deductively related propositions.)

Thus, all the way back from the highest-grade intellectual behavior to the earliest and simplest phases in language learning, we can see a common pattern of "signifacient procedures" (to coin a phrase), with fresh and more sophisticated constellations of behavior, both linguistic and nonlinguistic, being grafted onto earlier and simpler ones. These procedures confer meaning or significance on each separate behavioral element, whether linguistic or no, by associating it with a larger constellation. The ways in which we align our optical apparatus, the pencil marks we make in drawing a ray diagram, and the formula sin i/sin r = refractive index by which we calculate refraction all acquire significance together, as parts of the complete constellation of skills that we learn under the title of "geometrical optics." Likewise for simpler cases: in response to the words "Choose which dessert you want," one may utter the words "Strawberry ice cream, please," or one may point at the tub of strawberry ice cream, or one may simply take the appropriate plate, each of these responses having a significance cognate with that of the others. And, to anticipate a later argument, explaining the nonlinguistic elements in any constellation of skills or actions then involves "reading" them (i.e., recognizing their "meaning" or "significance") just as much as in the case of the linguistic elements. The alignment of the optical apparatus or the action of taking the strawberry ice cream plate is understood when we recognize its place in the broader constellation that also gives a linguistic meaning to Snell's formula for refraction or to the verbal expression of a choice.

We may accordingly conceive a possible collaboration between philosophers and psychologists, designed (a) to analyze our concepts, and at the same time (b) to show how they are acquired. This double task would involve reconstructing the standard ontogenies by which particular successions of characteristic language games, and forms of life, are progressively built up. For (on our present argument) such successions as these define both the typical constellations of adult human behavior and the associated concepts; and in doing so they determine what significance, or intelligible meaning, can be invoked to explain either an adult speech-act or the associated nonlinguistic actions. In a phrase, these ontogenies are at one and the same time behavioral and conceptual. Something of this sort is already implicit in the work of such men as Piaget, Michotte, and Bruner, who have studied the ways in which children develop conceptions of number, matter, space relations, causality, and so forth; and even more strikingly in the work of Luria, about which something will be said later. Yet much still needs to be done if we are to map exactly the constellations of behavior, both linguistic and nonlinguistic, that are developed or inculcated at each stage in the learning sequence; identify the thresholds of behavior that must be reached before the learner is ready to move on from one stage to the next; define the "logical grammar" characteristic of each stage in the development of the associated concepts; distinguish between the alternative learning pathways adopted in different cultures; and recognize the philosophical consequences flowing from each sequence of learning stages (e.g., how different presupposed forms of life find verbal expression in different "synthetic a priori" principles).

Seen from this point of view, the program that Piaget, Michotte, and Bruner set themselves has great merits; but it could be further refined if interpreted in the light of Wittgenstein's philosophy of language. The relevance of Wittgenstein's ideas is readily shown if one considers a well-known example discussed by Bruner (1966). At an early stage in his dealings with material objects and substances, Bruner reports, a child does not yet display any clear feeling for the conservation of matter: if presented with two one-pint glasses of water, one tall and the other squat (for instance), he is easily misled by the difference in shape into believing that the one contains more water than the other. Yet, in analyzing such an example —in particular, when attributing "beliefs" to a young child—it is important not to interpret his behavior in terms of linguistic distinctions that he is not yet ready to grasp. In dealing with material objects and substances in a new way for the first time, he will still be quite unfamiliar with distinctions that all adults draw without thinking. So far as the child is concerned, questions about height and bulk, volume and mass, will not yet have been given distinct meanings, since those distinctions are rooted in language games that he has not yet learned.

So it would be a confusion to speak, without qualification, of a child's "being misled" into "believing" anything about the relative quantities of water in the two glasses. (No one can *believe* something he does not yet even *understand.*) At the outset, the child has no way of differentiating considerations of shape, volume, bulk, and so on: his very acquisition of our adult concepts of "matter" and "conservation" proceeds by the progressive establishment of these distinctions, in his language, thought, and practical procedures alike. So, if we point to one of the two equal glasses at too early a stage, asking the child, "Is there more water in this one?," and he answers "yes," this reply need indicate nothing at all about his beliefs. Indeed, in terms of the language games he has learned hitherto, our question will probably still be ambiguous.

For intellectual psychology, the virtue of reconstructing our conceptual ontogenies analytically can be expressed in a twofold reminder. On the one hand, what new modes of behavior we are in a position to learn, at any stage, depends on our previous conceptual grasp; while, on the other hand, our linguistic performances and understandings at any stage can be no more refined or discriminating than the associated behavioral constellations yet allow. In development, as in actual use, the linguistic and nonlinguistic elements in our forms of life are complementary and interdependent.

III. Explanations of Human Action

Thus far, our discussion has had the following outcome. The term "significance" as applied to nonlinguistic human actions, and the term "meaning" as applied to linguistic expressions, are cognate notions and require to be characterized in the same way. In each case, the task is to diagnose the overall constellations (the forms of life) within which the actions or expressions are to be interpreted, and then to locate the specific action or utterance, by "placing" it in a particular context (behavioral and conceptual) within that wider pattern. An action whose significance remains problematic is, then, like a word whose meaning remains obscure: we do not yet see how it fits coherently into its context. And recognizing this significance —whether in the case of an action or of an utterance—is like spotting how a puzzling piece fits into a jigsaw. Its place in the larger-scale picture and its relations to all the rest of that picture thereby become clear.

A minor qualification is called for: one additional distinction can be drawn in the case of linguistic expressions, which does not apply to actions generally. Quite apart from the actual use made of an expression on some particular occasion of utterance, we can discuss also its standardized (conventional) use, which arises out of the standard language games in which it normally figures: this conventional use is what determines the "literal" or dictionary meaning of the expression. With nonlinguistic actions, by contrast, the distinction between actual and standardized uses has no application, except in the case of gestures and the like, which represent the border line separating language from other modes of behavior. With this one qualification, an utterance ceases to be obscure when it is related, first, to a relevant language game, and second, to an intelligible form of life—so that the "meaning" of the utterance is "explained." A nonlinguistic action ceases, likewise, to be problematic when it, too, is related to the relevant form of life, or constellation of behavior. In this one sense, at any rate, showing the "significance" of an action provides an "explanation" of the action in a way strictly analogous to explaining the meaning of a linguistic utterance.

The remaining sections of this essay will follow up some of the implications of this point. What bearing has the explanation of behavior, in this sense, on our wider understanding of human action? Does it throw any light on the proper aims and methods of a scientific psychology? And do the explanations of actions arrived at in this way show any likeness to the explanations of behavior given in everyday life, clinical practice, neurology or "operant" psychology, or all of these? Our purpose here will not be to dictate what form all psychological explanations *must* take: it will be, rather, to ensure that we have a broad enough conception of the different forms that psychological explanations *can* take.

A. Laws, Rules, and Learning

If the relationship between "meaningful" speech and "significant" behavior is as close as now appears, we are at once in a position to make a further important point. Any explanation we give, either of linguistic behavior or of the associated nonlinguistic behavior, must respect a fundamental distinction, namely, that between the *rule-conforming* character of such behavior and the *law-governed* character of natural phenomena. Let us see what is involved in this distinction.

Even today, many tough-minded academic psychologists regard human behavior as comprising just one more type of "natural phenomenon"; one that (to be sure) operates with its own mechanisms and is governed by its own laws, yet all of which (in principle) is capable of being analyzed scientifically by extending the simple physiological models involved in Pavlov's original work on conditioned reflexes. We are now in a position to challenge this assumption, and to question whether the program could be consistently carried through. As we shall see, in certain crucial respects the rules to which linguistic behavior conforms differ from the laws of the physical sciences, and the learning by which linguistic skills are acquired is essentially more complex than the conditioning by which law-governed reflexes are established. In the case of linguistic and language-associated behavior, then, any attempt to generalize the theory of conditioning threatens to destroy the essential character of language. And this same complexity must be respected also in the case of all those other skills, actions, and modes of behavior whose learning procedures in one way or another involve the use of language.

We can illustrate the differences between law-governed natural phenomena and rule-conforming human behavior by a purely linguistic example. In discussing languages, we have occasions to discuss both phonetic laws and linguistic rules: both laws and rules can sometimes apply in one and the same situation, and may even, in some cases, be stated in identical words. Thus, we can formulate a phonetic "law," or empirical generalization, about the *actual* pronunciation of Modern Greek: "Hard labiates such as *t* are [in fact] softened when they appear immediately after *n,* so that the combination *nt* is [in fact] sounded as *nd* or even as *d*." One can also formulate a corresponding "rule," or injunction, for the *correct* pronunciation of Modern Greek: "Hard labiates such as *t* are [to be] softened when they appear immediately after *n,* so that the combination *nt* is [to be] sounded as *nd* or even as *d*."

How can we tell whether such a maxim is being understood as a law or as a rule? The essential mark of rule-conforming behavior lies in the normative force of relevant rules. An agent who recognizes that he is deviating from a rule acknowledges (at any rate prima facie) a claim on him to correct his behavior. This criterion applies clearly enough to our example: the difference between law and rule is that between saying "Modern Greeks *habitually do* speak thus" and saying "To speak Modern Greek like a native, you should *make it a rule to* speak thus." Suppose that a speaker is deviating from the general practice—failing to soften *t* after *n*—and his attention is drawn to this fact: he may then respond in either of two ways. On the one hand, he may say, "No, I'm not a Greek myself": this reply treats the maxim as a law, not as a rule, and indicates why the law does not apply to him. Alternatively, he may say, "Oh, I made a mistake": this reply acknowledges a breach of the linguistic rule, and so accepts its authority. The pronunciation of foreign languages can, accordingly, be thought of as *either* law-governed *or* rule-conforming *or* both, depending on how far relevant maxims are accepted as having normative force and authority over the speaker's behavior.

By contrast, if we consider natural phenomena of a purely law-governed kind, no such distinction makes sense. For instance, the motion of the perihelion of the planet Mercury was observed, during the nineteenth century, to be deviating from the precise pattern astronomers had expected on the basis of Newton's dynamical theories. Yet scientists did not treat this deviation as a "failure" or "mistake" on the part of the planet: on the contrary, they regarded it as implying a failure or mistake on their own part, and mathematical physicists were at great pains to eliminate this error from planetary theory. It would have been laughable for them to talk of Mercury as "recognizing" that it was transgressing the "norm" set by the Newtonian "rules," and to say that it should "correct" its motion accordingly. It was, rather, the business of physicists to correct the Newtonian laws so as to conform more nearly to the norm set by Mercury itself.

The point can be generalized. When we speak of physical phenomena as "governed by laws," we do not imply that the natural phenomena in question are conforming to anything, since they are in no position either to conform or to fail to conform: instead, we imply that *we* have found (or expect to find) a law that conforms to the phenomena. In the case of law-governed phenomena, the only conformity to be looked for is a conformity of the theory to the phenomena, not one of the phenomena to the theory.

The far-reaching implications of this distinction for psychology are sometimes overlooked. Indeed, they are often actually concealed, through the sloppy practice of applying the term "behavior" indiscriminately, right across the spectrum from human actions to physical phenomena. Within the physical sciences themselves, it may do little harm to discuss (say) the "behavior" of iron filings in a magnetic field; for in purely physical cases the distinction between "phenomena" and "behavior" is trivial. In psychology, however, indiscriminate use of the term "behavior" can be very confusing, since it reinforces the tough-minded psychologist's temptation to play down the differences between rule-conforming human behavior and the law-governed natural phenomena of physics and physiology. Yet, far from being a phenomenon of a straightforwardly law-governed kind, a great part of human behavior is—manifestly—rule-conforming in the fullest sense; and this fact imposes certain limitations, or boundary conditions, on any comprehensive system of psychological explanation. In particular (as we shall now see), it rules out any program for explaining *all* human learning and behavior by extrapolating the model of simple Pavlovian conditioning.

The basic reason is that the classical concept of conditioning was inconsistent with the essential feature of rule-conforming behavior, namely, the relevance of "norms." As Pavlov conceived them, conditioned reflexes and associations were such that, once established, they were beyond the agent's capacity to control. Their subsequent recurrence became a purely law-governed phenomenon, for which straightforward physiological explanation was to be sought. Yet this is just what rule-conforming behavior can never become, without losing its essential character. For it is the crucial feature of such rule-conforming behavior that it remains within the agent's capacity to control: unless it did so, we could not speak of the agent's "recognizing a mistake" or "correcting" it. To the extent that the learning of rule-conforming behavior involves conditioning at all, it cannot therefore be the simple conditioning familiar from a study of reflexes. Rather, such learning is a double process, which proceeds on two levels at once: at one and the same time the agent learns both to behave generally in the relevant mode and to recognize and correct deviations from this required mode as occasion demands.

Neither element—regular performance nor the ability to recognize mistakes—is sufficient by itself. A man may be drilled to behave in some required mode so effectively that he ends up by doing so automatically, without having learned to notice whether he is acting as required or not. Such behavior as this ceases, however, to be rule-conforming: the concepts of a "rule," and of a "mistake" or "lapse," cease to be relevant to it. On the other hand, a man may learn to recognize that he has deviated from a rule only after the event, without learning to behave in the required manner any more frequently than before. In this case, the fact that he acknowledges the relevance of the rule to his behavior does nothing to ensure that his behavior will "conform" to that rule. So, insofar as learning to "behave" implies learning to "conform to rules," it essentially involves acquiring two groups of skills—performance and self-criticism—in conjunction. And when we talk (in this fullest sense) of a man's learning or of his conforming to a rule, we take it for granted that he possesses a capacity that planets and iron filings, crystals and cells all lack: namely, the capacity to understand what is going on when his attention is drawn to deviations from a rule, and to correct his behavior in the required direction.

We can now see why *some* linguistic grasp is indispensable, even in learning nonlinguistic behavior. For the crucial difference is not that between linguistic and nonlinguistic behavior, but that between rule-conforming behavior and (say) reflexes. Learning to conform to rules demands the capacity to understand when deviations are pointed out by others; so the learning of rule-conforming behavior presupposes interpersonal communication, whatever the actual content of the behavior. If, in point of fact, rule-conforming behavior is always associated with language use, this is no accident; for the control of behavior in conformity to rules involves an inescapable linguistic element. A behavioral constellation may, in itself, involve no linguistic elements; yet linguistic skills may nonetheless be required in order to learn the behavior and to correct it when necessary. At the level of learning, control, and correction, any constellation of rule-conforming behavior thus involves language games as well as nonlinguistic behavior.

B. LANGUAGE AS CONDITIONED VERBAL BEHAVIOR

With this distinction between rules and laws fresh in our minds, it is instructive to see what happens when the problem of explaining linguistic behavior is attacked in a way that ignores this distinction. What happens, for instance, if we attempt to apply psychological theories based on naive ideas of conditioning and reinforcement to behavior that is essentially of a rule-conforming type?

For purposes of analysis, we may consider the paper, "Conditioning Human Verbal Behavior," by Holz and Azrin (1966), published in a recent authoritative survey of Skinnerian operant psychology. There is an advantage in analyzing this particular paper, by two of B. F. Skinner's pupils, rather than Skinner's own William James Lectures on verbal behavior: Holz and Azrin take up unequivocally positions that Skinner, with his greater sophistication, takes care to qualify, and their paper discusses explicitly the experimental procedures required, in their view, for a truly "objective" study of verbal behavior.

Their essential points can be summarized briefly. Verbal behavior (they argue) is in particular need of investigation by operant methods because it has, by tradition, been closely associated with the "mentalistic conceptions" that good Skinnerians are so anxious to avoid.

Mentalistic causations can be dispensed with as superfluous for a major portion of animal behavior as well as for motor behavior of humans. To the extent that mental processes are unnecessary, verbal behavior loses importance as the method for explicating them. But what about verbal behavior? Can this too be accounted for in terms other than the subjective processes of thought and ideas? . . . The verbal behavior of humans is the last stronghold from which one can defend the necessity of mentalistic conceptions. The importance of this completely behavioristic analysis of verbal behavior cannot be overestimated. Investigators began utilizing Skinner's formulation by attempting to manipulate verbal behavior of humans in a wide variety of situations to determine whether the law of effects could provide an effective substitute for the mentalistic conceptions.

However, the problem of designing experiments in which linguistic behavior can be studied in a rigorously "objective" way proves a difficult one. One possible precaution is to eliminate interactions between the experimental subject and other human beings, and to "isolate the subject from a social environment with other types of stimuli being substituted for the role actually played by other persons." Another is "to avoid verbal responses which are part of the established language pattern"—by instructing the subject (e.g.) to use only one word—or alternatively "to define the verbal response according to its physical characteristics, rather than in terms of its content." All of these precautions appear necessary to the authors, so as to guard against the mentalistic implications implicit in the very conception of meaning itself.

Having discussed problems of experimental design and methodology, Holz and·Azrin end by reporting the results of recent experiments using such "objective" techniques. These experiments have to do, first, with stuttering; second, with the use of teaching machines to improve a speaker's articulation of the sound "s"; and finally, with attempts to modify the verbal behavior of psychotics in a mental ward. (The choice of topics is significant, as we shall see.) The authors express some encouragement at these results, but conclude:

> Though the experiments have emphasized objective methods, mentalistic explanations still occasionally creep into the studies themselves. We appear to experience great difficulty in studying verbal behavior in its own right and not as a reflection of some inner life.

Two features of this paper are particularly relevant to our central topic. First: when Holz and Azrin talk of language as conditioned verbal behavior, they understand the term in something very close to Pavlov's original sense. The associations created by this conditioning are (in their eyes) phenomena of a law-governed sort, like the association between the ringing of the dinner bell and a dog's salivating. They have nothing to say about the parallel conditioning process that we found to be characteristic of linguistic and other rule-conforming behavior, namely, that by which an agent learns to understand signals drawing attention to deviations between his behavior and the rules, and to correct these deviations.

This omission is understandable. Since their aim is to explain the use of language away—as just one more straightforward species of conditioned behavior, in which the behavior concerned happens to be "verbal"—they would find it profoundly unsatisfactory if they had to admit that the relevant conditioning process itself necessarily takes for granted some degree of linguistic understanding. For in that case, some capacity for linguistic understanding must be presupposed as a prerequisite of all rule-conforming behavior; and "understanding" is a prime example of the mentalistic notions from which, in Holz and Azrin's eyes, a scientific psychology must escape.

Second: Holz and Azrin's experimental methodology is deliberately and carefully designed to cut all links with "purposive" or "intentional" behavior patterns. (Once again, this is in their eyes the only way to escape from mentalism.) Yet the very steps they take to cut these links also have the effect of divorcing their subjects' utterances entirely from any significant context, since to leave "cues" for interpreting the utterances as "significant" would reopen the back door to mentalistic ideas like "understanding." Oddly enough, Holz and Azrin end by subjecting their human subjects to even more severe restrictions than they do in the case of rats: "The bar press with rats does not originally exist as an isolated unit, but rather it arises as part of a natural behavior chain." With rats, they are prepared to accept such "natural syndromes" of behavior as given; yet they do not discuss the possibility that some basic *linguistic* responses might be regarded, similarly, as parts of natural and legitimate behavioral chains in humans.

If one cuts all the links between verbal utterances and their contexts, however, what remains of "language" or of "linguistic" behavior? The answer is: nothing at all. The experimental procedures Holz and Azrin advocate are in fact adapted to the study not of linguistic behavior, but rather of bare vocalization. For, if an utterance is to be treated as anything more than a noise—if it is to be thought of as a word, and so as a verbal or linguistic unit at all—then some symbolic relation must exist between the utterance and its context, some relation to a specific language game, and through this to a broader form of life. When Holz and Azrin eliminate all references to purposiveness and intentionality, they eliminate also all definite relations to particular language games or forms of life, and so all possibility of the utterances they study *meaning* anything. It is no coincidence, therefore, that the only positive results they can report have to do with such things as stuttering, the enunciation of sibilants, and the learning of nonsense syllables. Given their experimental procedures, this is all they allow themselves to discover. By their own choice, they study human utterances qua sounds rather than qua words: and the category of "conditioned verbal behavior," as they define it, makes no distinction between language and prattle.

What impels operant psychologists to limit their enquiries into linguistic and other rule-conforming behavior so severely—to treat as "indispensable precautions for any objective scientific experimentation" restrictions that, to others, seem designed to destroy the whole significance of such behavior? Part of the answer is probably historical in character: in formulating his "objective" methodology for experimental psychology, B. F. Skinner was in revolt, both against earlier psychological theories and against earlier philosophical accounts of the relations between language and behavior. If this is so, the tirades against mentalistic explanations characteristic of his pupils' writings need to be understood as directed not so much against intentionality and understanding themselves as against rival theoretical analyses of those notions.

Certainly, such an answer would fit many of the historical facts. For Holz and Azrin's basic motive for eliminating references to understanding and meaning from their account of verbal behavior is clear: they want to make sure that everything involved in the experimental study is "publicly observable," and that no reliance is placed on appeals to "introspection." As they see it, understanding and meaning (like purpose and intention) are necessarily "subjective" notions and so inadmissible. How I *understand* an utterance, or what I *mean* by it, are—on their view—questions whose answers depend inescapably on introspection.

Given the accounts of intention and meaning current among philosophers and psychologists at the time when Skinner's methodology was being framed, such a view is perhaps understandable. Among psychologists, both Wundt and Titchener were committed to introspection as a basic tool of enquiry, while philosophers like Mach and Russell were writing in similar terms. (At one point, indeed, Russell went so far as to analyze "belief" as a "state of mind" comprising two elements: a mental image of the fact referred to by the proposition we believe, accompanied by a "yes-feeling" or a "no-feeling"!)

Such extreme reliance on essentially private entities was obnoxious not only to Skinner, but also to such philosophical critics as Wittgenstein. Their counterproposals, however, take quite a different form. Where Skinner's followers implicitly accept Russell's analysis of intention and meaning, forswearing all such notions as foreign to experimental psychology, Wittgenstein objected to introspectionist analyses as plain bad philosophy. Much of his *Philosophical Investigations,* in fact, comprises a sustained polemic against such analyses. To speak, say, of an action as having an "intention" (he argues) may be consistent with the agent's simultaneously forming a mental image of his goal, but such contemporaneous "introspectibles" are in no way necessary for intention, meaning, and the like; still less does the use of those terms presuppose them. Rather, calling an utterance significant or an action intentional locates it in a longer-term behavioral constellation, most of whose other essential elements are *not* contemporaneous with the particular action or utterance. No doubt, if we assume that whatever gives the action its intention or the utterance its meaning must be found among items contemporaneous with it, we shall end by falling back on such things as "mental images," "yes-feelings," and "no-feelings." But we can avoid this mistake by recognizing that the behavioral constellations involved in meaningful speech, or intentional action, are both complex and *extended in time.*

So we are not faced with a clear-cut choice between treating the unit of significant linguistic behavior *either* as a straightforward conditioned verbal response *or else* as that response together with contemporaneous images and feelings. (Faced with only those options, Skinner's preference is intelligible enough.) There is, in actual fact, a third option: that of relating the significance of particular actions to the wider constellations of behavior, linguistic and nonlinguistic alike, within which they are located. If we take up this third option (which is the one proposed throughout this essay), we can easily circumvent the fears of mentalism common among operant psychologists. For on this basis, we can continue discussing the significance of actions and utterances without being forced back on appeals to introspection: in all necessary respects, this significance, too, will be open to public observation and experimental study. When sufficient allowance is made for the essential complexity of rule-conforming behavior, and of the learning procedures by which it is developed, we need neither dismiss notions like meaning and motive as scientifically unobservable nor restrict our experimental procedures so severely that they become impossible to investigate.

C. The Diversity of Psychological Explanations

The proposal to treat language as conditioned verbal behavior thus represents a naive overextrapolation of simple Pavlovian ideas. Significantly, this mistake has not been made by Pavlov's own successors in the Soviet Union. For Pavlov himself had recognized early on that the simple conditioning of reflexes was only part of a much more complex story and, in his later writings on the development of higher mental activities, he placed equal emphasis on the role of "signaling systems." Vygotsky, working before the second World War and, more recently, Luria and his associates (cf. Luria, 1961) have fully confirmed the special character of such signaling systems as a distinctive and irreducible element in the development of human behavior; and their work makes clear the power of ontogenetic studies to reveal the roles of language in the development of behavior. Before the age of two, during the years from two to four, and then from the age of five onward, the young child responds to language in progressively more complex ways, so that after the age of five, he has normally learned to regulate his behavior in the light of interpersonal rules and can now apply these rules autonomously, for himself, without reminders from other people. Voluntary behavior (according to Luria) can be regarded as learned rule-conforming behavior, initially regulated by inner speech. This conclusion chimes in well with the analysis given in the first part of this essay, according to which the units of learned behavior are the constellations of behavior Wittgenstein christened "forms of life," and these are also the source of "significance" for both language and nonlinguistic actions. This is not to say that all human behavior is of one single kind, nor is it to deny that some actions—or bodily movements—are the outcome of simple conditioning; nor for that matter does it imply that every item of human behavior must be explained in the same way—by "locating" it in a learned rule-conforming "constellation." Undoubtedly, the simple conditioning of reflexes and associations plays an indispensable part in the development of human behavior; undoubtedly, too, we work with a basic repertoire of motor skills (e.g., the coordination patterns involved in the control of bodily posture) that reflect our genetic and physiological equipment (cf. Weiss, 1941), but when we turn to consider the higher mental functions, in particular, it is reassuring to find the experiments of Vygotsky and Luria bearing out the importance of learning, rules, and language in the regulation of behavior.

Even the category of "rule-conforming behavior" is too narrow to cover all higher mental activities. For it is—so to say—only the individual *atoms* or *units* of adult behavior that we learn to perform in a rule-conforming way, and that we perform "correctly" or "incorrectly." Free, voluntary behavior thereafter proceeds by building up these units into complex patterns and responses, having a flexibility and variety that cannot be reduced to "rules": the rule-conforming units of behavior then have specific usages —like letters or words—while spontaneous behavior is like the sentences and paragraphs we make up out of those letters and words.

So it would be unreasonable to look for one single model of explanation applicable equally to all kinds of human action and behavior. Rather, we should expect to find varied modes of psychological explanation applicable on different levels and in different situations. After all, the very procedure of explaining is itself one more general type of linguistic activity among others; and we have no right to assume beforehand that all the different language games covered by the general term "explaining" share any unique, necessary, or essential form. Among all the "prodigious diversity" of language games, indeed, we can find at least a dozen distinct procedures for explaining actions, intentions, states of mind, happenings, behavior, phenomena, and the rest. So the operative question is not: "Are psychological explanations of human actions *identical* in form and force with explanations of those same actions outside psychology, or with explanations in other sciences?" Rather, it is: "How far do the different varieties of psychological explanations *resemble* those other kinds of explanation, and one another?"

This diversity in our modes of psychological explanation is only one illustration of a more general point. For our modes of *describing* human behavior are themselves also manifold and distinct. We characterize a man's behavior in many different kinds of ways, according to the demands of the particular context. In isolation from all contextual cues, the question "How did so-and-so act?" is ambiguous. We cannot answer it until its force is made precise and explicit:

When you ask, "How did he act?", do you mean, "Was there anything odd or suspicious about his behavior?", or do you mean, "Did he betray any particular emotion?", or do you mean, "What sort of mood was he in?", or "How exactly did he move about the room?" or what?

To describe a man's actions may, accordingly, be to follow out any of a number of different language games; and in telling what any particular occasion calls for, we commonly rely on details of the context to provide us with the cues we need.

Correspondingly, the kinds of terms we use to describe behavior are complementary rather than in competition. A man's reactions, skills, and capacities; his performances, achievements, and intellect; his moods and propensities; feelings, emotions, and sensitivities; his character, disposition, and personality; and so on—all of these are not so many independent psychological constituents or processes going on within a man. Rather, they reflect our alternative ways of characterizing an agent, when we look at him from different standpoints and with different questions in mind. One may compare the dozen alternative ways in which we describe the weather: in terms of climate, season, variability, reliability, short-term episodes, mood (heaviness or freshness), feeling (geniality or oppressiveness), physical variables (pressure and humidity), and so on. With human behavior and weather alike, everyday life creates legitimate occasions for marking off many different aspects; and we have developed distinct terminologies and modes of description for dealing with all these different occasions and purposes.

The diversity in our everyday descriptions of human behavior is matched by a corresponding diversity in our *explanations* of behavior. We may be called on to explain our own actions, or we can volunteer explanations of other people's actions. The explanations we give of our own actions may be given "for our own parts" or "on our own accounts" (speaking from the point of view of agents: e.g., "I sneezed on purpose, to interrupt an embarrassing conversation"); alternatively, they may be hazarded as hypotheses, which happen to be about oneself rather than about someone else (speaking from the point of view of observers: "Perhaps it was the dust that made me sneeze"). And in either case several alternative modes of explanation may be used.

To begin with "self-explanations," in the strict sense: our upbringing normally involves learning to account for our own actions by speech-acts that have very different effects. (For a fuller discussion of this point, see Toulmin, 1969.) When asked, "Why did you do that?" we may explain our action by *signaling* the goal, destination, or "intention" that would complete the sequence of which that action formed one step: "I did it to interrupt the conversation." Alternatively, we may explain the action by *classifying* it, thereby relating it to some familiar routine or sequence: "I was saluting/scratching an itch on my forehead/waving goodbye. . . ." Alternatively, there are cases in which the question "Why?" implies criticism of a failure or contravention, and then we may explain our action by presenting an *excuse,* or extenuation. (The very notions of moral and legal "responsibility" presuppose the capacity to "answer for our actions" when challenged to explain such failures or contraventions.) Or again: in other contexts we may explain our actions by expounding the calculations or deliberations underlying them: "I moved Q to KB5, to take advantage of the missing pawn on that file."

These different modes of explanation are concerned with distinct aspects of our behavior, but they have one thing in common. They all relate the actions in question to broader constellations of behavior whose significance "goes without saying": and they all derive their power as explanations from that relationship. (The initial action then ceases to be problematic, provided that the broader constellation is accepted as self-explanatory.) The significance of an intentional action is understood in terms of its relevance to an intelligible goal; the classification of an action as, say, a "salute" accounts for it by placing it in a familiar syndrome; an excuse or extenuation, similarly, makes an objectionable action, at least, understandable, and so on.

Since the capacity to present such self-explanations is itself a linguistic capacity, it too is *something we have to learn:* one aspect, among others, of our socialization. Learning to explain chess moves, though not absolutely indispensable, is a normal part of learning chess. (A man *might* pick up the game intuitively, with the flair of a simple craftsman, but normally a chess player can explain "the ideas behind" his moves: i.e., the projected sequences into which they fit.) Learning what "explanations" are morally or legally relevant to some contravention is one aspect of a wider process: that of developing a responsiveness to moral and legal issues; while learning to classify one's actions, and to signal goals or intentions, are among the simplest and most basic language games we learn as part of a normal upbringing.

Likewise with our explanations of other people's actions: here again, the aim is to "place" the problematic actions within a constellation of behavior that we can presuppose as self-explanatory; and these constellations may be characterized by specifying the goals, excuses, or other significance of the actions. Or rather, we should say: they may be characterized by specifying the *presumed* goals, excuses, or other significance. For, our everyday modes of explanation being what they are, the reasons explaining why a man acted as he did are commonly "for him to say." Normally, at any rate, the relevant language games are ones in which the agent speaks with special authority. What he says, goes.

(In the case of lunatics and of the feebleminded, of course, this rule may be suspended: such people, we say, are no longer "answerable for" their actions. But in deciding that someone is not answerable, it should be noted, we are not describing his state of mind directly. Rather, we are taking a decision *in the light of* his state of mind: namely, the decision to withdraw the privilege every normal adult is allowed, of speaking "on his own account" when questions arise about his actions. Once a man's overall behavior has lost coherence, deliberateness, or directedness so completely that he cannot safely conduct his own affairs, we are no doubt justified in doing this; or alternatively, if his behavior acquires a kind of coherent direction and deliberateness that is too compulsively damaging to other people. Yet, when a man is deemed to be no longer "a responsible agent," this remains—essentially—a question of status, not one of fact. It is not that *he* does not continue to speak about his actions "for his own part": it is that *we* no longer take the same notice as we did before of the things that he says on these occasions.)

Our everyday nonscientific ways of explaining actions are, for the most part, pragmatic in character. Language, in general, is an *instrument in living;* and our different explanatory language games—declaring intentions, pleading extenuations, and so on—serve practical purposes of correspondingly different sorts. In "declaring intentions," for instance, our aim is that of "giving people to understand" what behavior they may expect of us. (We can successfully *lie* about our intentions only because, by and large, such declarations are reliable, and offered "in good faith.") All such explanations achieve their aims by relating the individual problematic actions to different types of longer-term patterns taking place over more extended periods. The action in question and the declaration of intention (say) may each take only a moment: their significance *as explained,* on the other hand, commonly derives from their place in a behavioral constellation occupying hours, or days, or even years.

Being pragmatic, such everyday explanations are neither inconsistent with, nor in competition with, causal or other scientific "explanations" of that same behavior. When I reveal my intentions, guess at your motives, or expound someone else's calculations, my resort to these language games implies nothing in the way of a diagnosis of the somatic causes of the behavior, nor of a hypothesis about the bodily mechanisms underlying it; still less need it be regarded as an abortive and ineffective *substitute* for those scientific activities. We are free to investigate the details of those bodily mechanisms, if we please; and if we do so effectively, the results will help us to understand better (e.g.) the limits to the scope of deliberate responsible behavior. But the resulting explanations, biochemical and physiological, are simply not in the same line of business as psychological explanations of motivation, intentionality, deliberation, drives, and so forth; and the creation of a fictitious rivalry between them can lead only to confusion.

D. Forms of Life as Paradigms

The genus *explanations* accordingly embraces half a dozen authentic psychological species, quite distinct from anything physicochemical or physiological: namely, those that seek to make an action intelligible by "placing" it in a larger behavioral syndrome or constellation. In this psychological sense (as we saw) "explaining" someone's actions means placing them not just in *larger* constellations of behavior, but in *self-explanatory* ones: constellations or forms of life whose significance "goes without saying." And these general forms of life play the same part in our explanation of human behavior that "paradigms," "themata," or "ideals of natural order" play in the explanation of physical phenomena. (See Kuhn, 1962; Toulmin, 1961; Mischel, 1966.)

In the physical and behavioral sciences alike, therefore, a puzzling action or phenomenon is accepted as *explained* when it is related to some more general pattern of happenings whose intelligibility can be *presumed*. To that extent, explaining a human action as "done out of jealousy" or as "the reduction of a hunger drive" resembles explaining the motions of a scrap of paper as "the influence of the charged amber rod" or "an effect of electrostatic attraction." Still, just because of the fundamental distinction between rule-conforming human behavior and law-governed phenomena, the resemblance between physical and psychological explanation is limited. For (a) the forms of life in terms of which the significance of human behavior is explained are not so much intellectual ideals as practical actualities; and (b) the "self-explanatory course of things" that they express is not some universal order of nature—in many respects, indeed, it is a cultural variable.

These two differences are worth illustrating. Thus, (a) when we explain some physical phenomenon in terms of a general theory or model—Newton's dynamics (say), or the Rutherford/Bohr planetary atom—our theory defines certain natural patterns of happenings that are "to be expected" in "the natural course of events." We use such theoretical patterns as instruments of analysis, in making consistent sense of physical phenomena; but just *how* we construct our theories involves a fair amount of arbitrary decision on our part. This is the force of characterizing the physicist's "paradigms," or "self-explanatory patterns," as *ideals* of natural order, and it reflects the Platonist element in the ancestry of mathematical physics.

By contrast, our explanations of human behavior function in an essentially Aristotelian manner. We do not *impose* patterns or ideal forms *on* human behavior, as instruments within an intellectual analysis: rather, we *recognize* such general patterns as operative factors *in* human behavior. We accept certain general modes of behavior as "intelligible" in an infant, an adolescent, a normal adult, or a moron, because we find them manifested generally, as expressions of different drives or ambitions, cultural habits or intellectual skills; and we then explain particular actions by relating them to such recognized modes of behavior.

In psychological explanations, therefore, our general self-explanatory behavior patterns are neither as abstract nor as idealized as the paradigms of the physical sciences. Nor are they so universal, either. For (*b*) when we explain physical phenomena in theoretical terms, our idealized conceptions define an order of nature having universal applicability: we seek to explain physical processes on Mars or Sirius by the same laws as apply to terrestrial phenomena, and to build up theories relevant equally on a cosmic and on a nuclear scale. With human behavior, on the other hand, actions that are "natural and intelligible" in one milieu may be mysterious in another. When, for instance, a man persists in driving at high speed down the left-hand side of the road, it may be appropriate to explain his behavior in terms relevant to all men, saying "He's in a reckless mood," or "It's a race, and he's clipping another second off his lap-time," or "He's just put on reversing spectacles, and is not used to them yet"; but it may, equally legitimately, be appropriate to reply, "After all, this *is* England!"—registering the fact that, in one country or culture, behavior of some kinds may not *need* explaining in the way they would in another.

Whole new behavioral subdisciplines are in fact growing up, which study the culturally relative aspects of behavior, for example, paralinguistics and proxemics, and these sciences are bringing to light, among other things, the diverse national ways of explaining people's behavior (cf. Sebeok, Hayes, & Bateson, 1964). Among the English, for instance, Italians have a popular reputation for "excitability": arguably, this originates in the different uses of gesture conventionally adopted by Italian and English speakers—Englishmen supplement speech by gesture *only* when excited. So, at this level of explanation, there can be no universal standards laying down what behavior is "natural," "intelligible," or "to be expected." Cultural conventions govern not only the language we use, but equally our paralinguistic and proxemic customs: the gestures we use, the distances we keep, and so on. To a substantial extent, therefore, the standard modes of "natural intelligible behavior" to which we appeal in explanation of human actions are relative to particular cultures. So even the "standard ontogenies" governing the development of our concepts must be expected to vary, in the details of the behavior they involve, as between one cultural group and another—and vary substantially, not merely in the particular words used to symbolize these concepts. Conceptual development, as much as social development, thus needs to be studied with cultural and anthropological aspects in mind.

IV. Conclusion

Even if we ignore the whole area of psychopathology, a comprehensive account of human behavior must be rich and complex enough to accommodate half a dozen contrasting and complementary modes of explanation. Certain aspects of our behavior reflect our basic genetic equipment; other aspects manifest the effects of simple reinforcement and conditioning; others again are essentially speech-regulated, intentional or voluntary. Some modes of rule-conforming speech-regulated (or voluntary) behavior are learned alike in all cultures: other types are learned in ways that vary from culture to culture; and the variety of such learned constellations ranges across a spectrum from simple object classification and color recognition to sophisticated technical and intellectual skills.

Correspondingly: as we move from one context to another, our "explanations" of human behavior are, properly and legitimately, given in very different terms. Neuroscientific theories about the physiological correlates of human behavior need not conflict with psychological theories about drives or reasons or motives (cf. Toulmin, 1969). Nor does the possibility of giving such physiological accounts prove that voluntary actions are any the less "voluntary": they simply provide the appropriate answers to questions of quite other kinds. In the long run, our task must be not to establish a monopoly in psychology for any one mode of explanation (whether in terms of neurons, or operant conditioning, or intersibling relationships), but rather to understand the mutual relevance of all these different legitimate modes of explanation.

How, for instance, does an adequate level of cerebral development become a precondition for acquiring certain behavioral or intellectual skills?

Why does the learning of some more complex conceptual syndromes depend on the previous acquisition of other simpler ones? What respective roles do our different styles of "explanation" play, in relating particular human actions to broader patterns of conduct—with human agents, characterized by their own genetic equipments, operating in specific personal and cultural contexts? The basic structure of a comprehensive picture cannot be laid down dogmatically—or all at once—by practitioners from any single natural or behavioral science; it is something that will be built up only gradually, through the modest (and analytical) collaboration of neuroscientists, psychologists, and philosophers.

The central aim of this essay has been to raise such questions as these, rather than to answer them. Can philosophers, after all, hope to "analyze" concepts without considering their ontogenies as well as their finished structures? And, if we do bring in these ontogenies, shall we not be compelled to see "conceptual" skills as all of a piece with broader constellations of behavior, embracing nonlinguistic skills as well as linguistic ones, practical skills as well as intellectual ones? Conversely, must we not recognize that the part played in all learning by linguistic and intellectual skills is larger than psychologists have sometimes recognized? Do not language games (in Wittgenstein's sense) play an inescapable part in the development of rule-conforming behavior of all kinds? In terms of these questions, the philosophical and psychological arguments of this essay meet at the point where Wittgenstein's philosophical work converges onto the psychological insights of Vygotsky and Luria.

Half a dozen further topics could have been pursued here, if the argument were not already overloaded. Very little has been said (for instance) about *perception,* though perception is undoubtedly one field where linguistic and sensory skills—seeing, recognizing, categorizing, naming—are very closely intertwined. (Something of this sort was implicit in our choice of colors to illustrate the nature and structure of "concepts": but a great deal more could be said.) Nor have we considered what happens where the sequence of learning stages normally involved in acquiring a concept is misperformed: that is, where the standard relationships between language games and nonlinguistic behavior are distorted in one way or another. (Here again, there are interesting possibilities. Certain Freudian psychologists, for instance, talk of "neuroses" as being rooted in "misconceptions": we do have to *learn,* e.g., how to express love, and how to recognize what we most seriously want; and the emotionally charged misconceptions generated if we do not form adequate conceptions of "love" or "wanting" may indeed have many of the characteristics of neuroses.)

Still, one final point is worth making. As Mischel (1967) has recently pointed out, Immanuel Kant used to deny the possibility of a "scientific psychology," and his grounds for doing so connect directly with the central argument of the present essay. For Kant's aim was not a pretentious or highfalutin one: he was not claiming that the human spirit has the power to exempt the bodily frame from the reign of causality or the laws of the phenomenal world. On the contrary, he courageously refused to make the significance of human behavior—including morality—dependent on any such "suspension of causality." (This point is repeatedly being overlooked, e.g., by those who seek a basis for free will in the "uncertainty relations" of Heisenberg's quantum mechanics.)

All that Kant claimed was this: that the rules and order appropriate to explanations of human behavior are of their own distinct kinds and operate on their own distinct levels. The rules are not like causal laws. The order is not like that of a physical theory. The explanations are not concerned with physical agencies whose influence is causally compulsive, but rather with considerations that an agent finds rationally compelling. So, in denying that a scientific psychology is "possible," Kant was not denying that one can give a systematic empirical account of human behavior: he was simply insisting that the structure, force, and implications of such an account will be quite unlike those of Newtonian physics, which was the model and ideal of a natural science for the men of Kant's day.

About this, he was surely right. In characterizing human behavior as rule-conforming rather than law-governed, we too have conceded that physiological, biochemical, and other scientific laws may well apply to the relevant phenomena underlying our behavior as strictly as they do to similar phenomena occurring outside the human body. The order of rule-conforming human behavior is thus not in conflict with the order of law-governed natural phenomena: it is an additional mode of order *super-imposed on* that natural order. A creature that is capable of self-awareness, and has the necessary linguistic capacity, will learn to select out certain standard modes of behavior from among an infinitely larger range of actions consistent with biochemistry and physiology. Where physiological defect frustrates the normal development of rule-conforming behavior, special considerations arise. Elsewhere, the explanations we give of human actions need not invoke their causal "infrastructure": they can take this for granted.

This essay has ended by arriving at a point very close to that of Kant himself. The natural units of human behavior are not law-governed phenomena: they are those constellations of language-regulated rule-conforming ("rational") actions that contribute, conjointly, to the development both of our concepts and of our practical conduct. The *Gesetzlichkeit* of human behavior must be identified, as Kant insisted, not in terms of physical "laws," but in terms of rules and "regulative concepts."

And it would be an interesting exercise in the history of philosophy to see just how far Kant's doctrines about the "noumenal world," in which the "pure" and "practical" reason have to operate, can be restated in terms acceptable two centuries later: as concerned with the behavioral constellations and systems of rules, concepts, or practical skills (or all three) in conformity to which our voluntary language-related behavior is developed and organized.

ACKNOWLEDGMENTS

The work on this article paper was supported, in part, by a National Science Foundation grant, No. GS-1589. The material discussed in Sections I, B and II, C owes much to the help I have had from Miss Nancy Baker. In places, it also recapitulates material already covered in my paper for the 1960 New York University symposium *Dimensions of Mind* organized by Professor Sidney Hook.

REFERENCES

Bruner, J. S. On the conservation of liquids. In J. S. Bruner *et al.* (Eds.), *Studies in cognitive growth.* New York: Wiley, 1966. Pp. 183–227.

Geach, P. T. *Mental acts.* New York: Humanities Press, 1957.

Geschwind, N., & Fusillo, M. Color-naming defects in association with Alexia. *Archives of Neurology,* 1966, **15,** 137–146.

Holz, W. C., & Azrin, N. H. Conditioning human verbal behavior. In W. K. Honig (Ed.), *Operant behavior.* New York: Appleton-Century-Crofts, 1966. Pp. 790–826.

Kuhn, T. S. *The structure of scientific revolutions.* Chicago: Univer. of Chicago Press, 1962.

Luria, A. R. *The role of speech in the regulation of normal and abnormal behaviour.* New York: Macmillan (Pergamon), 1961.

Mischel, T. Pragmatic aspects of explanation. *Philosophy of Science,* 1966, **33,** 40–60.

Mischel, T. Kant and the possibility of a science of psychology. *The Monist,* 1967, **51,** 599–622.

Sebeok, T. A., Hayes, A. S., & Bateson, M. C. (Eds.) *Approaches to semiotics.* The Hague: Mouton, 1964.

Toulmin, S. E. Concept-formation in philosophy and psychology. In S. Hook (Ed.), *Dimensions of mind.* New York: New York Univer. Press, 1960. Pp. 211–225.

Toulmin, S. E. *Foresight and understanding.* Bloomington, Ind.: Indiana Univer. Press and London: Hutchinson, 1961.

Toulmin, S. E. Reasons and causes. In M. Berger & F. Cioffi (Eds.), *Explanation in the behavioural sciences.* London and New York: Cambridge Univer. Press, 1969. In press.

Vygotsky, L. S. *Thought and language.* Moscow-Leningrad: Soc.-Econom. Izd., 1934. (Engl. Transl. by E. Hanfmann & G. Vakar. Cambridge, Mass.: M.I.T. Press, 1962.)

Weiss, P. Self-differentiation in the basic patterns of coordination. *Comparative Psychology Monographs,* 1941, **17,** No. 4 (Whole No. 88).

Wittgenstein, L. *Philosophical investigations.* Oxford: Blackwell, 1953.

CHANGE OF ACTIVITY

A New Focus for the Theory of Motivation *

JOHN W. ATKINSON

I. Introduction

There are no behavioral vacuums in the life of an individual except when he has lost all capacity for conscious thought and action due to illness or a blow on the head. Then he literally ceases to be a behaving

* This paper reviews, in outline, the conceptual analysis of motivation developed in collaboration with my colleague Professor David Birch in a forthcoming book on dynamics of action. This work was supported in part by grants NSF GS-9 and NSF GS-1399 from the National Science Foundation.

individual. Otherwise the behavioral life, the subject matter of interest to a psychologist, is, as Barker (1963) has argued, a continuous stream characterized by change from one activity to another without pause from birth until death. It now appears that the point of greatest theoretical interest and promise is the instant of change from the already ongoing activity to some other activity, and not, as supposed in traditional treatments of motivation, the analysis of separate goal-directed episodes into their beginning or initiation in a state of motivation; their middle, the vigorous and persistent pursuit of a goal; and their end, attainment of the goal or frustration of the attempt. The behavioral life of an individual is not such a series of discrete episodes, each of which, like the several events of a track meet, begins as a response to some stimulus such as the shot of a starter's gun. The persistence of an activity already in progress and the initiation of another activity, both traditionally viewed as basic but separate behavioral problems of motivation, are not separate issues but interrelated aspects of a single fundamental problem, two sides of the same coin, *a change in activity*. The focus of interest must turn from the initiation, persistence, and cessation of the single goal-directed episode to the juncture or joint between two episodes that constitutes the cessation of one and initiation of another.

The principle of motivation needed to account for initiation of an activity must include, in its systematic account of the conditions, an explicit reference to the activity already in progress when the stimulus or opportunity for the activity of interest arises. The principle of motivation needed to account for persistence of an activity already in progress (long viewed as a defining characteristic of purposive or goal-directed behavior) must include, in its systematic account of the conditions, an explicit reference to the activity that replaces it. This single principle will account for the time taken to change from an ongoing activity to the new activity in terms of variables that separately influence the strength of the tendency sustaining the activity already in progress and the strength of the tendency to undertake the alternative activity. The same clock reading will provide the measure of persistence in the initial activity and the measure of readiness to initiate the other activity that is traditionally called the latency of response.

This new principle, if it is to perform the integrative function expected of a principle of motivation, will provide a coherent account of the joint impact on behavior of the several major classes of determinants that have been identified and emphasized by psychologists in disparate fields of study where special interests and methods have tended to produce exaggerated estimates of the importance of one or another of these determinants. I refer to the effect of the immediate environment or stimulus, which has traditionally dominated the interest of experimental psychologists—probably because it is most easily manipulated; the effect of stable individual differences in personality, which has been a static interest of the mental test movement and its modern derivative having to do with assessment by diagnostic tests of the structure of personality; and the effect on current behavior of those persistent, unresolved tendencies that have a much earlier origin and can be attributed to inadequate expression in the past, whether due to inhibition or deprivation of opportunity. The latter is the factor that clinicians from Freud onward have always given the most emphasis, probably because these tendencies are most evident among the selected sample of individuals they have observed most closely.

These were my general conclusions a few years ago, following a historical survey of the evolution of the basic concepts of motivation within psychology since 1900 (Atkinson, 1964, Chapt. 10, pp. 295–314; Atkinson & Cartwright, 1964). They were based in part on an unavoidable recognition of the extent to which the stimulus-response mode of thought, originally anchored in the concept of reflex and studies of learning in a series of discrete trials, had produced a stimulus-bound paradigm for thought about the problem of the contemporaneous determinants of action even among critics like Edward Tolman and Kurt Lewin, who were outside the tradition. But these conclusions stem in larger part from actual confrontation with the limitations of the traditional scheme of analysis in empirical research on persistence in human achievement-oriented activities (Feather, 1962). Instead of again reviewing the arguments that seem to me to justify these conclusions, I shall outline some steps being taken collaboratively with my colleague, Professor David Birch, to change the focus of the conceptual analysis of the motivation of behavior [see also Atkinson and Birch (1967), Birch (1968), Birch and Veroff (1966)].

We have assumed the position of an external observer who can see and record the subject's overt activity but not his covert activity, that is, his conscious thought, unless it is revealed by the report of the subject. We have considered the general question of what is required to account for the main characteristics of molar behavior. Our conceptual analysis recovers old problems from a fresh perspective and discovers some new or previously neglected ones.

II. The Primitive Observation: A Change of Activity

When we begin to observe a subject, we note that he is always already doing something. An adequate taxonomy of behavior, if psychology had

such a useful descriptive coding system, would provide the basis for a
check mark on the protocol indicating that a particular activity, A, is in
progress at the beginning of the interval of observation. The subject is
eating his dinner, or playing the piano, or preening in the start box of
the maze, or working on mathematical problems, or perhaps sitting in a
chair and thinking. The observer can only know that he is thinking, and
about what, if the subject tells him. It is a fundamental methodological
problem for psychology that often, particularly of course in the case of
human behavior, the observer cannot adequately describe what is happening. It is as if in the course of observing the simpler activity of a rat
running a maze, a large black screen were to come down for a time to
hide the overt activity of the animal. The observer would obviously not
know what activity is in progress at that time. We begin, acknowledging
that the observer does not always know what activity is in progress, but
hopeful that useful principles can be evolved and tested under well-
controlled experimental conditions that do substantially increase, if not
guarantee, confidence in being able to describe the activities that are
actually occurring.

There is another possible complication at the outset. The subject may
be engaged in several different but compatible activities at the same time.
He may, for example, be driving his auto to work and talking to his friend
in the back seat, or smoking a cigarette while reading a novel. We have
something to say about the complication of compatible activities, a problem
that has been virtually ignored, but let us at the start and in this essay
confine our interest to incompatible activities, those that cannot be undertaken simultaneously, like playing the piano and playing golf or turning
to the left and turning to the right, because the individual we study is
constructed in a particular way. We assume that an individual would, if
he could, simultaneously engage in all the different activities he is then
motivated to undertake, but he cannot because certain activities are incompatible. And because of this, he must do one thing at a time.

III. Determinants of a Change of Activity

We shall refer to the initial activity of the subject during an interval of
observation as activity A. The fact that it, rather than some other activity,
is already in progress implies either that this is the individual's only active
tendency to behave at the time or that his tendency to engage in activity A
(T_A) is stronger than any other tendency. Thus we begin viewing activity
A, already in progress, as an expression of the then dominant behavioral

tendency (T_A) and assume that the intensity of activity A expresses the strength of T_A. Activity A will continue as long as $T_A > T_B \ldots T_X$, where $T_B \ldots T_X$ are tendencies to engage in other activities that are incompatible with activity A.

As we continue to observe the individual, we note, some time later, that activity A ceases. The individual is no longer eating his dinner, playing the piano, preening in the start box of the maze, working on the mathematical problems, or sitting in the chair and thinking about something. But when activity A ceases, the individual does not fall to the floor dead as if hit by a bullet. Rather, we observe that some other activity has replaced activity A. The subject has initiated activity B. And since we view the activity in progress at a particular time as an expression of the then dominant behavioral tendency, we must infer that now, at the end of this interval of observation, $T_B > T_A \ldots T_X$.

A. CHANGE IN DOMINANCE RELATIONS AMONG TENDENCIES

The change of activity from A to B during an interval of observation (t) implies a change in the dominance relations among tendencies from $T_{A_i} > T_{B_i} \ldots T_{X_i}$ to $T_{B_f} > T_{A_f} \ldots T_{X_f}$, where i and f designate the initial and final strength of tendencies in the interval of observation (t). Though somewhat oversimplified, the several logical possibilities are shown graphically in Fig. 1. Either T_B has increased more rapidly than T_A, T_A

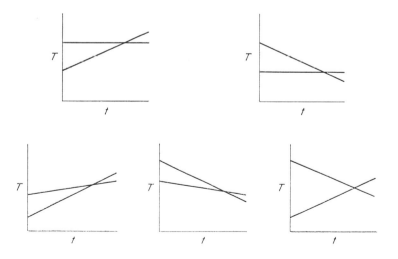

FIG. 1. Various ways in which a change in the dominance relation between T_A and T_B may come about during an interval of observation (t).

has decreased more rapidly than T_B, or T_B has increased while T_A has decreased during the interval of observation (t) to account for the change in dominance relations among tendencies and the observed change from activity A to activity B.

The main theoretical problem is to describe how these changes in the strength of a tendency come about. And, obviously, we must look within the interval of observation (t) for the empirical events that cause the increase or decrease in the strength of a tendency.

B. Determinants of Change in the Strength of a Tendency

We begin with the conservative assumption that the strength of a behavioral tendency does not change spontaneously. Something must happen during the interval of observation to bring about a change. We assume, in other words, that *a behavioral tendency persists in its present state until acted upon by some force that either increases or decreases its strength.* (The forces we have in mind are not, of course, physical forces but rather of the order of psychological forces.) When the observer considers what is happening during an interval of observation that might cause an increase or decrease in the strength of a behavioral tendency, he confronts the fact that the individual is exposed to a stimulus situation (S) throughout the period, and the individual is engaged in some molar activity or what has traditionally been called response (R). In those instances of change of activity that seem intuitively clear, like the change from eating dinner to reading the newspaper following a period of eating, or putting the newspaper aside to answer the ring of the front doorbell, certain activities (e.g., eating) seem to function to reduce the strength of the motivating tendency and certain stimuli (e.g., the doorbell) seem responsible for the sudden increase in the strength of a tendency.

We begin to construct our explanation supposing more generally that the *instigating force* responsible for increasing the strength of an individual's tendency to undertake some particular activity is attributable to his exposure to a stimulus and the *consummatory force* responsible for the decrease in the strength of his tendency to undertake a particular activity is attributable to the occurrence of the activity itself. The change in the strength of a particular tendency during an interval of observation (t) should then depend on the relative strength of the instigating force ($_sF$) to undertake the particular activity that is produced by a stimulus to which the individual is exposed and the consummatory force ($_RF$) of the activity, or response, in which he may be engaged and through which the tendency is being expressed: that is,

$$\frac{T_f - T_i}{t} = {}_sF - {}_RF. \qquad (1)$$

If the instigating force of the stimulus situation ($_sF$) is stronger than the consummatory force of the ongoing response ($_RF$), there will be an increase in the strength of the tendency to engage in the particular activity. If the consummatory force of the activity in progress ($_RF$) is stronger than the instigating force of the stimulus to undertake that activity ($_sF$), there will be a decrease in the strength of that tendency. If the two forces are equal, the strength of the tendency will not change during the interval of observation.

1. *The Effect of Instigating Force of a Stimulus*

When an individual is exposed to the stimulus or cue to engage in a particular activity B and that tendency is not, at the time, being expressed in behavior, the tendency to undertake the particular activity will increase, for there is no consummatory force. Consider, for example, the effect on appetite (i.e., the tendency to eat) of exposure to the odor of a steak on the charcoal burner while one is idly reading a book. In this case, the final strength of the tendency (T_f) at the end of an interval of time (t) will depend on the initial strength of the tendency (T_i), the magnitude of the instigating force of the stimulus to undertake the activity ($_sF$), and the duration of exposure to the instigating force (t): that is,

$$T_f = T_i + {}_sF \cdot t. \qquad (2)$$

The effect of continuous, periodic, and sporadic exposure to a stimulus producing an instigating force to engage in some activity is shown in Fig. 2. In each case, the magnitude of the instigating force of the stimulus ($_sF$)

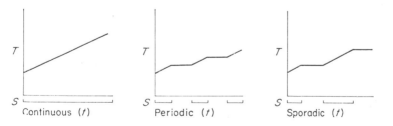

FIG. 2. The effect on strength of a behavioral tendency of continuous, periodic, and sporadic exposure to the instigating force of a stimulus when the tendency is not being expressed in behavior.

defines the rate of increase in strength of a tendency per unit of time. The magnitude of the instigating force depends, of course, on its implications for the individual as developed in his past experience with the same and similar stimuli (i.e., learning). A rapid increase in the strength of a tendency not currently being expressed implies that sooner or later it is likely to attain dominance over the tendency sustaining the activity already in progress, the condition needed for its overt expression.

Commonplace illustrations of the several cases shown in Fig. 2 are the continuous low murmur of voices in conversation in the next room that calls an individual from the work at his desk to affiliative activity; the periodic ringing of the telephone, producing an increase in strength of tendency to answer while it is on that persists, at a given level, while it is off, only to increase still further when the ringing begins again; the sporadic exposure one is likely to have to visual and olfactory temptations to eat while engaged in other everyday activities, producing sporadic increases in the strength of tendency to eat that persist until the next one, and so on. The latter, in brief, is our conception of the effect on the strength of tendency to eat of the conventional experimental operation called food deprivation, the phenomenon for which the concept of drive was introduced in psychology. The experimenter imposes one rule on the animal, namely, thou shalt not eat for a period of 1, 4, 8, . . . , n hours. This means the animal will not be exposed to the consummatory force of the activity of eating, which would function to reduce its tendency to eat, though it undoubtedly is exposed sporadically during the interval to various stimuli associated with eating since there is no other explicit control of environment. According to the present analysis, the longer the total time of exposure (t) to cues in the environment in any way similar to those associated with eating, without occurrence of eating, the stronger the tendency to eat should become. The effects of various temptations are cumulative. This is an implication of the concept of inertia applied to behavioral tendencies in our restatement of Freud's fundamental assumption that a wish, once aroused, persists until it is expressed and satisfied.

2. The Effect of the Consummatory Force of an Activity

It is more difficult to think of instances in which a tendency is being expressed in behavior but not, at the same time, being instigated by relevant stimuli. A hallucinatory activity such as the frantic running toward an oasis that is not there under conditions of very strong tendency to drink is illustrative. Perhaps the most common example, then, is dreaming, the expression of a tendency in the covert, imaginal activity that, according to Freud, functions to reduce the tendency. In the case of a dream, there is no immediately present instigating stimulus, merely the persistent unful-filled wish or tendency that has been aroused and strengthened on some earlier occasion and that now, without a stimulus, provides the motivation of the dream. We call this an *inertial* tendency.

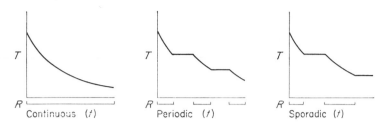

FIG. 3. The effect on strength of a behavioral tendency of continuous, periodic, and sporadic exposure to the consummatory force of an activity (or response) when the tendency is not being instigated by a stimulus.

Figure 3 shows the effect of consummatory force on the strength of a tendency. It is assumed that any activity, whether the kind traditionally called instrumental or consummatory, produces some consummatory force. We break with the traditional qualitative distinction between so-called in-strumental activity and goal activity, which suggests that eating but not walking to the restaurant will reduce the tendency to eat. We treat the difference as quantitative. As a first approximation it is assumed that the consummatory force of a particular activity ($_RF$) will depend on the nature of the activity (e.g., sitting down at the table, eating celery, eating custard pie) and the strength of the tendency that is expressed in that activity. This conception may be summarized

$$_RF = c \cdot T \qquad (3)$$

where c represents the consummatory value of a particular activity (i.e., its potential for reducing the tendency) and T represents the strength of tendency then being expressed in that activity. The decelerated, rather than linear, decrease in the strength of tendency as a function of duration of exposure to the consummatory force of an activity, as shown in Fig. 3, is attributable to the decline in the strength of T, one of the determinants of consummatory force, as the activity continues.

3. *The Joint Effects of Instigating and Consummatory Forces*

The third and perhaps most familiar case is when a particular activity is both instigated by relevant cues or stimuli in the environment and is being expressed in behavior. Then both the instigating force of the stimulus and the consummatory force of the response function simultaneously. This happens, for example, when an individual is exposed to the stimulus of food and is in the process of eating it, or when an individual is exposed to the stimulus of a challenging task and is actively engaged in the effort to master it. In this case, there will be no change in strength of T when $_sF = {}_RF$ or, to substitute the determinants for $_RF$, when $_sF = c \cdot T$, or when $T = {}_sF/c$. This is the general implication of our formulation: the strength of the tendency sustaining an activity in progress that is instigated by cues in the immediate environment that define a fixed instigating force will approach a limit during the interval of observation (t) defined by the ratio of the magnitude of the instigating force of the stimulus to the consummatory value of the activity or response (Fig. 4). This means that if the

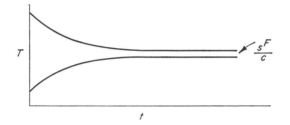

FIG. 4. The net effect on the strength of a behavioral tendency when it is continuously instigated by a stimulus and continuously expressed in behavior. The strength of the tendency approaches a limit at which $_sF = {}_RF$ and $T = {}_sF/c$.

tendency had exactly this strength at the beginning of the interval, there would be no change in its strength during the interval. If it was initially weaker, the strength of T would rise to a higher level, defined by $_sF/c$. If it was initially stronger, the strength of T would fall to a lower level, defined by $_sF/c$. This means, in general, that when an activity having very substantial consummatory value is initiated—the kind of activity traditionally called a goal or consummatory activity—the tendency will normally diminish to some weaker level. When an activity is initiated with relatively stronger $_sF$ and weaker consummatory value—normally the phase of so-called instrumental activity that constitutes pursuit of a goal —the strength of T will tend to rise to a higher level, defined by $_sF/c$ (unless, as mentioned earlier, the inertial tendency T_i is already that strong).

Perhaps the most important implication of the idea that the strength of a tendency that is both instigated by the stimulus situation and expressed in ongoing activity will stabilize at a particular level is that ultimate interruption of the ongoing activity and variability in behavior are virtually guaranteed. Since the dominant tendency (the one being expressed in the ongoing activity) stabilizes rather than tending to increase in strength indefinitely, some other subdominant tendency, one not then being expressed in activity but instigated either continuously, periodically, or sporadically by relevant stimuli, is sooner or later likely to become dominant and produce a change in activity.

C. THE PRINCIPLE OF CHANGE OF ACTIVITY

Having stated a principle that describes the change in the strength of a behavioral tendency as a function of exposure to the instigating force of the stimulus and the consummatory force of the response [see Eq. (1)], we can return to the fundamental problem of the change in dominance relations among tendencies that causes the change from activity A to activity B during the interval (t) and derive the principle of change of activity. At the beginning of the interval of observation, that activity A is in progress implies $T_{Ai} > T_{Bi}$. Some time later (t), at the end of the interval of observation, that activity A ceases and activity B is initiated implies $T_{Bf} > T_{Af}$ or $T_{Bf} = T_{Af}$ plus a very small quantity that for all intents and purposes can be ignored. Substituting the several determinants of T_{Bf} from Eq. (2) for T_{Bf}, we have

$$T_{Bi} + {}_sF_B \cdot t = T_{Af}, \qquad t = \frac{T_{Af} - T_{Bi}}{{}_sF_B}. \tag{4}$$

Equation (4) may be read as follows: the time taken (t) for cessation of an activity in progress (persistence of activity A), or initiation of an alternative activity (latency of activity B), or both, will be proportionate to the difference between the strength of tendency sustaining the activity in progress (T_{Af}) and the strength of inertial tendency to undertake the alternative activity (T_{Bi}) and inversely proportionate to the magnitude of instigating force to undertake the alternative activity $({}_sF_B)$. More simply, this means that persistence of an ongoing activity will be greater, and initiation of a new activity less immediate or less likely, when the tendency sustaining ongoing activity is very strong relative to the inertial tendency for an alternative activity, and the instigating force for the alternative is very weak. Initiation of the alternative will be most likely (or most prompt) when the strength of inertial tendency for that activity is strong relative to the strength of the tendency sustaining ongoing activity and the instigating force to undertake the new activity is also very strong. Thus we do not expect the professor back at his desk and deeply engrossed in his work shortly after a satisfying lunch to be interrupted and called from his work by the aroma of a neighbor's charcoaled steak. But later in the day, after a long period of work in which he has made substantial progress and after a series of sporadic exposures to the familiar sounds of dinner in preparation and tempting kitchen aromas, the explicit call to dinner should produce a fairly prompt cessation of work and initiation of preparations for eating.

We can see the role of immediate environmental or situational determinants of motivation, which function to sustain the activity already in progress and to provide an inducement to change, by considering the special and simple case in which the initial activity has been in progress long enough for T_A to have stabilized at the level defined by $_sF_A/c_A$. In this case we substitute $_sF_A/c_A$ for T_{Af} and get

$$t = \frac{(_sF_A/c_A) - T_{B_i}}{_sF_B}. \tag{5}$$

In the previous illustration, $_sF_A$ is produced by S_A, the stimulus of the work immediately before the professor; c_A is produced by activity A, the work in progress; and $_sF_B$ is produced by S_B, the explicit call to dinner.

IV. The Behavioral Measures of Tendency and Force

It is apparent that the same aspects of behavior, namely, willingness to initiate an activity (latency of response), persistence in an activity, and vigor or intensity of activity, provide alternative measures of instigating force and tendency when the other determinants are held constant. The principle of change of activity defines ideal conditions for measurement, but it remains a difficult experimental task to approximate these conditions in empirical study. Finally there is the more complex problem of choice between explicitly defined alternatives, as in the choice point behavior of the rat in a maze or of the human subject in a decision experiment. We tend to view the traditional paradigm of choice as one in which the observer is prepared to record the initiation of one or another of several designated activities, and the critical matter is which among the several competing tendencies attains dominance over the tendency sustaining the activity already in progress (whatever it is) and the other alternatives. That tendency will be expressed in behavior and recorded by the observer as the preference.

The concept of inertial tendency carries with it the interesting implication that when an individual has been exposed to $_sF_B$ and $_sF_C$, instigating forces to undertake incompatible activities B and C, and then chooses to undertake one of the activities, B, there is subsequently likely to be greater inertial tendency to undertake the other alternative (T_{C_i}) since the latter has not been expressed in behavior and exposed to consummatory force, which would reduce its strength. The general idea that the effects of temptations to engage in activities, when not actually expressed in behavior, will persist to influence subsequent behavior provides a foundation for explanation of the kind of variability in behavior that sometimes seems irrational. As an example we may consider the fact that individuals in decision-making experiments sometimes make choices that fail to maximize the expected value of alternatives. When fully developed, the implications of the concept of inertial tendency, related as they are to Freud's general notions concerning the persistent influence of the unfulfilled wish, may begin to meet a need emphasized by Miller (1959, p. 262) for a theory of motivation that can provide an equally adequate account of both intelligent behavior and stupid behavior.

V. Displacement and Substitution

The basic concepts needed to provide a coherent account of the dynamics of a change of activity refer to specific activities, the tendencies to engage in them, and the instigating and consummatory forces produced by the stimulus for the activity and the activity itself. Now we must take account of the more general effects of particular stimuli and particular activities. The tantalizing aroma of a charcoal-broiled steak increases not only the specific tendency to eat a charcoaled steak but also tendencies to eat potato chips, pickles, a variety of other foods, and to engage in many different activities that are instrumental in bringing about the occasion for eating something. And eating a charcoal-broiled steak tends to reduce not only the specific tendency to eat a charcoal-broiled steak but also tendencies to eat other foods and to engage in a variety of other different activities that have in the past culminated in an opportunity to eat. If we did not already know this, we could discover it empirically using the principle of change of activity as a guide. If exposure to the aroma of a broiling steak has the effect of decreasing the latency of initiation of the act of reaching for a potato chip, we infer that direct instigation to eat the steak has produced an *indirect* or *displaced instigating force* to reach for and eat a potato chip. If actually eating the charcoaled steak has the effect of increasing the latency of initiation of the act of reaching for a potato chip, we infer that the consummatory force of eating the steak has produced an *indirect* or *substitute consummatory force* on the tendency to reach for and eat a potato chip.

Displacement and substitution begin to define what is meant by the functional equivalence of different activities and provide a justification for referring to a whole family of interrelated action tendencies that suffer a common fate by the family name. Thus we may employ a kind of short-hand and say that the individual is expressing the tendency to eat or the tendency to achieve or the tendency to affiliate or the sexual tendency when, in fact, the individual is engaged in some very specific activity, such as looking for an orange, trying to solve a mathematics problem, talking to a friend, or watching a girl in a bikini.

By *displacement* we mean: Direct instigation of one activity ($s_X F_X$) may produce an indirect or displaced force to engage in some other functionally related activity ($is_X F_Y$):

$$is_X F_Y = s_X F_X \cdot \alpha_{XY} \tag{6}$$

where α_{XY} represents the degree of relationship (0 to 1.00) between activities x and y.

By *substitution* we mean: The consummatory force of a particular activity ($R_X F_X$) may produce an indirect or substitute consummatory force on the tendency to engage in some other functionally related activity ($iR_X F_Y$):

$$iR_X F_Y = R_X F_X \cdot \gamma_{XY} \tag{7}$$

where γ_{XY} represents the degree of relationship (0 to 1.00) between x and y.

In many cases the interrelatedness among different activities derives from the fact that they represent alternative means to the same goal or substitutable goals. Other hypotheses suggested in the psychoanalytic literature have to do with the symbolic equivalence of different activities, or their accidental association in the life history of the individual, or both.

VI. Some General Implications of the Conceptual Scheme

A. EMITTED BEHAVIOR AND VACUUM ACTIVITIES

Perhaps, before continuing, it would be useful to take stock of some general implications of this conceptual scheme. Most obvious is the implication that the time to change from one activity to another (which embraces the traditional interest in the initiation or occurrence of an activity) is not completely determined by the immediate stimulus situation. Behavior is not stimulus bound. It depends as much on the already active and persisting tendency to engage in activity B, which would continue to be an influential behavioral disposition of the individual even if he were suddenly transported from his present environment, as defined by S_A and S_B, to some other environment, S_X. The general implication that the latency of some particular activity or response in a given stimulus situation may range from very short to very long, depending on conditions other than the mere presentation of the stimulus (viz., the activity already in progress and inertial tendency), embraces the fundamental idea in Skinner's concept (1953) of operant behavior as distinguished from respondent behavior. It is the lack of correlation between stimulus and response that distinguishes operant or *emitted* behavior. One can see, referring back to Fig. 1, that the extreme case of operant behavior, when an activity is, so to speak, spontaneously emitted without anything resembling an appropriate external goad or stimulus (a phenomenon referred to by ethologists as a *vacuum activity*) should occur when the tendency sustaining an ongoing activity is reduced by its occurrence for some time and a strong persisting tendency to do something else, not then in any sense attributable to or strengthened by an immediately present stimulus, attains dominance by default and is expressed in behavior.

B. TOLMAN VERSUS FREUD ON PERSISTENCE

It should also be apparent that the present scheme implies that Tolman, in his effort to give the term purpose a respectable, objective meaning, was wrong in stressing that *behavior,* once initiated, persists until an objectively defined goal is reached. A goal-directed sequence of activities once initiated, like activity A in our discussion, does not always persist until the goal is attained. Just as often it is interrupted by some other activity, B. Normally, it might persist until an activity having a substantial consummatory value c occurs if the tendency sustaining it is very strong relative to inertial tendencies to engage in other activities and if the other environmental inducements to which the individual is exposed are relatively weak. But if particular goal-directed activities were as persistent as the argument of Tolman once suggested, the professor sitting down in his study to finish the chapter for a book would have no need to close the door and instruct his wife to intercept all phone calls; no need, in other words, to take appropriate preparatory actions to prevent his exposure to the instigating forces for other, incompatible activities (Tolman, 1951).

The present scheme emphasizes the distinction between the argument of Tolman that behavior persists, and the assumption of Freud that the *tendency* (i.e., motivation) persists even when not overtly expressed in behavior. It is the Freudian concept of persistence, persistence of the unfulfilled wish, that is represented in the concept of inertial tendency and the redefinition of the functional significance of stimulus (environment) and response (activity) in the present scheme.

The general observation of "purposivists" like McDougall (1908) and later Tolman (1932) that behavior persists until an objectively defined goal is reached (e.g., Thorndike's cats and dogs continued to struggle, with attendant trials and errors, until the food outside their problem box was reached) is recovered from a new perspective. The present scheme suggests that some activities, for whatever reason, have substantially greater consummatory value for the tendency that produced them than others. This means, given the present analysis, that gross qualitative changes in the nature of activity will more often be evident to an observer *after* one of these activities has been going on for some time than shortly *before* the occurrence of the activity. It is easier, in other words, to bring about a change in an individual's behavior after he has been sitting at a table eating for some time than when he is hurrying to a restaurant or walking from the living room to the dining room to eat. Witness the typical reaction to the call from a friend to hurry off to a movie when it is received just as one is about to begin dinner versus just as one is about to finish the dessert. The traditional identification of the goals of behavior may be in part attributable to the fact that some activities have substantially greater consummatory value than others so that qualitative changes in the nature of behavior, a precondition for developing the concept of different kinds of activity, are much more frequently observed following certain activities than others.

C. Drive and Psychogenic Need

The traditional problem of drive, grounded in observations of the cyclical nature of certain activities like eating and drinking, is also recovered from a different vantage point. Without explicit reference to metabolic activities that use up the supplies of vital commodities, creating a bodily need (though this possibility is not excluded), it is argued that the traditional experimental operation called food deprivation, which has the general effect of increasing an animal's willingness to initiate a particular kind of activity (viz., eating or some other activity that has normally eventuated in eating in the past), consists of preventing the occurrence of the particular kind of activity (e.g., eating) that would, because of its consummatory value, produce the greatest consummatory force and reduction of the tendency. But there is no comparably tight control of the environmental cues to which the individual is exposed during the period of deprivation. Hence, according to well-known principles of learning (viz., stimulus generalization) and the present scheme, all that should be required to produce an increase in the tendency to eat is sporadic exposure to environmental cues that are in some degree similar to cues closely associated in the history of the animal with eating. These constitute instigating forces to eat, or to engage in certain preparatory activities and then eat. It follows from the present analysis that even if the tendency to eat were to become dominant during the period of deprivation and expressed in a search for food, that is, activities that have in the past been followed by the presence of food and the opportunity to eat, the consummatory value of such activities would be substantially less than that of eating and so the strength of tendency would continue to rise to a relatively high level defined by the ratio $_sF/c$.

Suggested by this application of the scheme to the classic issue of the effect of food deprivation on the tendency to eat is the more general implication that when an individual is deprived of an opportunity to engage in some activity that has substantial consummatory value for him, but is not protected from environmental inducements and temptations to engage in that activity, there should be an increase in the strength of inertial tendency. A person deprived of the opportunity for friendly commerce with others, but not protected from reminders of the possibility that produce instigating force, should experience a rise in the inertial tendency to engage in affiliative activity. The entrepreneurial businessman on vacation and therefore prevented from engaging in the kind of achievement-oriented activity that is central in his life, but not protected from the Wall Street Journal and so on, should experience a heightened tendency to achieve. This provides a general paradigm for discussion of what clinical psychologists have tended to mean when using the term *psychogenic need*. Most often, the past deprivation implied in their use of the term is attributable to frustrated effort or an individual's self-imposed deprivation, that is, the inhibition of a particular activity that is attributable to resistance, a stronger tendency *not* to undertake the particular activity.*

* Though not included in the present discussion because it is too complicated to develop in limited space, the concept of resistance that Professor Birch and I are

To illustrate, we refer to the experimental results of McClelland, Atkinson, Clark, and Lowell (1953), which provide an empirical basis for the assumption that content analysis of imaginative activity provides a valid method for measurement of the strength of tendency to achieve or n Achievement. College students were exposed to an instigating force to achieve, instructions to undertake a particular intelligence test. Then, in some conditions, they were given misleading norms with which to compare their own scores. This provided an occasion for reactions of success or failure. Assuming that success would reduce the already aroused need to achieve more than failure (here called a difference in the consummatory value c of success and failure for the tendency to achieve), McClelland *et al.* also assumed that if motivation was expressed in imaginative behavior, as so long presumed by clinical psychologists, the particular symptoms of need for achievement could be identified by systematic comparison of the content of stories written following failure versus success. The significant differences in content of imaginative stories produced under these and other related experimental conditions has, since 1949, provided a foundation for study of effects of individual differences in motive to achieve.

D. Time as the Duration of a Dynamic Process

The conceptual analysis of change of activity, with its fundamental assumption that a tendency to engage in an activity persists until changed by the influence of some force, and its redefinition of the functional significance of stimulus and response, views time as the duration of a dynamic process in which the relative strengths of behavioral tendencies are constantly changing. These tendencies are expressed in both overt and covert activities. We shall turn, now, to the issue of covert activity (conscious experience or thinking) as distinct from overt activity (action) and the programmatic view we now take concerning the relationship between the phenomenological and behavioral aspects of motivation.

developing is consistent with the general logic of earlier Expectancy × Value theories of motivation and decision: viz., a tendency *not* to undertake a particular activity is produced and strengthened when an individual is exposed to an inhibitory force implying that the activity, if performed, will produce a negative or noxious consequence. Tendencies not to undertake activities (resistance) oppose and dampen the strength of action tendencies. It is, in our conception, the resultant action tendency that appears in the principle of change of activity. To simplify this presentation, T_A and T_B have been treated as tendencies to undertake activities A and B rather than as resultant tendencies as in the more complete statement of the theory.

VII. The Relationship between Overt and Covert
Expressions of a Tendency

From the perspective of an external observer, conscious thought can be described as covert activity. The observer cannot know that it is going on unless he is told about it by the individual, who has the position of privileged observer. A covert perceptual, imaginal, or conceptual activity A in progress implies $T_a > T_b \ldots T_x$, where $T_b \ldots T_x$ refer to other covert activities that are incompatible with activity A. We start, in other words, with the same notion employed in the analysis of a change of overt activity, that there is constant competition among tendencies, but now for conscious attention. It is again assumed that the dominant, or strongest tendency and others compatible with it and each other are expressed.

The content of conscious experience, that is, covert activity, is derived from sensory experience. A physical stimulus, quite apart from any conditioned force it may exert on the individual to undertake a particular motor activity, will always produce an unconditioned instigating force to engage in a particular perceptual activity. This will increase the strength of the perceptual tendency. If the latter becomes dominant, it will produce the covert, perceptual activity we refer to as hearing the click of the metronome, seeing the rainbow, feeling the warmth of the sun, noticing that the clock now says five o'clock. Since every overt activity, traditionally called a response R, immediately produces a certain distinctive sensory consequence or feedback stimulus S, every overt activity will produce, via this sensory route, an instigating force for the perceptual activity that constitutes the conscious experience of being engaged in that activity. Thus, when there is no serious conflict among imaginal tendencies for conscious attention, the sequence of events recorded by an observer of the behavior of another individual as $S_1R_1S_2R_2S_GR_G$ (e.g., the traditional animal behavioral sequence of start box–run–choice point of maze–turn right–food–eat) should have, as its subjective counterpart in the individual being observed, a sequence of covert perceptual or imaginal activities corresponding to $S_1 \ldots R_G$. These are all to be considered expressions of tendencies produced by the instigating forces of physical stimuli. We should describe this sequence of covert activities as $r_{s1}-r_{r1}-r_{s2}-r_{r2}-r_{sg}-r_{rg}$, to remind ourselves that the chain of thought is a stream of covert activity (r). But having made the point, we shall find it less cumbersome to describe the sequence in terms of whether the source of the stimulus is the

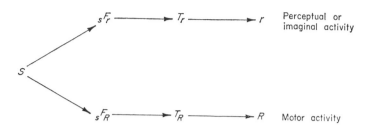

FIG. 5. The dual instigating function of a stimulus (S). The same S produces an instigating force to engage in a particular perceptual or imaginal activity ($_sF_r$) and an instigating force to engage in a particular overt action ($_sF_R$). The tendencies to engage in perceptual or imaginal activity (covert activity) and to engage in overt activity, and the activities themselves are, as a result, highly correlated.

environment (s) or the activity of the individual (r) as in $s_1-r_1-s_2-r_2-s_g-r_g$.

The reader is reminded that s_1 is not a stimulus but a perceptual activity resulting from the instigating force of an *environmental* stimulus to have the thought or image or perceptual activity appropriate to that environmental stimulus (S). And the reader is reminded that r_1 is also an imaginal or perceptual activity, but one caused by the response-produced stimulus of one of the subject's own activities (an R).*

The point of importance for the present discussion of the relationship between primitive thought (covert activity) and action (overt activity) is that the very same sequence of historical events that accounts for the fact that the originally ineffective stimulus of the start box of a maze will take on the property of producing a conditioned instigating force to run and eat ($_sF_{Run, Eat}$) for a particular rat, one that is capable of strengthening the tendency to run and eat ($T_{Run, Eat}$) and ultimately promoting the overt activity of running, also accounts for elaboration of the perceptual or imaginal activity of the animal such that the stimulus of the start box, after training, also produces an instigating force to have the thought of the start box and the anticipatory thoughts of running, food, and eating (i.e., $_sF_{start box, run, choice point, right turn, food, eat}$).

The dual instigating function of a stimulus, as here conceived, is presented schematically in Fig. 5. The stimulus produces instigating force to

---

* We mean to imply, though I shall not develop the argument here, that physical properties of the stimulus define the strength of unconditioned instigating force to engage in the perceptual activity appropriate for that stimulus. This is why, e.g., recognition of a stimulus occurs with only short exposure when intensity of illumination is very strong but requires much longer exposure when intensity of illumination is weaker, etc. So-called effects of motivation on perceptual sensitivity or imagination are thus viewed as special cases of the influence of inertial tendencies on activities—in this case, covert activities.

engage in a particular perceptual activity and instigating force to engage in a particular motoric activity. These distinct instigating forces are correlated because they have a common origin. One produces an increase in the tendency for a certain perceptual or imaginal activity, and the other increases the tendency to engage in a certain motoric activity. When the perceptual tendency attains dominance over other incompatible perceptual tendencies, the relevant perceptual activity occurs. When the action tendency attains dominance over other incompatible action tendencies, the relevant overt activity is initiated. Normally, the tendency for the covert imaginal activity (e.g., $T_{\text{start box, run, choice point, right turn, food, eat}}$) and the tendency for the overt locomotor activity (e.g., $T_{\text{Run, Eat}}$) will both attain dominance, one in the domain of covert activity (thought), the other in the domain of overt activity (action). So the rat will initiate the activity of running toward the food while, it is supposed, also experiencing the correlated thought sequence (or intention) of running to eat the food and other phenomenological characteristics, such as expectation of the goal and attractiveness of the goal.*

The traditional commonsense explanation of human behavior refers overt activities to the intentions (covert activities) of the individual (Mischel, 1966). This is the foundation of an intuitive understanding of behavior, we are tempted to argue, because the covert activity called intention or wanting and the corresponding overt activity so often occur together. They are produced by different specific tendencies that belong to the same family. According to the principles of displacement and substitution, these tendencies suffer a common fate. Perhaps the notion that intention (covert activity) causes action (overt activity) is central in the traditional view of motivation as, for example, in the ideomotor theory of volition described by James (1890) because the covert expression (thought) so often precedes the overt expression of a tendency (action). The tendency to engage in the covert activity attains dominance more easily than the tendency to engage in the correlated overt activity. And in many cases the occurrence of the overt activity requires the concurrence of the related covert activity: for example, the activity of hitting a golf ball requires constant conscious attention and intention. But sometimes an overt activity is compatible with some other unrelated covert activity, as in the case of driving an automobile to work while deeply engrossed in thinking about something else with little awareness of driving. And almost as often one's reasons for initiating a particular activity, if conscious at

* Further analysis suggests that instigation to overt activity ($_sF_R$) is mediated by the perceptual tendency (T_r) whether or not the latter is dominant and covertly expressed. This would be illustrated by removing the arrow between S and $_sF_R$ in Fig. 5 and drawing the arrow from T_r to $_sF_R$ instead.

all, become so only after the activity has been initiated. One comes to know, after the fact, what supposedly was the intention that motivated the action.

Treatment of the relationship between phenomenal and overt aspects of motivation becomes more complicated and interesting when resistance, the tendency not to undertake a particular activity, is included in the discussion. But it must be sufficient for this presentation to outline a preliminary position concerning the relationship between conscious thought and action. The main point of the argument is that normally there is a good correlation between covert activity (conscious thought) and overt action, enough at least to suggest theories of conscious volition, even though, according to the present view, there need be no casual relationship between the two. They can be viewed as different consequences of the same physical events. Thought and action are different mediums for expression of different tendencies that belong to the same family. It thus makes sense to speak of the phenomenal and behavioral aspects of the tendency to eat (family name) because the specific tendencies involved share, to some extent, a common fate, increasing in strength (by displacement) following exposure to the instigating force of certain stimuli and decreasing in strength (by substitution) following the occurrence of one or another activity having consummatory value.

This very rudimentary treatment of the nature of the relationship between covert activity (thought) and overt activity (action) tends to emphasize the perceptual and imaginal stream of consciousness in the primitive case of a rat in a maze to make its point. Very much neglected is the stream of conceptual activity that is comprised of covert verbal activity. The latter we view as much more akin to overt action except for the matter of its often not being overtly expressed. At issue, and not satisfactorily resolved at this writing, is the general question whether or not the expression of a tendency in consciousness (e.g., the thought, "I want to eat") has some additional implication for overt action, one not already implied in the fact that the tendency to eat, i.e., to engage in activities that will culminate in eating, must already be relatively strong to account for the very fact of having the thought "I want to eat."

VIII. Description of Individual Differences in Personality in the Context of a Theory of Motivation

An impetus for development of the conceptual scheme outlined here was provided by actual confrontation of the inadequacies of the traditional stimulus-bound mode of thought at the frontier of empirical research on achievement motivation (see Feather, 1962; Atkinson, 1964, pp. 295–314). It should be of some interest, in this final section, to consider the way in which the conceptual analysis of a change of activity relates to the theory of achievement motivation that has evolved in systematic study of the effects of individual differences in strength of motive to achieve (n Achievement) on behavior (Atkinson & Feather, 1966).

One of the central concerns in the research on achievement motivation has been an effort to bridge the gap between "the two disciplines of scientific psychology" (Cronbach, 1957) that have developed in relative isolation, namely, the study of individual differences, preoccupied with the development and use of diagnostic tests; and the analysis of basic behavioral processes within experimental psychology with the major emphasis on experimental manipulation of conditions. With our new conceptual spectacles in place, we shall consider the behavioral implications of the concept of motive that has evolved in study of achievement-oriented activities. This will help to provide a fresh basis for evaluation of the potential utility of descriptions of personality in terms of general dispositions of the sort called motives and the progress made toward conceptual integration of the two disciplines. It will also help to sharpen understanding of the differences between the technical sense and the common sense of the term *motive*.

A. The Concept of a Goal-Directed Disposition

Current interest in describing individual differences in personality in terms of general goal-directed dispositions is probably rooted in McDougall's (1908) treatment of the individual as a bundle of instincts. Parting with the notion that a psychogenic need was necessarily instinctive, Henry Murray (1938) developed the concept programmatically and introduced the thematic apperception method, in which an individual provides fantasies in response to picture cues, for clinical diagnosis of his underlying, often unconscious needs. Murray argued that description of personality in terms of the *effects* an individual generally strives to bring about yields a better understanding of his behavior than description in terms of general habits or traits, which tell little of an individual's aims or goals.

McClelland (1951) has advanced a number of sound hypotheses concerning the way in which relatively universal (i.e., transcultural) motives might be acquired early in life, before the development of language, as a result of socialization practices the world over that deal with the common problems of adjustment, such as relations with other people and mastery of the environment.

B. DETERMINANTS OF ACHIEVEMENT MOTIVATION

The effort to achieve a useful description of personality in terms of dimensions common to all men spurred the work by McClelland *et al.* (1953) to develop a valid method for measurement of important social motives, beginning with the studies of effects of experimentally induced motivation to achieve on imagination (or thematic apperception) that have already been cited. Then followed a decade of experimental study of the behavioral effects or correlates of individual differences in strength of achievement motive as measured by the individual's thematic apperceptive *n* Achievement score. The constant aim of this work was to specify the nature of the interaction between personality (P) and the immediate environmental (E) determinants of motivation that Lewin had summarized in the programmatic equation $B = f(P, E)$.

It soon became apparent in this work that the effect of the immediate environment or situation could be described in terms of the cognitive expectations it aroused in an individual, given his history, concerning the consequences of particular actions in that situation and the incentive value of those expected consequences (Atkinson, 1958, Pt. III). These basic concepts, introduced earlier by Tolman (1932) and Lewin (1938) and currently formalized in decision theory (Edwards, 1954), together with the concept of motive as a relatively stable and general disposition of personality, were represented in a formulation of the determinants of the strength of tendency to undertake an activity in order to achieve success:

$$T_{r,s} = M_S \times P_{r,s} \times I_s \tag{8}$$

where M_S represents the strength of the relatively general and stable motive to achieve, $P_{r,s}$ represents the strength of expectancy, or subjective probability that the consequence of undertaking a particular activity will be success, and I_s represents the incentive value of success at that particular activity.

This conception contains a hypothesis concerning what has been called the subjective value, utility, or valence of a goal in the other statements of the Expectancy $\times$ Value principle, namely, to use Lewin's term, that the valence of a goal depends on both the incentive offered in a given situation and the strength of motive in the individual:

$$V_{a_g} = M_G \times I_g. \tag{9}$$

The general logic of decision theory, that the subjectively expected utility of a particular activity involves the summation of the products of subjective probability and utility over all possible outcomes, is apparent in an equivalent assumption in studies of motivation: the total strength of the tendency expressed in a given activity is the algebraic sum of separate component motivational tendencies, each attributable to a different kind of expected consequence and itself the product of a motive, expectancy, and incentive. Thus the general premise in studies of achievement-oriented activity has been

$$T_r = T_{r,s} - T_{r,-f} + T_{r,\,ext}, \tag{10}$$

in which $T_{r,\,-f}$ represents the tendency to avoid the negative consequence of failure, and $T_{r,\,ext}$ represents a summation of separate extrinsic motivational tendencies to undertake the achievement-oriented task (e.g., to gain social approval or a monetary reward).

C. MOTIVE AS A DETERMINANT OF INSTIGATING FORCE

Now, having argued that a stimulus situation does not elicit a tendency to respond from a state of rest, as was certainly implied in this earlier formulation [Eqs. (8)–(10)], but rather functions to define an instigating force that acts on an already activated inertial tendency to undertake a particular activity, we see the need for a simple reformulation to integrate the earlier theory of achievement motivation and the new conceptual analysis of determinants of a change of activity. Motive, expectancy, and incentive value are to be considered the determinants or components of an instigating force; that is,

$$_sF_{R,G} = P_{r,g} \times V_{a_g} = M_G \times P_{r,g} \times I_g. \tag{11}$$

Motive (M_G) is still conceived as a variable that influences a whole family of functionally related activities, namely, those activities that are expected to lead to the same kind of goal. The strength of an individual's motive to achieve, for example, functions to influence a whole family of instigating forces to engage in activities that are expected to eventuate in a successful evaluation of one's performance in relation to some standard of excellence, but to have no influence on instigating forces to engage in affiliative activity or sexual activity or to eat, and so on.

Now viewing motive as a relatively general and stable characteristic of personality that is a determinant of, or a component of, the strength of the instigating force of a stimulus to undertake a particular activity, we may look at the principle of change of activity to see whether or not the behavioral implications of motive, as now specified by that principle, are consistent with experimental evidence. Given the general principle stated in Eqs. (4) and (5), we can consider the behavioral effects of differences in the strength of a particular motive by assuming, as suggested in a very simplified and truncated version of this principle, that the situationally defined inducements, which also influence the strength of $_sF_A$ and $_sF_B$, have a constant value of 1; that is,

$$t = \frac{(M_A/c) - T_{B_i}}{M_B}. \tag{12}$$

We can see that a strong motive sustaining an activity already in progress (M_A) will, like the somewhat analogous concept of inertial mass in physics, tend to produce greater persistence in that activity than would a weaker motive. And the same strong motive, but now considered as a determinant of $_sF_B$, in the position of M_B when the individual is engaged in some other kind of activity, should promote greater readiness for prompt initiation of activity B than would a weak motive. In this position, its function is somewhat analogous to that of the gravitational mass of physics. Thus, other things equal, the person described as strong in achievement motive should be more willing to initiate achievement-oriented activities when presented with challenging opportunities in his environment and should be more persistent in them when confronted with opportunities to engage in other kinds of activity than the person described as weak in achievement motive. And since the strength of the tendency expressed in an ongoing activity will approach a limit defined by $_sF_A/c$, or M_A/c in the truncated expression, we expect that a strong motive will also often be expressed in a higher level of achievement-oriented performance, that is, a more intense and vigorous pursuit of the goal. (It is worth noting that sometimes the more intense and vigorous pursuit of the goal may produce inefficiency, as in the confusion of problem solving under pressure, and therefore a lower level of achievement-oriented performance as measured by society's standard.)

The achievement motive, conceived as the common determinant of the strength of a whole family of instigating forces to achieve for a given individual, should generate correlations between behavioral measures obtained from the same individuals on separate occasions and in different activities when the situational determinants of instigating force to achieve and the inertial tendency to achieve are relatively constant within the group of subjects. This is the general character of the empirical evidence: individuals who express a great deal of achievement imagery in imaginative stories produced in response to one kind of picture also express it in response to another kind of picture; individuals who express a great deal of achievement imagery on one occasion also express a great deal of achievement imagery on another occasion, even when the average response of the whole group is significantly higher. And these individuals who score relatively high in thematic apperceptive need for achievement should and do tend to display higher level of performance and persistence in achievement-oriented activities. The specification of the functional properties of a motive, conceived as determinant of family of instigating forces, is consistent with the available empirical evidence (McClelland *et al.,* 1953; Atkinson, 1958; Atkinson & Feather, 1966).

D. PERSONALITY CONCEIVED AS A HIERARCHY OF GENERAL MOTIVES

If the implication of a strong motive is that an individual will be eager to initiate a particular kind of activity and resistant to change from the kind of activity once it has been initiated, the more general implication of a description of an individual's personality in terms of a hierarchy of motives is that it constitutes a specification of how that individual will distribute his time among different kinds of activity. The person strong in motive to achieve but weak in motive to affiliate will spend much more of his time in work than in friendly commerce with others. A reversal in the relative strength of these two motives implies less time in work and more in affiliative activity. We are led by the conceptual analysis of the determinants of a change of activity and of the determinative role of particular motives to the more general and molar implications of individual differences in personality.

Allison (1963) has already studied the way animals distribute their time when given equal opportunity to engage in the activities of eating, having commerce with another rat, or playing with a wire grid in separate compartments of a small maze. The preference for the activity of eating (under a constant condition of food privation) was measured by the proportion of the total time spent eating or in commerce with the food. This proportion ranged from 0.12 to 0.85 for different animals, indicating the range of individual differences in personality. Of particular interest in the present context is the fact that this measure of the relative strength of a motive to eat was positively correlated as expected, with the speed of initiation of eating on the first occasion and the level of performance in pursuit of food in another setting.

One can overemphasize the determinative role of an individual's motives as here conceived, and we have been doing that for purposes of the discussion in assuming that all other things are equal. But the other major determinants of selectivity in behavior are seldom, if ever, equal among a group of individuals who may differ in strength of motive. So it is of some importance, in closing, to call attention to the potential integrative function of the principle of change of activity. It identifies, in a coherent statement, the motivational properties of the several major classes of determinants that have been accentuated, to the neglect of the others, in the relatively disparate subfields of psychology. The impact on behavior of the immediate environment, the stimulus situation, which has been a central interest of the experimentalist, is represented in the concept of the instigating force of the stimulus. The effect of relatively general and stable individual differences in disposition, as typically measured by the mental tester, is represented in the concept of motive as a determinant of a family of instigating forces. And the persistent effect of previously aroused but inadequately satisfied tendencies, of central importance in the clinical psychologist's analysis of behavior, is represented in the concept of inertial tendency. The latter is the foundation stone in this step toward a theory of an *active* individual.

REFERENCES

Allison, J. Preference for food, magnitude of food reward, and instrumental conditioning. Unpublished doctoral dissertation, Univer. of Michigan, 1963.

Atkinson, J. W. (Ed.) *Motives in fantasy, action, and society.* Princeton, N. J.: Van Nostrand, 1958.

Atkinson, J. W. *An introduction to motivation.* Princeton, N. J.: Van Nostrand, 1964.

Atkinson, J. W. and Birch, D. *The dynamics of action.* In preparation (mimeo), 1967.

Atkinson, J. W., and Cartwright, D. Some neglected variables in contemporary conceptions of decision and performance. *Psychological Reports,* 1964, **14,** 575–590.

Atkinson, J. W., & Feather, N. T. (Eds.) *A theory of achievement motivation.* New York: Wiley, 1966.

Barker, R. G. (Ed.) *The stream of behavior.* New York: Appleton-Century-Crofts, 1963.

Birch, D. Shift in activity and the concept of persisting tendency. In Spence, K. W. and Spence, J. T. (Eds.) *The psychology of learning and motivation: Advances in research and theory,* Vol. II. Academic Press, 1968.

Birch, D. and Veroff, J. *Motivation: A study of action.* Belmont, California: Brooks/Cole, 1966.

Cronbach, L. J. The two disciplines of scientific psychology. *American Psychologist,* 1957, **12,** 671–684.

Edwards, W. The theory of decision making. *Psychological Bulletin,* 1954, **51,** 380–417.

Feather, N. T. The study of persistence. *Psychological Bulletin,* 1962, **59,** 94–114.

James, W. *The principles of psychology.* Vol. II. New York: Henry Holt, 1890.

Lewin, K. *The conceptual representation and measurement of psychological forces.* Durham, N. C.: Duke Univer. Press, 1938.

McClelland, D. C. *Personality*. New York: Sloane, 1951.

McClelland, D. C., Atkinson, J. W., Clark, R. A., & Lowell, E. L. *The achievement motive*. New York: Appleton-Century-Crofts, 1953.

McDougall, W. *An introduction to social psychology*. London: Methuen, 1908.

Miller, N. E. Liberalization of basic S-R concepts: Extension to conflict behavior, motivation, and social learning. In S. Koch (Ed.), *Psychology: A study of a science*. Vol. 2. *General systematic formulations, learning, and special processes*. New York: McGraw-Hill, 1959. Pp. 196–292.

Mischel, T. Pragmatic aspects of explanation. *Philosophy of Science*, 1966, **33**, 40–60.

Murray, H. A. *Explorations in personality*. London & New York: Oxford Univer. Press, 1938.

Skinner, B. F. *Science and human behavior*. New York: Macmillan, 1953.

Tolman, E. C. *Purposive behavior in animals and men*. New York: Century, 1932.

Tolman, E. C. *Collected papers in psychology* (also called *Behavior and Psychological man*). Berkeley, Calif.: Univer. of California Press, 1951.

MOTIVATION, EMOTION, AND THE CONCEPTUAL SCHEMES OF COMMON SENSE

R. S. PETERS

I. Introduction

In reflecting upon what contribution I might most usefully make to a symposium of philosophers and psychologists on a conceptual framework for human actions, I came to the conclusion that I would attempt a bridging and synoptic one. Presumably the psychologists will approach this topic from the vantage point of the conceptual scheme that they have found to be most fruitful in research. The philosophers, on the other hand, are likely to concern themselves with less heuristic conceptual and methodological matters to do with action, reason, cause, and the status of teleological explanations. I thought it might be useful, therefore, to try to relate psychological theories of motivation and emotion, especially those favored by the psychologists contributing to this symposium (insofar as I am familiar with them), to the conceptual scheme of human actions the "logical geography" of which philosophers of the analytic school try to map.

This is a vast and ambitious undertaking that would tend to meander from one theory to another unless some connecting thread were provided. I have therefore attempted to provide one by developing a unifying thesis about the indispensability in psychological theory of what I call the conceptual scheme of common sense. This has helped me to get a bit clearer about what has puzzled me profoundly on and off for the past twenty-five years, which is the problem of the relationship between psychological theories and the less specialized knowledge that enables us most of the time to make sense of each other's behavior and of our own.

II. Psychology, Common Sense, and the Institutional Framework

One of the sources of George Kelly's * dissatisfaction with psychological theories of motivation, which have been in fashion during the last half century, has been that such theorists seem to propound two theories (Bannister, 1966, p. 361). The first deals with the behavior of the organism, which is characterized as impelled by drives, reacting to stimuli, or at the mercy of unconscious wishes; the second relates to the psychologist himself, who constructs theories and derives and tests hypotheses in the endeavor to understand, predict, and control his environment. Although the first is usually called a scientific theory and the second an account of scientific method, both are thought to have application to human behavior. Kelly's own theory of "personal constructs" derived from his attempt to take the second type of account of man seriously. He extrapolated the notion of "man the scientist" from this type of situation and conceived of human behavior generally in terms of the attempt to understand, predict, and control the environment. Personal constructs are conceptual templates that enable individuals to anticipate events (Kelly, 1955, Chapters 1–3).

The suggestion that psychologists should think seriously about a typically human activity, such as thinking scientifically, as well as atypical animal activities, such as running mazes and pressing levers, is one with which I have great sympathy; for my belief is that much of the work done in this century by psychologists reveals very little about the psychology of animals, let alone of men. But I do not think that Kelly has pursued far enough the implications of his initial insight. Many, of course, would object to the emphasis on control and prediction in his account of the scientist,

---

* The device of launching this paper from the pad provided by Kelly's theory was first adopted when it was thought that Kelly was to be a participant in the colloquium. His untimely death, however, prevented this. Nevertheless it was thought fitting to retain this way of introducing the topic.

and many would demur at the extrapolation of this type of human activity rather than some other; but my objection to a possible interpretation of this starting point is much more deep seated. It is that man the scientist might be postulated in isolation from the rules and procedures that are constitutive of this form of activity. Science is one of the most rule-ridden of all human activities. One must listen to what other people say; one must accept nothing as true unless evidence is produced; one must state one's hypotheses as clearly and in as impersonal a way as possible; one must not cook the evidence or misrepresent other people's assumptions. Men only come to think "scientifically" if they have been brought up in this kind of critical tradition, with the overriding value that it places on truth and, as Francis Bacon argued so forcibly in his *Novum Organum,* this way of thinking goes against inveterate tendencies of the human mind.

If, therefore, one pursues the implications of Kelly's starting point, one comes to see not just that scientific thinking is only possible within a certain type of tradition, but that it is only intelligible to us as a form of human activity because we have been initiated into such a tradition. This is how we are placed in relation both to science and to all typically human activities. For most of us, however, most of the time the preoccupations of the scientist are pretty remote, unless notions like "control" and "prediction" are extended so that they cease to distinguish scientific from any other typically human activity. This is because much of our time is spent in making different forms of judgment within various human activities rather than in systematically trying to understand them in a more detailed way. On occasions we state our intentions, make promises, and justify our conduct; on other occasions we praise and blame people, we give advice and warnings, select some for jobs and reject others. We listen to music, perhaps; appreciate pictures; watch and participate in games. We make love, money, and cakes. Sometimes we even give people orders. All such activities presuppose distinctive structures of rules and distinctive types of languages. No doubt within these public forms of life we develop our own criteria of importance, our personal constructs, if you like. But these arise as personal emphases out of a public stock, and they are made on situations that are intelligible to us only because we have developed a shared system of concepts and ways of behavior.

What is called our commonsense knowledge consists largely in what we possess when we have learned our way around this complex heritage. It comprises no set or fixed body of beliefs; in content it is, to a large extent, culture bound, depending on the level of differentiation and complexity that a society has attained. It may include deposits of scientific theories that have been incorporated in a popular way into the common stock of assumptions; it may vary from group to group within a society. Its main characteristic is its intimate connection with the practical concerns of a society, the particular rules and purposes of its institutions, and the more personal relationships of its members. When, therefore, psychologists speak sometimes rather disparagingly about what they call common sense (see, e.g., Atkinson, 1964, Chapter 1), they usually ignore and oversimplify the richness and complexity of the understanding that it contains. This is the first aspect of common sense for which it is difficult to see how psychology could provide an adequate substitute. For this sort of understanding is revealed in the *identification* of behavior as well as in its explanation, there being no hard and fast line between them (see Melden, 1961, *passim*). To revert, for instance, to the case of the scientist: we could ask why Galileo was rolling balls down an inclined plane. If we were told that he was doing this in order to test a scientific hypothesis, we could then, in some other context, refer to what he was doing as "testing a scientific hypothesis." An action with a low-level purpose would be classified as one having a higher-level purpose. Similarly, in a means–end type of situation, an end like "getting a promotion," which can be appealed to as an explanation of a person's hard work, could be used to characterize his behavior at work. This is because both the explanation and the identification of actions depend on the aspect under which the agent views what he is doing: as conforming to some standard or as bringing about some end. And this can be stated at different levels of generality or located at different points of prevision. To identify human behavior, therefore, as well as to explain it in a commonsense way, we must know not only the general rules and purposes governing the type of activity under scrutiny; we must also know the agent's view of the matter, his information, what he sees as important in the situation. Whatever would we make of a person sitting down and moving bits of wood around unless we knew something about the rules of chess and the point of the game?

These are not particularly outlandish examples; for my contention is that much of human behavior is like this. It is constituted by human beings maneuvering within a complicated network of purposes and rules that are appealed to for both the explanation and the identification of behavior, depending on the context (cf. Winch, 1958, Chapter 11). The same sort of point can be made, too, about performances in which psychologists are interested, such as perception and memory, as has been made about activities, such as doing science, or actions, such as moving a piece of wood. For both perception and memory involve standards of reality, claims about what is really there or about what really happened; both involve classification of things or events as falling under concepts that are related in complicated ways to each other. All these presuppose elaborate conventions worked out over centuries, which are incorporated in our language. If we understood nothing of these elaborate conventions, human behavior would be as unintelligible to us as it is to small children and to animals.

Of course, we do understand it, more or less. And this is not because we have learned any psychology; it is because we have been initiated from childhood onward into the various rules and purposes that are constitutive of human life (see Peters, 1966, Chapter 2). In learning to behave as human beings we at the same time take into ourselves the structure of concepts and categories without which we could make no sense of human life. In learning a language we gradually structure our consciousness with these rules for making sense of the world and relating ourselves to aspects of it in various ways. Our ability to reason scientifically, for instance, depends not only on gradually acquiring categories like those of enduring object, reality, and causality, but also on the incorporation of a critic into our consciousness so that we look for counterexamples to our expectations. All this has to be laboriously learned.

It is not surprising, therefore, if the psychologist can contribute very little to the understanding of particular actions and if his ability to predict what an individual will do in particular circumstances is little better than that of his nonprofessional colleagues. This is because success depends much more on detailed knowledge of the society and the individual in question, including his history and belief system, than on the devising of any new general laws. Lewin, it is true, emphasized the importance of the life space of a person at a given time; but he devised no satisfactory way of including all that would have to be known about this in his Galilean system. Indeed, how could he have done so? Furthermore, he neglected the importance of knowledge of the enduring attributes of a person, which only familiarity with his history could provide.

A similar point can be made about more recent work on achievement motivation. It is suggested that "the motive to achieve success (M_s), which the individual carries about with him from one situation to another, combines multiplicatively with the two specific situational influences, the strength of expectancy or probability of success (P_s), and incentive value of success at a particular activity (I_s) to produce the tendency to approach success that is overtly expressed in the direction, magnitude, and persistence of achievement-oriented performance" (Atkinson, 1964, p. 242). Atkinson points out that, whereas the first variable is a relatively general and stable characteristic of the person, values of the other two variables P_s and I_s depend on the individual's past experience in specific situations that are similar to the one that he now confronts. Assigning values to these variables must therefore depend on a fairly intimate knowledge of the individual concerned. This presents far greater difficulties than does formulating the commonsense assumptions enshrined in the generalizations. Indeed, I am inclined to say that if people in American society were not alive to these generalizations about achievement, one would ask questions about their general education rather than about their attendance at psychology courses!

Of course in coming to understand why individuals do what they do, or to predict what they will do, we make use not just of our detailed knowledge of their past and their individual systems of beliefs, purposes, and appraisals; we also rely, as I have emphasized before, on our familiarity with the general rules and purposes of the various activities and social institutions (such as science) that they have internalized in varying degrees. Much of this type of knowledge is specific to particular activities and institutions. It is because of this that we know what people are doing and roughly what to expect of them in restaurants, hotels, colleges, churches, and golf clubs. It is because of the importance of this sort of knowledge that, on getting to know people, we first orient ourselves to them by finding out their profession, marital status, and other affiliations. In this area of knowledge, social psychologists have much to contribute, which falls under the rather too general concept of role playing. It is difficult to see how any developments in psychology could reveal the unimportance of this sort of general knowledge; for as I have argued before, it is largely constitutive of the form of life in which we are engaged most of our waking lives. To dispense with it would be to put ourselves in the positions of dogs trying to take part in or to understand the proceedings of a law court.

It might be thought that much store is being placed on what might be called the conventional wisdom of the tribe. But the thesis here advanced is not about the indispensability of all the *content* of common sense; rather it relates to the indispensability of the types of concepts that it employs, namely, those belonging to the family of which "wanting," "following a rule," "deciding," and so on are members. Particular assumptions embedded in common sense (e.g., about what people invariably want) may well be mistaken and it is an important function of empirical psychology to provide evidence that may falsify such assumptions. Similarly, evidence should be provided as confirmations of common sense, though on occasions this might seem rather otiose.

Psychological theories, too, may extend and attempt to make more precise assumptions that are embedded in common sense (e.g., the work done by Atkinson and McClelland on "achievement") and to suggest ways in which factors involved in such assumptions are combined and related to each other. Doubts of a conceptual sort might, of course, be raised about the type of relationship envisaged. It is not altogether clear, for instance, how far the use of algebra in a system like that of Lewin or Atkinson advances our understanding until the basis of the measurement is clear and one is sure that commensurables are being combined. The way in which "beliefs," for instance, are related to "wants" in giving an account of action is distorted if these are thought of as separable variables that can be quantified and causally related to each other; for to want something is always to want it under some aspect and the aspect falls under beliefs. (If I want to eat something, my seeing it under the aspect of "food" is connected with various beliefs about its properties.) The connection, in other words, between beliefs and wants insofar as both are involved in "motivated behavior," is conceptual rather than causal. The strength and persistence of certain wants can, of course be measured. But if an attempt were made to isolate and quantify the belief component, all sorts of problems would break out. What could be done about the content of beliefs, for instance, and the grounds on which they are held? "Strength" of beliefs is a notion that suggests quantification; but it is unintelligible apart from notions like "evidence" and "good reasons"; and how are logical notions of that sort to be expressed algebraically?

This general sort of point can be made with particular reference to the problem of quantifying a variable, such as P_s in Atkinson's system, which is a situational variable relating to the strength of expectancy or probability of success. Probability theorists have always found these sorts of sums very difficult; but when they occupy a twilight zone between rational grounds of belief and actual psychological potency, the algebra becomes even more problematic. And the more the notion of "strength of expectancy" approximates to psychological potency, the nearer it gets to the notion of the "incentive value of success" (I_s), which is represented as a distinct situational variable. Nevertheless, whatever one thinks of the algebra by means of which Lewin and Atkinson summarize their theories, the attempt to give more precision to commonsense assumptions is laudable enough. It would be more laudable still if it were accompanied by an attempt to break down further conceptually such commonsense notions as achievement, which incorporate at least three rather different notions, namely, the desire to master or succeed in anything that one attempts, the desire to master or succeed in anything that one thinks important, and the desire to do anything better than one's fellows.

III. Motives, Traits, and Attitudes

Mention of the achievement motive brings to the fore the fact that there are, even at the commonsense level, a whole range of explanations of human behavior that do not seem so clearly bound up with *specific* activities and institutions. We interpret a range of behavior as directed toward making good a deficit of things such as food, water, and affection. Other types of behavior are classified in terms of character traits, such as honesty, punctuality, selfishness, and considerateness, which are internalized rules widespread in society rather than confined to particular institutions, or in terms of higher-level traits, such as persistence, integrity, consistency, and conscientiousness, which pick out the manner in which people stick to lower-order rules (Peters, 1962). At this general level, too, talk of motives is apposite; for this is a term that we use to ascribe purposes to people of a *personal* rather than specifically institutional sort. An ambitious man is one who is moved by the thought of getting ahead of others; a jealous man is one who is moved by the thought that someone else has something to which he thinks he has a right; an envious man is one who is irked by the thought that another has something that he wants.

The points that I have made about the dependence of our understanding of behavior on the cognitive content that pervades particular forms of social life applies to this more general area of conduct as well. The difference is in the lack of specificity of the cognitive content, not in the essential features of the type of understanding that is involved. Without moral education and the development of a fairly sophisticated grasp of interpersonal relationships we would not know how to apply these concepts. How, for instance, would we know when to say that a person was jealous, as distinct from envious, unless we grasped notions to do with possession? How would we begin to understand the difference between remorse, guilt, and shame unless we could make fairly sophisticated moral distinctions?

What I have said, too, about the different functions of the discourse of common sense applies very much to concepts at this level; for our general terms, such as motive, intention, need, and interests, reflect the complexity of our preoccupations. When, for instance, we say that somebody needs something—a bath, for instance, or oxygen or affection—we are combining a value judgment about the desirability of being clean, alive, or mentally healthy with the assertion that there is something absent, namely, a bath, oxygen, or affection, without which the desirable condition cannot be attained. Diagnostic remarks of this sort combine empirical hypotheses with value judgments. Similarly, as I have argued elsewhere (Peters, 1958, Chapter 2, and 1967), remarks about people's motives usually combine the suggestion that somebody's behavior is up for assessment with a certain type of explanation of it. I was delighted to have confirmation of this point from an unexpected source when I read that one of Kelly's objections to the construct of motives is that he thinks that it is widely used as "part of the language of complaint about the behavior of other people" (Kelly, 1958, p. 46). The same sort of point can be made about the term "intention," whose general function is to identify rather than to explain actions, usually in some kind of justificatory context, often where there is a suggestion of a mistake having been made. Stephen Toulmin, in a recent paper, has developed this point about the justificatory as distinct from the explanatory use of language (Toulmin, 1968).

Common sense also has concepts that operate at an even more abstract level than that of motives and traits. Sometimes we interpret people's behavior in terms of attitudes, such as optimism, pessimism, cynicism, and fearlessness, which exert a general influence on whole areas of their behavior. We also talk about people's ideals and aspirations. There is little point in probing into the distinctions between these sorts of concepts. All that need be noted, for the purpose of the present argument, is their obvious connection with affectively tinged beliefs; they have a wide-ranging cognitive content.

I need hardly mention that in this area, much important work has been done by psychologists to supplement common sense. The work of McClelland and Atkinson on the motives of achievement and affiliation, as I have already noted, makes more precise use of commonsense concepts. Kelly's theory of personal constructs operates also at this level and, like most theories of this sort, is very important for the understanding of individual differences. It suggests that individuals tend to anticipate and to interpret the behavior of others in terms of very general dichotomies, such as "loving–hating." The key to the general style of a person's behavior is to be found by unearthing the system of constructs with which he operates. Other theories of personality types, such as those of Adler, Fromm, and Horney, make use of similar types of concepts. So do theories of attitudes such as those of Allport and Campbell. Such theories in no way supersede explanations in terms of the purposes and rules that structure the consciousness of members of a particular society. Rather they suggest that there are certain general orientations toward others and toward oneself that determine individual differences in behavior within such systems. And this may well be true; for one of the important ways in which man differs from animals is that he acts not just in the light of a concept of his own nature and relationship to others, but in terms of a variable concept of these.

The view that we have of ourselves and of others as *persons,* as distinct from as occupants of a variety of institutional roles, is as important in influencing our behavior as it is variable between people. That it should be so is not a notion unfamiliar to any keen commonsense observer. Psychol-

ogists, however, provide an additional dimension to this type of understanding by constructing causal-genetic theories about the origins of such
general orientations in childhood. Freud's theory of character traits, for
instance, was a theory about the genesis of certain exaggerated and distorted styles of rule following (Peters, 1962). It presupposes a pattern of
rules operative in a society but suggests that individuals, because of early
social influences, adopt a characteristic style of exhibiting them. This way
of looking at such theories seems to me much more helpful than to suggest
that the content of the individual's rule-governed behavior can be deduced
from such high-level orientations, that from one such "genotype" many
"phenotypes" may be deduced (Brown, 1940, p. 79).

Such theories seem highly plausible on general grounds; for given the
established importance of early learning, and given the fact that in early life
interpersonal rather than institutional relationships predominate, it seems
highly plausible to suggest that the early stances that we adopt in this
interpersonal sphere, especially at crucial stages of conflict where we en-
counter general social norms, are likely to persist and to be of an all-
pervading influence throughout our lives. One need not go along with many
of the details of the Freudian scheme in order to accept the general plausibility of this imaginative idea. The problem in this area is not the dearth of
interesting theories to supplement the conceptual scheme of common sense,
but the intractable difficulties involved in devising tests to decide between
them. There is the additional difficulty, too, that some of the theories in
this area are expressed in too woolly a way to be testable.

IV. Theories of Motivation and the Abstract Postulates of Common Sense

At this juncture psychologists may well be feeling rather fidgety; for they
will be thinking, nothing yet has been said about more ambitious theories
of motivation that operate at a much more abstract level than common
sense. Before passing to these, however, I want to point out that this is an
oversimple contrast. Common sense is often thought of as a very mundane
low-level system of beliefs. Yet a little thought about its presuppositions
scarcely supports this stock assumption. This is particularly true in the
sphere of human behavior; for insofar as we are concerned in ordinary life
with explaining what people do, as distinct from praising them, cursing
them, advising them, selecting them, giving them orders, and so on, we take
for granted some very abstract assumptions in ascribing purposes to people
and in classifying their behavior as being cases of following certain rules.

We assume that, other things being equal, a person who wants something, and who has the information about means necessary to attain it, will take what he judges to be the means. Deviations require some special explanation. We assume, too, certain postulates about rule following. There are appropriate as well as efficient ways of performing most actions. In our society, for instance, we do not expect people, without some special reason, to slam doors, but to shut them in an appropriate manner. Similarly, in activities that are, in the main, constituted by rules of appropriateness, we assume that a person who knows what the rules are and who voluntarily participates in an activity will act in the light of his knowledge of these rules, other things being equal. We assume, as I have argued before (Peters, 1958, Chapter 1), that man is a purposive rule-following animal, who acts in the light of what Popper has called "the logic of the situation" (Popper, 1945, p. 90). A lot more work, of course, needs to be done to tidy up these assumptions and express them more precisely, which would not be either appropriate or possible in an article with as broad a coverage as this one. There have, however, been several other philosophers who have attempted this (e.g., Hempel, 1962; Ayer, 1964; and Mischel, 1966). We do not, of course, learn such basic postulates of human action by having them explained to us like the postulates of mechanics. We learn them as what Freud calls "the ego" begins to be superimposed on "the id"; they are gradually built into us by others and by our transactions with the world as we learn to want things in a full sense, which involves taking means to ends, as we learn to interpret the world in causal terms, and as we learn to follow rules. We learn these abstract postulates without first being able to formulate them by being initiated into a form of life that exhibits them.

Atkinson (1964, pp. 4–7) admits the intuitive validity of what he calls the "common-sense of motivation." He claims, however, that psychological theories transcend it in the same sort of way as Galilean explanations transcended the common sense of Aristotle. This, of course, is a familiar claim made by psychologists not just since Lewin wrote his notorious chapter on the subject (Lewin, 1935), but ever since Hobbes set himself up as the Galileo of psychology in the seventeenth century and suggested very much what Atkinson himself suggests at the end of his most erudite and illuminating book: that psychological phenomena could be deduced from the law of inertia (see Peters, 1956, Chapters 4 and 6). But nothing that Atkinson produces in the way of a plausible theory ever shows that these sorts of postulates about human behavior have in fact been superseded; all that psychologists have done, who have been concerned with human behavior rather than with pipe-dream extrapolations from animal movements, is to translate such assumptions into a more technical (and often pretentious) terminology. Lewin's dreadful jargon about life space, vectors, and valences, for instance, enshrined first of all the astounding discovery, which he shared with Koffka and Köhler, that the behavior of individuals is to be interpreted in terms of how they see a situation and their information about it, rather than in terms of the purely physical or geographical properties of their environment. Second, it translated familiar assumptions about wanting and avoiding things into a language that added nothing to what we already know and that suggested no deductions that would not readily be made from postulates expressed in the commonsense language. Was anything added, for instance, to the suggestion deriving from Freud that unfulfilled wishes tend to persist and to influence thought and action by translating all this into the language of tension systems and psychological forces? Did not Zeigarnik's work on interrupted tasks and subsequent work on substitute activities owe more to Freud's speculations, which could be expressed in commonsense language, than to the elaborate conceptual superstructure that Lewin erected in order to demonstrate that the Galilean era was dawning?

The same sort of point could be made about technically expressed decision theories that are now becoming fashionable. Admittedly they permit mathematics to be used, which may be useful in dealing with some areas of human behavior. But do not assumptions about "subjectively expected utility" make use of postulates belonging to the old commonsense family of wanting, having information about means to ends, deciding in terms of the relative attractiveness of alternatives, and so on? And does not all the valuable work done by McClelland and Atkinson (McClelland, Atkinson, Clark, & Lovell, 1953; Atkinson, 1964) on achievement and affiliation motivation itself make use of most of the concepts connected with a purposive rule-following model?

My point is not, of course, to deny that a great deal of additional light has been thrown on phenomena of motivation by all the work that has been done under the aegis of these elaborate conceptual schemes. It is only to query the assumption, often made, that the conceptual scheme of common sense has been superseded. As far as I am aware, there is no important theory of human motivation that has seriously suggested that we can dispense with the family of concepts of which "wanting," "taking means to ends," "following rules," and "deciding between alternatives" are members. Some theorists (e.g., Tolman, Lewin) have verbalized these concepts in terms that sound more scientific; others (e.g., Hull) have suggested that postulates in this conceptual scheme could eventually be deduced from postulates about "colorless movements" which, as I have argued before, is a piece of metaphysics at least as old as Hobbes (Peters & Tajfel, 1955); others (e.g., Freud) have admitted its validity for a certain range of behavior (the theory of the ego) but have supplemented it by another conceptual scheme (the theory of the id) to account for phenomena that it does not fit; others (e.g., McDougall) have been so impressed by this conceptual scheme that they have argued that behavior is to be explained in terms of a finite number of innate purposes, thereby exalting a conceptual insight into a superfluous genetic doctrine; others (games and decision theorists) have elaborated this scheme and tried to quantify some of the variables; others (cyberneticians and information theorists), impressed by the similarities between purposive behavior and self-regulating machines, have honored such machines, and the human brain, with terms such as "plans," "standards," "information," "memory," and "knowledge of results" in order to theorize about them.

Given, then, that the applicability of this conceptual scheme has usually been granted at some level of explanation, with what have theories of motivation usually been concerned? Surely with what have been thought to be further and more fundamental questions. Unfortunately, however, most of the work on motivation in the first half of this century has been dominated by the postulation and gradual refutation of an all-inclusive theory that provided answers, albeit mistaken ones, to most of these further and more fundamental questions. Koch gave a splendid caricature of this when he remarked in 1956 "there was a time not too many years ago when a direct pipe-line extended between Cannon's stomach balloon and the entire domain of motivational psychology" (Koch, 1956, p. 78). What he was referring to, of course, was the old homeostatic theory, the metaphysics of drive or need reduction, whose conceptual confusions and empirical mistakes I tried to catalogue in *The Concept of Motivation* (Peters, 1958). There is no need to go over any of that hallowed ground again. Nevertheless, most of the questions raised by the theory were legitimate enough, except perhaps that of a special explanation for the initiation of behavior, which presupposed an antiquated view of the nervous system. Fundamental questions still remain about the energizing and directedness of behavior. In singling out hunger, thirst, and sex, the classical theory was not on a wrong track; for there do seem to be very special conditions here that sensitize behavior and make talk of drives not inappropriate. The mistake was to generalize the concept and to think of all behavior as in some way "driven."

It was also a mistake to think that all other behavior patterns are acquired by being conditioned on these basic drives. Unfortunately, those who established that some forms of behavior are not so acquired tended to postulate other drives, like "the drive to know" or "extero-ceptive drives" or, as in the case of modern hedonists such as Young and McClelland, to generalize the model appropriate to positive preferences (e.g., for sugar). Worse still, even more metaphysical overall tendencies toward "self-realization" and "growth" were postulated by people such as Rogers and Maslow to provide a more positive supplement to the old overall model of deficiency motivation (see Peters, 1958, Chapter 5). I suspect, too, that a similar hankering for an overall supplementary postulate to drive reduction prompts Hunt's recent suggestion that all these more positive aspects of motivation, covered by concepts, such as curiosity, novelty, competence, and pleasure seeking, that are inconsistent with the old model of the organism stimulated into activity, and driven ultimately by biological needs, can be encompassed within some general postulate of intrinsic motivation "inherent in information processing and action" (Hunt, 1965, pp. 196–197). It is also very strange to equate *this* assumption with what Hunt calls "the ancient doctrine of rationality" (Hunt, 1965, p. 270), though it is encouraging to learn that he thinks that there might be something to be said for the ancient notion that man is a rational animal!

For anyone who accepts the indispensability of the purposive rule-following model in the explanation of actions, there are not only important further questions about how particular wants are acquired, but also questions about how children learn in general to want things and to follow rules, including especially those involved in the use of language, and to interpret the behavior of others by means of these concepts. Psychologists have devoted little attention to this because of their concentration on animals, whose motor systems mature very quickly; philosophers tend to ignore it because of their preoccupation with language games and with concept formation. But the use of words in a language as distinct from babbling and reacting to words as mere noises presupposes that children already understand what "wanting" is, at least in an intuitive sort of way; for they come to grasp that noises are made to mean something, that is, that they are at least instrumental to human purposes. It is interesting to note that Hunt spends a lot of time dealing with this in his reinterpretation of Piaget's account of the development of action in terms of his own all-inclusive theory of "intrinsic motivation" (Hunt, 1965, pp. 246–260).

Once a child has learned to see things as instrumental to other things and to classify things in terms of important aspects, the role of motivation in learning becomes ubiquitous. For all sorts of things can be seen as related to something that is wanted, such as food, warmth, and affection. How important this sort of extrinsic motivation is in the development of new wants, as distinct from forms of social learning such as imitation and identification, would be difficult to determine. Its importance in accounting for *persistence* in behavior and for *change* in behavior is also obvious enough; for to talk about motivation is to talk about the aspects under which things are wanted that explain some kind of persistence of activity or change of activity in respect of them. Obviously much of the detailed empirical work on motivation must consist in trying to answer such further questions about wants. Most of our actual daily behavior, as I have argued before, is to be explained by reference to the myriads of rules and purposes that are constitutive of life in our particular society. But appeal to more general purposes is in place in asking further general questions about their acquisition and about individual differences in persistence and vigor within them and about changes from one pattern of behavior to another. Perhaps one of the most important things that McClelland and his co-workers have done is to devise tests for studying the influence of a few important wants in noncontrived and complex situations such as that of the classroom (McKeachie, 1961; Atkinson, 1964, p. 255) and even during remote periods of the past (McClelland, 1961).

In the realm of human as well as animal motivation much is made nowadays of various forms of intrinsic motivation, such as the tendency to explore, master things, and search for novelty. White's article, "Competence and the Psycho-sexual Stages of Development" (White, 1960) and Hunt's "Intrinsic Motivation" (Hunt, 1965) are perhaps two of the most interesting expositions of the emergence of these forms of motivation in childhood. These developments are certainly most encouraging in their rejection of the old model of extrinsic motivation; certainly, too, the new emphasis on cognition is salutary, whether or not theorists try to unify these tendencies by means of rather formal cognitive notions, such as familiarity, dissonance, and incongruity. But what these types of theory tend to neglect is the valuable element in the old doctrine of hedonism that has been somewhat obscured by modern attempts to revive the doctrine by Young and McClelland (Young, 1955, 1961, Chapter 5; McClelland *et al.,* 1953). There is no time here to enter into all the complications associated with the notion of "pleasure" (see Kenny, 1965; Taylor, 1963). Suffice it to say that one of the main functions of the concept is to draw attention to things that are done or indulged in for what there is in them as distinct from things done out of habit or for some extrinsic reason. Given that there are things of this sort, it is very important to make a detailed study of the intrinsic features of various activities in virtue of which they fall into this category. Koch threw out this suggestion at the end of his contribution to the Nebraska symposium of 1956 (Koch, 1956). But as far as I am aware, no detailed work has been done to follow this up.

This may sound an academic sort of investigation to suggest, but for anyone actively engaged in education, it is far from academic in the pejorative sense of that word. In my view one of the main objectives of education is to get children going on various worthwhile activities so that they come to pursue them and continue with them for what there is in them as distinct from what they offer in the way of instrumental value. I need not elaborate on the difficulties of this enterprise in a consumer-oriented society in which most things are viewed in an instrumental sort of context, with wants of rather a material sort providing the most widespread reasons for doing things. It may well be that various forms of extrinsic motivation (e.g., grades, approval) have to be used to get children going, combined with appeals to the types of general intrinsic motivation in which there has been so much recent interest. But I doubt whether those sorts of motivation do much to get children really on the inside of activities so that they continue with them after they leave educational institutions. What we need to know is what is specific to, say, biology or cookery, toolmaking or astronomy, that will provide reasons for pursuing them that are not entirely idiosyncratic (see Peters, 1966, Chapter 5). If we knew more about this, we might come to know better how to present them to children. General talk about problem solving, discovery, mastery, curiosity, novelty, and even more general talk about incongruity and dissonance, is about as much use in this context as is talk about self-realization and growth in the context of educational aims.

V. Commonsense Clues to Phenomena Requiring Special Explanation

A further feature of common sense that is important for psychological theories is that it makes all sorts of distinctions in a variety of dimensions that intimate that there is something untoward, faulty, or lacking in a piece of behavior that makes us unwilling to classify it as an action, activity, or performance in a full sense, or to apply one or other of the postulates of the rationality model to it. We have words, like "involuntarily," "unintentionally," and "accidentally," that make distinctions in a rather different dimension from words like "inadvertently," "impulsively," "carelessly," and "automatically" (see Austin, 1955–1956). We distinguish between jumping on purpose to avoid a puddle, jumping automatically when skipping, and jumping involuntarily when a face appears at the window or in response to a loud noise. Even the Greeks realized that dreams, visions, deliria, and certain emotional states could not be accommodated within their commonsense explanations; indeed, they often accounted for them by suggesting that they were due to the agency of gods and goddesses. A strict behaviorist, of course, imposes a self-denying ordinance on himself that forbids him to take cognizance of such distinctions; but I think it would be extremely foolish for a less Puritanically minded psychologist to refuse to avail himself of these clues provided by common sense. Indeed, one of the troubles about ordinary language is that some of the distinctions that we make in it are too subtle to be coped with by science, not that it is too crude as a form of communication. Psychology might be wiser to "home in" on some of the important distinctions between phenomena suggested by common sense and develop special theories to explain groups of phenomena rather than to try to develop one type of theory to encompass all phenomena. A good example of such a special theory is that developed by Freud.

I have argued elsewhere (Peters, 1958, Chapter 3), following Ernest Jones, that Freud's originality as a thinker lay not in his discovery of "the unconscious" but in his suggestion that it worked according to *different principles,* and in his use of it mainly to explain not everything but a special group of phenomena that had previously not been explained in psychological terms and among which a certain kind of "family resemblance" is discernible. The phenomena are "related to facial and other expressive movements and to speech, as well as many other processes of thought (both in normal and in sick people), which have hitherto escaped the notice of psychology because they have been regarded as no more than the results of organic disorder and of some abnormal failure in function of the mental apparatus. What I have in mind are 'parapraxes' (slips of the tongue or pen, forgetfulness, etc.), haphazard actions, and dreams in normal people, and convulsive attacks, deliria, visions, and obsessive ideas or acts in neurotic subjects" (Freud, 1955, p. 166). The family resemblance between these phenomena that Freud's theory explained is not that they are abnormal in the popular sense; for what, in this sense of "abnormal," is abnormal about dreams and slips of the tongue? They are rather abnormal in the more recondite sense of not being explicable in terms of the norms of the rule-following purposive model. Slips of the tongue, motor slips, and lapses in memory represent "fallings-short" of standards of performance of which the agent is assumed to be capable and Freud himself gave careful criteria for the range of such phenomena (Freud, 1914, pp. 192–193). Conversely, compulsive and obsessional behavior require special explanation because they are *excessively* rule ridden; either there seems no point to the exaggerated pattern of rule following, or the behavior seems unduly influenced by the predominance of one sort of purpose. The rationality model cannot be applied in any straightforward way to such phenomena. Dreams, deliria, visions, hysteria, and so forth, on the other hand do not rank as actions, activities, or performances at all. They are states that prima facie fall completely outside the range of application of the purposive rule-following model. Freud's genius consisted in seeing links between this wide range of phenomena requiring special explanation and relating them all to his hypothesis of unconscious wishes.

This introduces the second main point of Freud's originality, his use of the concept of "wish"; for, as I have argued, Freud explained these phenomena in terms of wishes, not motives. In developing his theory of the primary processes of thought, Freud combined both a negative and a positive characterization of them. Negatively he argued that they are unchecked by logical contradiction and causal association; they are unhampered by a proper sense of time, space, and reality. Positively they are ruled only by a vague idea of emotional congruence based on the association of ideas with a discharge of tension. One cannot discuss his positive suggestions without going into his whole theory of sexuality and his antiquated tension-reduction model of psychic functioning; but his negative characterization of wishes is instructive in that he reports, on the basis of introspection and clinical evidence, certain important points about wishes that could also be arrived at by conceptual analysis. For when we talk about wishes we are prepared to withdraw the applicability of a range of categories that go along with the rationality model. Typically we wish for things, like the moon, where realistic questions of taking means to ends do not have to be raised. We can even have wishes for states of affairs that are logically impossible, as in the case of an old colleague of mine who wished that he was monogamously married to eight women at once. Freud postulated that this form of cognition still persists in us, after we learn to think and act in accordance with the purposive rule-following model, the stages of which have been mapped by Piaget. Because of this, some of our more rational behavior is "overdetermined" when it follows the lines of such wishes which are consistent with more realistic wants; but forms of "abnormal" behavior, namely the classes listed above, which require special explanation, are to be explained in terms of the persistence of such wishes and the "mechanisms of defense" that are adopted to deal with them.

When I first defended this interpretation of Freud's theory in *The Concept of Motivation* (Peters, 1958), my concern was mainly to attack the notion of an all-inclusive theory of motivation. I argued that Freud saw himself as putting forward a special theory to explain a limited class of phenomena. It was left to others, like Hartmann and David Rapaport (Rapaport, 1959, 1960), to say more about the development of the ego and to link this with developmental theories, such as that of Piaget, that elaborate in detail the stages at which the various categories characterizing rational forms of behavior are acquired. But when I came to do some work on emotions a few years later, I was struck by the similarities between this range of phenomena and those that Freud tried to explain. This suggested a possible extension of this type of explanation to cover a whole range of what I called "passive" phenomena. I will now pass to the details of this suggested extension.

VI. Common Sense and Psychological Theories of Emotion

I have argued throughout this article that in the sphere of our understanding of human behavior, as distinct from that of our understanding of the natural world, we are in a special position that should make us beware of taking too cavalier an attitude toward common sense and the distinctions that we have found it important to make in ordinary language. This is also true in the sphere of emotional phenomena, and the history of psychological theories of emotion is an embarrassing reminder of what can happen if this rough and ready source of understanding is neglected.

If we ask ourselves, first of all, what we might naturally call "emotions," we would give quite a long list that would include fear, anger, joy, sorrow, jealousy, envy, pride, wonder, shame, guilt, remorse, and the like. We would not include hunger, thirst, pain, pleasure, and an interest in symbolic logic. What sort of criteria are implicit in this selection? Surely the connection between "emotion" and a class of cognitions that might conveniently be called "appraisals." These consist in seeing situations under aspects that are agreeable or disagreeable, beneficial or harmful in a variety of dimensions. Fear, for instance, is conceptually connected with seeing a situation as dangerous, anger with seeing it as thwarting, pride with seeing something as ours or as something that we have had a hand in bringing about, envy with seeing someone else as possessing what we want. We would not call hunger or thirst emotions because, although they too involve seeing the world in a certain light, this tendency is cyclic, depending on definite internal conditions; emotions, on the other hand, seem to be appraisals elicited by external conditions or by things that we have brought about or suffered. We do not think of pain and pleasure as emotions unless they are connected with some determinate aspect of a situation that is appraised as affecting us in the agreeable or disagreeable ways indicated by "pleasure" and "pain." An interest in symbolic logic would be ruled out for many reasons, one of them being that emotions do not seem to be connected with specific activities but with general ways in which we view ourselves as related to others and to environmental conditions.

It is a depressing fact that most of the psychological work done on emotion during this century has taken little cognizance of this peculiarly intimate connection between emotions and specific forms of cognition, in spite of the fact that attempts to differentiate emotions in other ways have proved abortive. Ever since Darwin conducted experiments with photographs on facial expressions connected with emotions, attempts to distinguish them in this way have failed, although some general differences in terms of variables such as "pleasant–unpleasant" and "attending–rejecting" seem to be discernible (Woodworth & Schlosberg, 1954). Attempts to distinguish emotions by reference to physiological conditions have proved equally abortive, starting from the highly confused hypothesis about the relationship between emotion and changes in the viscera put forward in the James–Lange theory. Another connection also favored by James and many other psychologists has been that with actions or tendencies to action that were alleged to be criteria of emotion. This connection, like that between emotion and specific facial expressions, was also asserted by Charles Darwin in his *The Expression of the Emotions in Man and Animals* (Darwin, 1872).

The explanation of this widespread neglect by psychologists of this most obvious lead-in to the study of emotion is not very recondite. Ever since the latter part of the nineteenth century, psychology has been trying desperately to make itself scientifically respectable. Physiological psychology had long been established as a scientifically respectable form of enquiry that was based on publicly observable "data." It was thought that concentration on facial expressions or on overt actions (e.g., flight in the case of fear) would provide equally reliable data, which were not dependent on the hazards of introspective reports. It is, I suppose, encouraging to read a long recent article by Leeper (Leeper, 1965), which elaborates the startling discovery that emotions are connected with cognitive cues, though they are not quite the same as perceptions! But his labored explanation of how psychologists have been led to ignore this palpable point because of the general tendency of scientists to concentrate on what is palpable scarcely holds water (Leeper, 1965, pp. 37–40). What Leeper never brings out squarely into the open is the skeleton in psychology's cupboard, namely, behaviorism, which as a methodological doctrine has exercised a stranglehold on academic psychology since the early part of this century. It was the concept of "palpability" that went with this particular brand of dogmatic methodism, with all its conceptual confusions and antiquated notions of scientific method, that both restricted the questions that psychologists felt they could respectably raise about emotions and that occasioned them to ignore the obvious point that we cannot even identify the emotions we are talking about unless account is taken of how a person is appraising a situation. This is not to deny, of course, the importance of work done on the physiology of emotion. It is only to assert that the investigation of emotional phenomena has been hamstrung by a widely influential methodological dogma.

Another important facet of this very restricted approach to the study of emotion has been the tendency to take fear and anger as paradigms of emotion rather than, say, sorrow and pride, which probably cannot be experienced by animals that lack a developed conceptual scheme. This tendency had a highly respectable ancestry in Darwin's work, which gave prominence to these emotions, which have an obvious biological utility. These emotions, too, have palpable facial expressions connected with them and are accompanied by palpable signs of changes in the autonomic nervous system, such as goose pimples, sweating, and flushing, some of which, such as the psychogalvanic response, are measurable by instruments. Also, if any emotions are closely connected with typical action patterns, these two are. If sorrow were taken as a paradigm, as it could not be by psychologists who concentrate on rats, the connection with action is, to put it mildly, difficult to discern. And what distinctive facial expressions are connected with envy or pride? Is it plausible to suggest that highly specific physiological changes, of the sort that often accompany fear and anger, accompany remorse?

These restricting influences on the study of emotion are still with us. Witness George Mandler's pronouncement, which provides the keynote to his chapter on emotion in *New Directions in Psychology:*

> Since antiquity, students of man have emphasized two facets which, in conjunction, appear to differentiate emotion from other human experiences: First, emotion involves action which is strongly influenced by certain environmental goals and events, and second, it usually presupposes bodily, visceral, or physiological reactions (Mandler, 1962, p. 270).

In his treatment of emotion there is thus a significant contrast between the specificity of the references to the physiology of emotion and the amount of space devoted to the viscera, and the woolly and brief references to prior experience and to the "content of our emotions," which "is determined by the sort of things that go on around us, particularly the things people do and say to us" (Mandler, 1962, p. 338), which relate to "social induction, and a vast category of presumptive stressors or emotional situations, mostly social in nature" (Mandler, 1962, p. 312). Consciousness is mainly considered in relation to the specific role played by the subject's awareness of his own physiological state. The complicated and highly ingenious experiments of Schachter were designed to exhibit the importance of consciousness in emotional behavior only in this limited respect (Mandler, 1962, pp. 279–298). The distinctive appraisals connected with the different emotions receive no specific attention whatever.

Suppose that, resisting these historic influences in the scientific study of emotions, we stick to common sense and insist on both the connection between emotions and distinctive appraisals and a broad sample of emotions rather than only fear and anger. An interesting point then emerges if we study the list, namely, that most of the terms in the list can also be used to characterize motives, and obviously, as the terms "motive" and "emotion" suggest, there is a close family resemblance among these terms. Indeed this may be another reason that has led countless theorists to postulate an intimate connection between emotion and motivation, culminating in the dispute between Young and Leeper about the facilitating or disrupting effect of emotion on motivated behavior. I have elsewhere summarized most of the important attempts to establish such a connection (Peters, 1961–1962, Section 3) and do not wish to elaborate this theme here. What is of present interest is the proper way to conceptualize this undoubted overlap between the concepts.

In attempting to do this, I think, again, that the common sense that is embedded in ordinary language can help. For surely, in ordinary language we only talk about motives in certain contexts, when we are demanding an explanation of actions; we do not ask for motives for feeling cold, indigestion, or mystical visions. We talk about emotions, on the other hand, in contexts where things come over people, where individuals are passive rather than active. The phrases in which the term "emotion" and its derivatives are not only natural but also indispensable are those used when we speak of judgments being disturbed, warped, heightened, sharpened, and clouded by emotion, or people being in command of or not being properly in control of their emotions, being subject to gusts of emotion, being emotionally perturbed, upset, involved, excited, biased, and exhausted. In a similar vein we speak of emotional outbursts, reactions, and upheavals. The suggestion in such cases is that something comes over people or happens to them when they consider a situation in a certain kind of light. This passivity frequently occurs when we appraise situations as dangerous and frustrating. Hence the obviousness of fear and anger as emotions and hence our slight reluctance to regard benevolence or remorse as emotions; for there are rarely marked symptoms of passivity when we think of people or situations under the aspects connected with these terms. What is common to both motives and emotions on this view is the distinctive appraisals that are necessary to characterize the states of mind as being cases of fear, jealousy, joy, and so on. The difference lies in the fact that "motive" is a term that we use to connect these appraisals with things that we do, "emotion" with things that come over us. And we need not, of course, always connect these appraisals with either. We may, for instance, simply feel remorse or regret without being disposed to do anything in particular and without being particularly affected by our view of the situation. In such cases we simply view a situation under the aspect connected with the appraisal.

To put the difference between the concepts in this way is to suggest a conceptual connection between motive and action and between emotion and passivity. There is thus no conceptual connection, as many maintain, between emotion and action. Indeed, when such appraisals are related to emotion, they are typically connected with the functioning of our autonomic nervous systems, about which we usually speak in a metaphorical way, but in metaphors that are consonant with our passivity. We boil and fume with anger; we tremble and sweat with fear; we swell and glow with pride; we blush with shame and embarrassment; our eyes dilate with fear, sparkle with delight, and moisten with sorrow. Often, of course, the motor system is involved, but when it is, the manifestations typically take on an involuntary character. Our knees knock with fear, our teeth chatter with fright, and sometimes our limbs are paralyzed.

There can, of course, be a *de facto* rather than a conceptual relationship between fear, anger, and so forth, as emotions and action in the sense that they can disrupt, heighten, and intensify motor performances. We can act in fear as well as out of fear. The preposition "in" draws attention to the manner of acting rather than to the reason or motive for acting. "He acted in anger" is different from "he was angry," which merely interprets the action as being of a certain sort, as well as from "he acted out of anger," which gives a reason or motive for acting beyond the initial characterization of the action as being of a certain sort. A man can act in anger who is also acting out of pity. His manner of acting is affected by considering aspects of the situation, considerations that may distort or intensify his actions. And it is very nice when such gusts of emotions, as it were, speed us on our way rather than deflect us from our path. Thus there is no reason why fear or anger should not function both as motives and as emotions at the same time.

There are, too, the intermediary class of cases where people do not act altogether with reason, but where their reaction, which is typically of an uncoordinated protopathic type, springs from an intuitive type of appraisal of a situation. An example would be when a person lashes out in anger or starts with fear. These are not reactions to stimuli, like jumping when one receives an electric shock, because of their cognitive core. Neither are they actions in a full-blown sense; for there is no appraisal of means to an end, no careful consideration of the end to be achieved. They are what we call "emotional reactions." They are dissimilar, too, from acting on impulse; for we act on impulse when there is no such appraisal of a situation as is involved in emotional reactions. To say that a man acts on impulse is at least to deny that he acts deliberately. But it is not necessarily to class what goes on as being subsequent to the sort of appraisal that is involved in emotion. A hungry man might put his hand out and grab a banana in a store. This might be an action on impulse but it would be very strange to describe it as an emotional reaction.

In a similar way, there can be and often is a *de facto* relationship between perception, memory, and judgment on the one hand and emotion on the other. In such cases, the suggestion is that the appraisal that is conceptually connected with the emotion in question acts on the person so as to cloud or distort, or heighten or sharpen, the assessment that he is making. The appraisal of a situation as being in some way agreeable or disagreeable, which is involved in emotion, takes the attention away from or clouds over the relevant features of the situation, "relevance" being defined in terms of whatever criteria are involved in the type of judgment that is being made. Or maybe it goes along with the criteria of relevance and thus enhances or sharpens the judgment, as in the case of a terrified sentry who spots an approaching enemy long before anyone else.

The widespread tendency to postulate a conceptual connection between emotion and action, which is shared by philosophers and psychologists alike, is due not only to the overlap between the concepts but also to the tendency to concentrate on some emotions rather than others. If sorrow, wonder, and grief were taken as examples, this connection would surely be most implausible; for, as Koestler puts it: "The purely self-transcending emotions do not tend towards action, but towards quiescence, tranquillity and catharsis" (Koestler, 1966, pp. 273–285). There are, of course, plenty of passive phenomena connected with the autonomic system that go with these emotions, for example, weeping, catching one's breath, a lump in the throat, and so on. But one cannot *act* in any specific way out of wonder or grief; one is overwhelmed by it. Furthermore, even appraisals that can function both as motives and as emotions do not necessarily lead to action, or even tendencies to action. Jealousy, for instance, may affect one's judgment or memory; but it may not issue in action in the sense in which psychologists have thought of action.

The tendency to connect emotion with action is the main feature that I reject of the treatment of emotion by Asch and Arnold, whose writings on this subject I have otherwise found most illuminating. They above all psychologists have taken the cognitive aspect of emotion seriously and Asch's writings reinforced my conviction of the connection between emotion and passivity. Nevertheless, Asch seems to me to connect emotion too closely with motivation when he says

> Emotions are our ways of representing to ourselves the fate of our goals. They are a direct consequence of the understanding of our situation. One may say that emotions mirror the course of motivational events (Asch, 1959, p. 112).

Similarly, Arnold, to whose erudition and insight on the subject of emotions I am greatly indebted, comes to the view in the end that an emotion is "a felt tendency towards or away from an object" that is preceded by an appraisal of a situation as being of a sort that is harmful or beneficial to the agent. This attraction or aversion is, on her view, accompanied by a pattern of physiological changes organized toward approach or withdrawal (Arnold, 1961, Chapters 9–12).

VII. Emotions, Wishes, and Passive Phenomena

I have argued against the prevailing tendency to postulate a conceptual connection between emotion and actions or dispositions to action, although I have been ready enough to admit widely prevalent *de facto* connections in the case of some emotions. There is, however, an additional explanation of the closeness of this connection if we follow a previous suggestion that I have made (Peters, 1961–1962, Section 4), that emotion is conceptually connected with the concept of "wishing" rather than with the concept of action via the stronger and more determinate notion of "wanting." Wishing, I suggested, is a bare teleological notion whose object is some state of affairs that can be very indeterminately conceived. "The moon" is the sort of object that can be wished for, because questions about what one would do with it if one had it do not have to be pressed. Also, mundane questions of "taking means" to get it, which go along with wanting, need not be raised. Obviously, however, the concepts are very intimately connected, and if emotions are conceptually connected with wishes, the tendency to connect emotion with action via the notion of wanting would be readily explained.

My contention is that there is such a connection. If we consider emotions such as grief and wonder, which are the most intractable ones for those who try to connect emotion conceptually with action, the connection with wishes is quite obvious. A wife who is mourning her dead husband fervently wishes that he were alive. But what action could consummate a want of this sort? A lover overwhelmed by his love may wish himself to be fused into one with his beloved; but he cannot, strictly speaking, want what is logically impossible. Yet this is just the sort of way in which those deeply in love do express their feelings. And, surely, it is just because there is no appropriate action with which these sorts of appraisals can be connected that there is what we call a "welling up" of emotion and some kind of discharge in internal visceral and glandular processes connected with the parasympathetic system. Similarly, a person strongly affected by fear or anger certainly has wishes such as "Would that I were away from here" or "Would that he were dead." Such wishes may or may not follow the lines of wants exhibited in actions.

Magda Arnold has drawn attention to some other aspects of emotion that are very relevant in this context. She notes what I call its connection with passivity when she says

Emotion seems to include not only the appraisal of how this thing or person will affect me but also a definite pull towards or away from it. In fact, does not the emotional quale consist precisely in that unreasoning involuntary attraction or repulsion? (Arnold, 1961, p. 172).

She stresses its immediate or "here and now" character and its connection with wild and intuitive judgments that often are inconsistent with our more rational understanding. These features of emotion are the ones to which Sartre paid most attention. He regards emotion as "an abrupt drop into the magical" (Sartre, 1948, p. 90): "Thus the origin of emotion is a spontaneous and lived degradation of consciousness in the face of the world" (Sartre, 1948, p. 77). This brings out well the connection between emotion and wishes; but it also emphasizes a feature of appraisals connected with fear, jealousy, pity, and so forth, when we employ the concept of emotion to connect them with our passivity. A jealous man's appraisals are not always wild or intuitive, any more than are those of a man who quite sensibly experiences fear when he hears the shriek of a bomb descending toward him. But the more we think of these appraisals as emotions, the more we tend to think of the appraisals as immediate and "intuitive" and of our reactions as having an involuntary character. What we call emotional reactions provide a good example of both these features. For if we jump when we see what we take to be a face at the window, our appraisal is immediate and intuitive and our jump has an involuntary protopathic character. It is quite unlike the deliberate jump of a high jumper. When we "jump for joy" we express a highly indeterminate wish; it would be difficult to describe us as wanting anything in particular. "Lashing out" in anger is another good example of this type of phenomenon. The appraisal is not very discriminating and the movements do not attain the level of coordination and grasp of means to ends for them to qualify as actions that exhibit our wants.

The character of the appraisals in cases of emotion is very similar to that of those noted by Dember in his more stimulus and response ridden account of perceptual vigilance and perceptual defense (Dember, 1964, pp. 313–325). His problem is that of the "mechanism" by reference to which the responsiveness to stimuli below the identification threshold could be explained. Dember's speculative solution is that identifying and affective responses are not learned in identical fashions. Affective responses are learned much earlier in childhood, before children have developed the conceptual apparatus necessary for identification, and can be aroused by stimulation that is not sufficiently informative to arouse the appropriate identification responses. When, however, the stimulation can arouse the identification responses, it will probably also arouse affective responses. If Dember's solution is generalized, it can be postulated that after the conceptual apparatus essential to life as a rule-following purposive agent has been developed, the individual still retains his capacity to respond much more "intuitively" to affectively significant signs that may be fragmentary or well below the threshold of conscious discrimination. Such "intuitive" awareness can have either a disrupting or a facilitating effect on more rational forms of appraisal, depending on whether the cues to which the individual is sensitive at the different levels are consonant or dissonant. This links some of the phenomena of perception with the type of distinction that Freud made between primary and secondary processes of thought (see Hilgard, 1966).

If these affective responses are connected at the start with strange wishes such as Freud postulated, then a link between emotional phenomena generally and those that Freud's theory was designed to explain can readily be suggested. The "mechanisms" that Freud postulated as defenses against such wishes have the same character. They are activated by an immediate type of appraisal and then strange things happen to us that cannot be categorized as actions or performances. In conversion hysteria, for instance, a man's arm becomes paralyzed or he finds that he cannot see. In repression the memory of a traumatic experience just passes out of his mind; he does not intentionally suppress it. Similarly, a man who projects his fears onto something does not wittingly or purposely rig his environment; he just comes to see it under a different aspect. The phenomena are indubitably "mental" because of their cognitive core; that is why the description of them as mechanisms is really inappropriate; but they fall into the category of passivity because of their unintentional involuntary character.

VIII. Conclusion

If the sort of conceptualization presented in this article is not completely off-beam, it gives rise to a whole cluster of fascinating problems: for example, about the possibility, suggested by many past theorists, of there being a few primitive types of appraisals at the basis of our more sophisticated ones, about the transition from one level of appraisal to another and the connections established between them and actions that issue in motives, and about the whole subject of "the education of the emotions." But I must leave these and cognate problems for consideration on some other occasion.

For present purposes I hope I have succeeded in indicating the lines along which some of the phenomena that cannot be accommodated within the purposive rule-following model might be unified by being explained by this supplementary model of mental passivity. To suggest a further generalization of the Freudian type of explanation to cover emotional phenomena is not, of course, to accept all the details of the Freudian conceptual scheme, much of which I find objectionable—especially the tendency to physiologize mental concepts. Perhaps one of Freud's greatest insights was to hit upon the importance of the concept of "the wish" in the explanation of this realm of phenomena—another commonsense concept! To characterize the ways in which wishes work, however, our ordinary forms of description will not do, almost by definition; for the latter are couched in categories of what Freud called "secondary processes." From a commonsense point of view, too, the connections suggested between wishes and phenomena such as facial tics, parapraxes, paralysis, and a host of psychosomatic phenomena seem anything but obvious. Indeed, as I have argued before (Peters, 1965, p. 381), because there does not seem to be such a close conceptual connection between beliefs and passive phenomena as there is between beliefs and actions, there seems much more scope for the development by psychologists of novel empirical generalizations in the sphere of passivity than there does in the sphere of action.

It might be reasonably argued that I am not really suggesting two conceptual schemes. For insofar as these wilder types of appraisal are connected with bodily phenomena such as facial tics, paralysis, and stomach ulcers, the connection is no more and no less intelligible than that between wanting to do something and the movement of our limbs. In this respect wants and wishes are equally mysterious in their mode of operation. On the other hand, insofar as such appraisals are connected via wishes with dreams, distorted judgments, and perceptions, and the phenomena referred to as "the mechanisms of defense," we dimly understand them by starting with secondary processes and thinking away the categorizations involved until we are left with the bare notion of a fulfilled wish. That is why we find notions like that of "displacement" difficult to understand save by analogy with the lower-level operations of animals (Austin, 1956–1957, pp. 29–30). The parasitic character of such descriptions explains the tendency to talk of the unconscious in terms of "as if," or to say that it deals with the sort of things that one might want if a more determinate description of them were specified (MacIntyre, 1958). There are also phenomena, such as when we are "driven" by hunger, or when actions are overdetermined, for example, when a surgeon takes obvious delight in using his instruments, that fall between the two models. Such considerations should encourage us to look at the various phenomena to be explained as lying on a continuum rather than as having always to be placed unambiguously as falling under the activity or passivity models.

Certainly, too, there are other phenomena that cannot be accounted for in terms of either of these two models. Reflexes, pains, and nonemotional reactions are also passive phenomena; but they cannot be explained in terms of appraisals linked with wishes. Perhaps a more mechanical type of model is required to deal with these. Two conceptual schemes, however, are quite enough for one article. Indeed it might reasonably be said that they are at least one too many. It might have been better to dwell longer on the details of one of them and discuss more thoroughly many of the points that have been raised. But there is something to be said for a synoptic view at times—especially if it can be linked with common sense.

REFERENCES

Arnold, M. *Emotion and personality.* Vol. 1. London: Cassell, 1961.
Asch, S. *Social psychology.* Englewood Cliffs, N. J.: Prentice-Hall, 1959.
Atkinson, J. W. *An introduction to motivation.* Princeton, N. J.: Van Nostrand, 1964.
Austin, J. L. A plea for excuses. *Proceedings of the Aristotelian Society,* Vol. LVII, 1956–1957.

Ayer, A. J. *Man as a subject for science.* (Auguste Comte Memorial Lecture) London: Athlone Press, 1964.

Bannister, D. A new theory of personality. In B. M. Foss (Ed.), *New horizons in psychology.* Harmondsworth, Middlesex, England: Penguin, 1966.

Brown, J. F. *The psychodynamics of abnormal behaviour.* New York: McGraw-Hill, 1940.

Darwin, C. *The expression of the emotions in man and animals.* London: Murray, 1872.

Dember, W. N. *The psychology of perception.* New York: Holt, Rinehart & Winston, 1964.

Freud, S. *The psychopathology of everyday life.* London: Benn, 1914.

Freud, S. The claim of psycho-analysis to scientific interest. In *Collected Papers.* London: Hogarth Press, 1955.

Hempel, C. G. Rational action. *Proceedings and Addresses of the American Philosophical Association,* 1962, **35,** October.

Hilgard, E. Impulsive versus realistic thinking. In R. N. Haber (Ed.), *Current research in motivation.* New York: Holt, Rinehart & Winston, 1966.

Hunt, J. McV. Intrinsic motivation. In D. Levine (Ed.), *Nebraska symposium on motivation.* Lincoln, Neb.: Univer. of Nebraska Press, 1965.

Kelly, G. A. *The psychology of personal constructs.* Vol. I. New York: Norton, 1955.

Kelly, G. A. Man's construction of his alternatives. In G. Lindzey (Ed.), *The assessment of motives.* New York: Holt, Rinehart & Winston, 1958.

Kenny, A. *Action, emotion and will.* London: Kegan Paul, 1965.

Koch, S. Behaviour as "intrinsically" regulated. In M. R. Jones (Ed.), *Nebraska symposium on motivation.* Lincoln, Neb.: Univer. of Nebraska Press, 1956.

Koestler, A. *The act of creation.* London: Pan Books, 1966.

Leeper, R. W. Needed developments in motivational theory. In D. Levine (Ed.), *Nebraska symposium on motivation.* Lincoln, Neb.: Univer. of Nebraska Press, 1965.

Lewin, K. Aristotelian and Galilean modes of explanation. In K. Lewin (Ed.), *A dynamic theory of personality.* New York: McGraw-Hill, 1935.

McClelland, D. C. *The achieving society.* Princeton, N. J.: Van Nostrand, 1961.

McClelland, D. C., Atkinson, J. W., Clark, R. A., & Lowell, E. L. *The Achievement Motive.* New York: Appleton-Century-Croft, 1953.

MacIntyre, A. *The unconscious.* London: Kegan Paul, 1958.

McKeachie, W. J. Motivation, teaching methods and college learning. In M. R. Jones (Ed.), *Nebraska symposium on motivation.* Lincoln, Neb.: Univer. of Nebraska Press, 1961.

Mandler, G. Emotion. In G. Mandler & E. Galanter (Eds.), *New directions in psychology.* New York: Holt, Rinehart & Winston, 1962.

Melden, A. *Free action.* London: Kegan Paul, 1961.

Mischel, T. Pragmatic aspects of explanation. *Philosophy of Science,* 1966, **33,** March–June.

Peters, R. S. *Hobbes.* Harmondsworth, Middlesex, England: Penguin, 1956.

Peters, R. S. The concept of motivation. London: Kegan Paul, 1958.

Peters, R. S. Emotions and the category of passivity. *Proceedings of the Aristotelian Society,* 1961–1962, **62.**

Peters, R. S. Moral education and the psychology of character. *Philosophy,* 1962, April.

Peters, R. S. Emotions, passivity and the place of Freud's theory in psychology. In B. Wolman & E. Nagel (Eds.), *Scientific psychology.* New York: Basic Books, 1965.

Peters, R. S. *Ethics and education.* London: Allen & Unwin, 1966.

Peters, R. S. More about motives. *Mind,* 1967, January.

Peters, R. S., & Tajfel, H. Hobbes and Hull: Metaphysicians of behaviour. *British Journal of the Philosophy of Science,* 1955, May.

Popper, K. R. *The open society and its enemies.* Vol. II. London: Kegan Paul, 1945.

Rapaport, D. The structure of psycho-analytic theory: A systematizing attempt. In S. Koch (Ed.), *Psychology: A study of a science.* Vol. 3. New York: McGraw-Hill, 1959.

Rapaport, D. On the psycho-analytic theory of motivation. In M. R. Jones (Ed.), *Nebraska symposium on motivation.* Lincoln, Neb.: Univer. of Nebraska Press, 1960.

Sartre, J. P. *The emotions.* (Transl. by B. Frechtman) New York: Philosophical Library, 1948.

Taylor, C. C. W. Pleasure. *Analysis,* 1963, **23,** Supplement.

Toulmin, S. Reasons and causes. In R. Borger & F. Cioffi (Eds.), *Explanation in the behavioral sciences.* London and New York: Cambridge Univer. Press, 1969.

White, R. W. Competence and the psycho-sexual stages of development. In M. R. Jones (Ed.), *Nebraska symposium on motivation.* Lincoln, Neb.: Univer. of Nebraska Press, 1960.

Winch, P. *The idea of a social science.* London: Kegan Paul, 1958.

Woodworth, R. S., & Schlosberg, H. *Experimental psychology.* (Rev. ed.) New York: Holt, Rinehart & Winston, 1954.

Young, P. T. The role of hedonic processes in motivation. In M. R. Jones (Ed.), *Nebraska symposium on motivation.* Lincoln, Neb.: Univer. of Nebraska Press, 1955.

Young, P. T. *Motivation and emotion.* New York: Wiley, 1961.

HUMAN EMOTION AND ACTION

MAGDA B. ARNOLD

I. Introduction

In this paper I would like to attempt a short sketch of my theory of emotion and show how it is connected with action, motivation, and personality. Essentially, this theory starts with a phenomenological analysis of the sequence from perception to action. Granted that we do not start afresh with every perception; but by and large, we must see, hear, or otherwise experience something, know what it is, interpret its significance, decide on the best possible action, before we can do what is necessary to cope with it. We do not throw a ball before we have it in the hand, nor do we ordinarily open an umbrella before we notice that it is raining. There is a natural sequence from perception to action, and this sequence cannot be reversed. A phenomenological analysis should give us the psychological functions as they follow one another in this sequence, even though they are often so contracted as to be almost instantaneous. With this sequence as a clue, it should be possible to identify the neural structures and circuits that mediate each function and so trace the connection from sensory cortical areas to the motor area. In this way, we should be able to describe not only psychological functioning but the brain structures that make it possible.

II. Phenomenological Analysis

This analysis necessarily has to start with human experience. At the same time, at this point we are not concerned with the fullness of human experience but rather with the psychological functions that make such experience possible. In other words, I want to describe the "psychic apparatus," as Freud would call it, before we investigate how this apparatus is used to live a human life, to establish human goals in science, art, business, or industry. This psychic apparatus includes many functions we share with animals: animals also can see, hear, taste, smell, touch; they want food, drink, mate; go about getting them in various ways; and show considerable ingenuity when these things are not readily available. Animals, like human beings, dislike things that hurt, and avoid them; they attack what threatens them; they can and do learn when motivated by hunger, thirst, or pain. Consequently, they must be able to *remember*. Moreover, they *expect* food and expect to avoid harm by running a maze or pressing a bar in the laboratory, or by the various activities they undertake in their natural habitat.

Since these activities are common to man and animal, it will often be convenient to refer to animal experiments to demonstrate some of the points in this discussion. Just because animals have no access to the highly complex experience of a civilized human being, it is easier to show on their example what are the basic functions of the psychic apparatus.

A. Perception

In recent years, it has been the fashion to include a grab bag of functions in "perception." To listen to modern psychologists, one might think that perception is the only kind of experience and leads directly to action. Though perception is based on sense experience, many psychologists also include meaning, learning, and, at least in one theory (Leeper, 1963), emotion in it. Perhaps we have settled on this wastebasket category because we are afraid that other categories are too "mentalistic" to be respectable. But perception surely is as mentalistic as is memory, learning, or emotion; all are recognizable experiences that do not gain in precision by being taken altogether-all-at-once. If to be mentalistic is so disgraceful, perhaps we had better exclude perception also and return to Watsonian behaviorism with its aridity. On the other hand, if we have reached the point where we cannot do without perception in our theorizing, as I think we have, it surely is better to take a careful look at the kind of experience we are dealing with. For that, we need a careful phenomenological analysis.

When we look at a bear, we not only have a visual experience, we also *know* that this is a bear and *remember* that this animal is wild. We *see* that the bear is behind a fence in the zoo, we *recall* that this kind of fence is strong and *expect* that it will keep the bear from breaking out. Finally, we *assess* the bear behind the fence and his potential for us and *decide* that we are in no danger. We might even throw food to him, though we realize it is inadvisable to hold it out to him. The whole complex is a "perceptual" experience for most psychologists. But actually it includes sense experience, conceptual thinking, inference, memory, and imagination; it also includes the appraisal that the bear is not dangerous here and now.

B. APPRAISAL

In the human being, such an evaluation is of two kinds, deliberate and intuitive. It is deliberate because it depends on conceptual knowledge that is recalled at will: that this is a bear; that bears are dangerous; that the fence is intended to keep the bear away from the visitors to the zoo. On the basis of such knowledge, we judge that the bear cannot attack us. This deliberate judgment is accompanied by an immediate intuitive appraisal that this bear is harmless, so that we approach the fence with confidence, unafraid. That there are these two kinds of evaluation is best seen in cases where one appraisal is positive, the other negative.

For instance, a child may be told that the bear cannot break out, and may have confidence in his father who tells him so. But the bear looks very big and fierce and the child is afraid, despite his reflective judgment. An even better example is the child on the beach who is afraid to go in the water. His father may have taken the little boy by the hand or held him in his arms while he walks with him into the shallows. The child knows that nothing harmful is happening to him, but he does not stop crying as long as he is in the water and cannot be persuaded to go in again.

Another example is the fear of a man suffering from obsessive-compulsive neurosis who washes his hands incessantly whenever he has touched anything. He is afraid of contamination, but he knows that his skin will be roughened by frequent washing and so offer a more vulnerable surface. He is so afraid of germs that he feels compelled to wash his hands despite his conceptual and reflective knowledge that his fear is exaggerated and that washing will only increase the danger. It is his unconscious intuitive appraisal that produces the fear and the conscious reflective evaluation that is impotent against it. Just as we have to distinguish between sense experience of objects and conceptual knowledge, which enables us to talk about them, so must we make a distinction between intuitive appraisal (which could be called sense judgment) and deliberate judgment.

This intuitive appraisal is not an emotion, though it can give rise to an emotion; nor is it what James has called a "cold perception." Sheer perception only establishes what is there. It takes an evaluation to relate what is perceived to the perceiving subject. Something is either good for me or bad for me, and that in varying degree. If it is appraised as neither good nor bad, it is indifferent and will be disregarded.

In contrast to conscious deliberate judgment, the intuitive appraisal is not consciously experienced. It is experienced as no more than a feeling, a favorable or unfavorable attitude to this thing, a liking or disliking. Such an appraisal is possible for the animal as well as for man. Some psychologists may quarrel with this statement on the grounds that the animal cannot report his experiences. But this objection misses the point. The human being also cannot report his intuitive appraisals because he experiences them only as favorable or unfavorable attitudes. He can report that he likes and wants one thing and not another, but only by reflection can we infer that this constitutes an intuitive judgment. Liking something is not an experience of sensory qualities like seeing or hearing or touching. But it is just as immediate, it completes sensory experience and links it with action. The human being (unlike the animal) also makes deliberate judgments (practical judgments, as they are often called), which are conscious.

The animal does not have conceptual knowledge in the sense that he cannot abstract the essential feature of a thing and use a symbol to refer to it. If he had conceptual knowledge, he would have no difficulty developing or learning a conceptual language. Accordingly, the animal cannot make deliberate judgments, which are based on conceptual knowledge. But he can and does evaluate intuitively. He likes this thing and dislikes that, and so approaches the one while he avoids the other. Foods preferences in the white rat, for instance, have been painstakingly investigated by P. T. Young (1961). Thus to anyone but an adamant behaviorist, the statement that animals have likes and dislikes needs no apology. We can call this liking or disliking a feeling.

1. *Appraisal for Action*

Such an intuitive estimate, experienced as liking or disliking something, brings about an immediate urge to action. What is liked, attracts. But the type of approach will depend on another intuitive appraisal answering the question: "What is it good for?" The monkey likes a banana for eating, a female for mating. Both banana and mate have a positive valence, but the action tendency produced by each of the two appraisals is quite different. Both things are "good here and now," but there is a specific approach for each. In fact, this appraisal for action has many dimensions. The animal is aware that he sees the food, and gauges the distance he must cover before he can take it. When he can touch it, however, he simply opens his mouth and bites. Every situation requires not only an estimate of its value for the subject but also a gauging of the action required to approach or avoid it. The first estimate leads to an urge to approach (or escape), the second, to an urge to approach in a particular way. It is the whole appraisal complex, the thing-appraised-as-good-for-a-particular-action, that produces the desire to do something in particular, that arouses a specific appetitive tendency.

C. Appetitive Tendency, Instinct, and Emotion

Any appetitive tendency, then, is based on the appraisal of something as good for a particular action here and now. There are some appetitive tendencies, however, that seem to be based on an innate appraisal. If the cheek of a newborn infant is touched, the infant will turn its head and seek to grasp the touching finger with its mouth. In the same way, any neonate mammal will seek with its mouth until it finds something to suck, and the newly hatched chick will start to peck at something small, before mammal or chick can have acquired any experience that nipple or grain can provide satisfaction.

It is usually assumed that "instinct" provides the impulsion behind such behavior, though the mechanism of such impulsion has never been spelled out. I venture to suggest that instinct works through the same mechanism of appraisal and appetitive tendency discussed above, a mechanism that is set in motion by various hormonal changes. Apparently, hormonal changes in the composition of the blood are detected by the hypothalamus (e.g., in hunger, thirst) and bring about a sensitivity to certain objects such that at this time, and neither before nor afterward, these objects become attractive. Only the hungry infant will seek with its mouth, only the hungry chick will peck, and only the sexually mature animal will react to a female in heat. Though the hormonal change accounts for the attractiveness of the instinctive object, it must still be found and appraised as good for a particular action before it can be approached and obtained. Thus appraisal and appetitive tendency are the psychological functions that make instinctive action possible; and "instinct" becomes a species-specific sequence of activities rather than the impulsion behind each action in the sequence.

In emotion, there is no such hormonal change that sensitizes perception. Rather, the object or situation is appraised as to its effect on the individual here and now. If that effect is pronounced, the appetitive tendency (toward or away from the object) develops into an emotion. Actually, an emotion is a strong appetitive tendency toward or away from something appraised as good or bad for the person here and now that urges to appropriate action and is accompanied (but not initiated) by physiological changes.

D. Memory

The neonate does not experience emotions because he is not as yet capable of an appraisal for action. He does, however, experience feelings in all gradations from pleasure to pain.* Feelings, as mentioned before, are the experiences of the beneficial or harmful effects of stimulation or, put differently, the experiences of intuitive appraisal. Pleasure and pain can be experienced immediately: colic, hunger pain, discomfort from a pinprick or a chafing diaper are the most usual pain experiences of the infant. The only pleasures he seems to feel are the pleasure of satiety and the pleasure of gentle touch. According to Watson, the newborn baby has only three "emotions": fear, when it is dropped; love, when it is stroked or handled gently; and anger, when it is restrained. None of these is an emotion. What Watson calls fear is really startle, though the newborn needs a more intense stimulus than does an older child or adult. What Watson calls love is the plea-

---

* Pain has been considered a sensation in recent years because it is known that pain is mediated by fine somesthetic fibers that are found, together with thicker beta fibers, in somesthetic nerves. But from various reports it can be inferred that these fine fibers mediate the *intensity* of somesthetic stimulation (i.e., its effect) rather than its *quality* (like touch, stretch, etc.).

sure of touch, and what he calls anger, the simple dislike of restraint with no attempt to retaliate.

On the basis of such experiences of pleasure and pain, the infant later develops emotions. Because he remembers what has brought pleasure or pain, he hopes for the one and fears the other. Without such memory, anything that is as yet distant, anything that is merely heard or seen, could not be appraised either as beneficial or dangerous, and so could neither be approached nor avoided. Without memory, only direct somesthetic experience can bring either pleasure or pain. Only memory makes it possible to anticipate pleasure or pain and act accordingly.

The memory necessary to appraise something seen, heard, or smelled as good or bad is not merely visual, auditory, or olfactory memory. Over and above such modality-specific memories there is also what could be called "affective memory," a reliving of past likes and dislikes as soon as the same situation recurs. When something has brought pain, it is disliked on sight the second time. This dislike is a recurrence of the earlier appraisal and is experienced as a "here-and-now feeling" rather than a memory. Since this dislike is felt immediately, yet obviously cannot be aroused by something that is still in the distance, it must be the residue of previous appraisals of its effect on us as soon as it came near us: it must be *affective memory*.

1. *Affective Memory*

Such affective memory is aroused not only by what has actually hurt us in the past. Anything similar may have the same effect. The burnt child is afraid of fire, any fire, even St. Elmo's fire or a magnesium flare. A child who has once felt pain in the dentist's chair will be afraid of the dentist, even though he may never have seen this particular dentist before. Freud suggested that a traumatic memory is repressed and goes on working underground, to explain why the emotion aroused by the traumatic experience recurs in similar situations though these have no connection with the original trauma. However, an emotion often recurs even when the traumatic experience is well remembered: A man who nearly drowned when his boat capsized may be afraid of boats ever after; a boy who was thrown by a horse may never go near a horse again. In addition, emotional experiences do not need to be traumatic to leave an affective memory. An emotional situation encountered repeatedly may have the same effect. A child who experiences repeated failure may finally refuse to try even when he is assured of success. All these cases can be explained by affective memory, that is, the spontaneous reliving of an experienced liking or dislike on encountering a similar situation, which leads to the same impulse to approach or withdraw as did the original appraisal.

What Freud has explained as the effect of a repressed traumatic memory has been explained by academic psychologists as "emotional conditioning." It has usually been assumed that emotional conditioning is based on the same association of unconditioned with conditioned stimuli that occurs in ordinary conditioning. But there are some important differences: ordinary conditioning requires repeated exposure of the unconditioned stimulus following upon the conditioned stimulus, until the CS arouses the same response as the US. But in emotional conditioning, one exposure to the unconditioned, "traumatic" stimulus may be sufficient for man or animal to react in the same way to a number of stimuli that have never been formally associated with the unconditioned stimulus. Think, for instance, of the fear developed by little Albert when he was frightened by a loud noise as soon as he stretched out his hand for a white rabbit (Watson, 1929). Soon he was afraid not only of the rabbit but of his mother's white fur coat and the white beard of Santa Claus. This is usually explained as "stimulus generalization." But just what does happen in stimulus generalization?

When an animal has been trained to go through a door marked with a square rather than a door marked with a cross to find food, it will also choose a door with an octagon, polyhedron, a circle, and even a triangle, rather than the door with the cross. The animal apparently appraises anything with a white center and black outline as good, but anything with a black center as bad, provided his choice is confirmed by finding food behind one door and not the other. His response is governed by affective memory, the immediate liking for and approach to anything with a white center behind which he has found food. Thus affective memory actually takes precedence over visual memory and so determines the animal's response. Similarly, little Albert experienced an instant dislike as soon as he saw anything white and furry, anything similar enough to the white rabbit to arouse the affective memory.

2. *Motor Memory versus Kinesthetic Memory*

The appraisal for action depends not only on modality-specific and affective memory but also on motor memory. Psychologists have often identified motor memory with kinesthetic memory, that is, with the memory of the sensations experienced as a result of various movements. Though kinesthetic memory undoubtedly exists, I do not believe that it is the only or even the most important factor in learning a motor skill. Rather, kinesthetic memory seems to be involved in the "feel" of learned movements.

When they are correct, they also "feel" right, so that the sensory feedback of movement seems to be a confirmation or check on learned motions rather than a template according to which movements are organized. Every golfer or baseball pitcher knows this feeling of "right" movement and knows as soon as he has made his drive or pitched his ball whether he has done well, long before the ball has landed. He also knows that the harder he tries to achieve this feeling, the worse his drive or pitch will be. But if he keeps relaxed and confident and lets his trained muscles take over, he will make the right movements and have their correctness confirmed by kinesthetic sensations that are familiar and appraised as right.

If kinesthetic memory really were the deciding factor in learned performance, patients with parietal lesions that destroy somesthetic memory should lose their motor skill. Such patients will have tactual agnosia, that is, they can no longer recognize an object by touch alone, but they are still able to write, play tennis or golf, and engage in other skilled performances. Motor skills (particularly speaking and writing, which depend exclusively on motor memory) are severely impaired by lesions of the lateral prefrontal cortex (e.g., Broca's area). This is consonant with the notion that the prefrontal area is a motor association area and that skilled performance depends on motor memories registered in this region.

By motor memory I mean the disposition to move in a particular pattern, which is strengthened by every correct movement. As such a pattern is repeated, it is executed more smoothly, more speedily, and becomes a fluid effortless performance that proceeds almost automatically. The small child has great difficulty formulating speech sounds but within a very few years he becomes so proficient that he can direct his attention exclusively to what he wants to say, confident that his pronunciation will take care of itself. Though we experience such increased facility in performance, we do not immediately recognize this facilitation as motor memory. Indeed, the only memories we immediately recognize as such are visual and auditory memories because we are able to recall visual images and auditory patterns at will. We remember something we have seen as a memory *picture,* and remember something we have heard as an auditory pattern, a sentence or a melody. It is much more difficult to recall a fragrance or a taste, though we may recognize it without difficulty. Similarly, we easily recognize the touch of velvet or sandpaper, but when we try to recall it, we find ourselves visualizing velvet or sandpaper rather than recalling the touch experience directly.

Motor memory does allow recall, but usually only in its complete temporal pattern, just as visual recall is not of one feature but of the complete picture. We can recall a dance step by making it, a poem by saying it, a word or letter by writing it, either actually or in imagination, though visual recall is often involved as well. We usually have to repeat the whole poem, however, though we can easily recognize any line that is quoted from it. Motor memory, like auditory memory, has a temporal pattern. Motor imagination (to imagine doing, saying, or singing something) is just as vivid as visual imagination. The very fact that motor imagination is possible proves the existence of motor memory; indeed, Jacobson has found that motor imagination activates the muscles actually used in the imagined action, while visual imagination activates the eye muscles. Motor imagination, like visual imagination, depends on the appropriate memories and can, in the case of motor imagination, even improve motor learning. For instance, it has been reported that imagining throwing a dart at a bull's-eye, and practicing such imaginary throwing, is as effective as actual practice in dart throwing (Beattie, 1949); and Gasson (1967) found that basketball players increased their scores at the free-throw line by shooting with their eyes closed (during practice session) and simply imagining the flight of the ball.

In fact, motor memory and motor imagination are necessary for action, whether in man or animal. Unless an individual knows what actions have been successful before, in similar situations, and unless he imagines what to do in the situation here and now, he cannot act appropriately. Without motor memory, he could not acquire his daily habits or cherished skills; and without motor imagination he could not change his habits when a changing situation requires it. Of course, the human being does not depend on motor memory to quite the same extent the animal does because he can often use concepts to guide his action. Instead of depending on an acquired habit of turning to one side or the other in a maze, he can remember to "turn once left, twice right" and learn the maze in this way; and such self-instruction can be recalled as a visual or auditory pattern as easily as by speaking the words (which would again be a motor pattern). After Goldstein insisted that brain-injured patients had lost the "abstract attitude" because they were unable to pretend to drink a glass of water or to comb their hair, later investigation disclosed that these patients could use and recognize concepts as well as normal people. They were still able to make abstractions and use abstract concepts, but they were apparently unable to *imagine* what to do. When they saw the actual glass or the actual comb, the objects recalled their use without further difficulty.

3. *Feedback versus Motor Memory*

Cyberneticists insist that organismic movement follows the procedure of the feedback apparatus; that is, we aim, begin to move, and predict a miss upon sensory feedback information, and so correct our aim. This makes a chopped-up and jerky zigzag out of what is in practice a fluid movement. Actually, modern tracking mechanisms need a computer to do the tracking effectively. The aim has to be corrected by computing the direction in which an airplane or ship travels, its speed, and that of the missile, so that the missile is dispatched to the point the vessel will have reached at the exact time the missile will arrive. To aim by such feedback information requires the lightning speed of a computer. Our mental processes of computing speed and direction are considerably slower.

Yet the Western gunman could draw and shoot practically in one movement without loss of accuracy. The new technique of "quick kill" in the Vietnam war has revived this method of using the weapon as an extension of the arm in pointing because this method of aiming gives the only assurance of hitting the enemy before being hit. Obviously, this technique does not employ feedback information for aiming. Since it is far more accurate and speedy than deliberate aiming, feedback cannot be the sole or even the best method for hitting the target. Imaginary practice, as described above, also dispenses with feedback information, yet markedly improves the learner's aim. What holds for aiming applies to other movements as well. Any movement that depends on feedback information is necessarily slower than a movement that is executed by focusing on the goal and letting the muscles do the rest. The quick draw, like any other practiced motion, depends on motor memory that is activated as the movement is started; if correct, it "feels right" without any attempt to modify it.

4. Emotion and Motor Memory

Emotion as a felt appetitive tendency partakes of the nature of movement, at least to some extent. There is "facilitation" in emotion as in movement. Not only will someone who is apprehensive appraise a new situation as dangerous more easily than his more courageous fellow, (affective memory), his tendency to withdraw will become a habit if he never tries to go against his fear, so that he will find it more and more difficult to act courageously. This is true not only for the felt urge to keep away from danger but also for the physiological changes that go with it: such a man will feel more "nervous" as time goes on, will tremble more easily, feel a greater malaise, have a fast heart rate even in trivial situations.

I noticed in one of my classes that one student sometimes seemed to be completely abstracted, was very pale, and kept grimacing as if in pain. When I finally asked him what was the matter, he explained that he was

afraid he had heart disease because he noticed that his pulse began to race
as soon as he started counting it. He had done this for a few weeks and
found his pulse faster every day. When I pointed out that it was his increasing fear that produced the acceleration, he did not believe it. However, he
did agree to leave his pulse alone for a while. When he took it again some
days later, he found it had slowed down considerably. Now he was ready to
admit that his lessened fear had something to do with the improvement.

5. *Memory and Imagination*

Appraisal is not based on spontaneous recall alone. If it were, the reaction to a situation would be completely stereotyped and would repeat the
original response as dictated by the original appraisal. Actually, we not
only recall what has happened and what we have done, and relive the
appropriate feeling and emotion; we also take account of various differences in the present situation, gauge their possible effect, and then estimate
whether the situation as it is here and now is good or bad for us. Similarly,
we plan our action to fit the present circumstances, that is, we imagine it
and appraise its possible effects. Memory and imagination together make it
possible to learn from past experience and to adapt our performance to
present requirements.

III. Appetitive Tendencies and Action

An appetitive tendency produced by appraisal will lead to action unless
a new round of appraisal, based on different aspects of the situation, produces a different or even contrary response tendency. If that happens, there
is a conflict, which has to be resolved by one or more reappraisals until the
strongest response tendency wins. In the animal, appetitive tendencies (toward both instinctive and emotional actions) are the only available response tendencies. There is no conflict between two such tendencies urging
toward different *instinctive* objects: an animal that is hungry and thirsty
will drink until its thirst is slaked sufficiently to start eating, and vice versa.
Buridan's ass would first eat the one bundle of hay and then turn to the
other. The only conflict possible is between a positive (instinctive) and a
negative (emotional) tendency. An animal that is hungry wants to approach the food box. But if it has been given an electric shock on beginning
to eat, it may hang back the next time—make a few steps and then stop, or
not approach at all, depending on the intensity of pain he has experienced

before. Since pain is more urgent than hunger, the fear of pain, if intensive enough, usually wins out over instinctive tendencies.

With human beings, more is involved in a conflict than two kinds of appetitive tendencies. The diabetic may want sweets but refrain from indulging because he knows what the consequences will be. The smoker knows the long-range effects of smoking but he may take a chance and hope that he will be one of the lucky ones. In both cases, there is an appetitive tendency that urges one course of action and sober reflection that urges another. There is conflict only when both alternatives are as desirable in some way as they are undesirable in another. The final decision may not necessarily be the most attractive alternative, nor is it always the most prudent choice. Because we know from personal experience that it is possible though difficult to choose the unattractive but useful course of action, it has been maintained that man is free to act in one way or the other, to act or not to act. What this means is that a man is able to choose something that he knows at the moment of choice is less than the absolute best for him. By his choice he just "shuts his eyes" to the other alternative, refuses to consider it further, so that only one "good" course of action is left for him to take. It is the choice that makes the chosen action the better one at the moment.

At any rate, it will be generally admitted that human evaluation and judgment is not only intuitive but can be deliberate or reflective. Man has sources of information the animal lacks. Is it too much to suggest that therefore the impulse to action that is produced by an intuitive appraisal will be different from the impulse to action produced by a deliberate or reflective appraisal? Granted that even the deliberate appraisal must have a modicum of attraction or we would never judge anything as good for us here and now, or feel urged to approach it. But that admixture of appetition is so slight that it does not carry us into action unquestioningly, as is the case with a strong emotion. It may be necessary again and again to call to mind the reason for an unattractive course of action to persevere in it. On the other hand, if there is a strong conviction in favor of an unpopular course of action, there will be enough emotional appeal to carry it through. What I am trying to say is that without an appetitive tendency there could be no action; but the strength of this tendency does not determine what action a man will take.

Because human beings must often act against strong emotional desires, I cannot fully agree with Lazarus (1966), who speaks of emotion only as *coping* processes. True, emotional or appetitive tendencies are indispensable for actions, including coping actions. But the actions to which strong emotions urge us are not always those that will really cope with the situation. Indeed, they often defeat the purpose for which they are done. The alcoholic or drug addict has a strong desire, yet he can, with help, resist it. Only by subduing his desire will he cope with the difficulties his addiction has created for him. If emotions are so intense that they must be obeyed (as in obsessive-compulsive and anxiety neuroses), coping becomes impossible—and this is not merely a semantic quibble.

A. Neural Mediation

A phenomenological analysis of the chain of psychological activities from sense experience to appetitive tendency and action should give us some hints as to the brain structures and circuits that make them possible. What has always prevented a genuine theory of brain function is the difficulty of finding the connections between the cortical receptor areas, which, as we know, mediate sense experience, and the cortical motor areas, which produce muscular contractions. We know that such a circuit must go through the subcortex because cutting around any sensory area has no effect, while undercutting it prevents sensory discrimination in this particular modality. Our analysis would indicate that the connection is not a simple neural linkage from receptor to motor areas but consists of several circuits corresponding to recall, imagination, appraisal, and appetitive tendency, including emotion.

First of all, the appraisal of an object or situation as good or bad (which, as I have indicated, completes perception and initiates a response tendency that leads to action) seems to be mediated by the limbic system. Olds (1955, 1956) has called this a "reward system" because self-stimulation in this area may be kept up indefinitely without any other reward; and "reward" is an objective term for the subjective experience of pleasure or satisfaction. The limbic system consists of a simple three-layer type of cortex (in contrast to the six layers of sensory and motor cortex) and borders on all the sensory and motor areas in the cortex. Accordingly, the appraisal of things seen, heard, touched, smelled, tasted, and the appraisal of movements seem to be mediated by connections to the neighboring limbic cortex.

Since most situations require memory and imagination before they can be fully appraised for action, there should be connecting circuits that make recall and planning possible. It is curious that scientists have expended much thought on the problem how various sense impressions are preserved, but none on the question how these "engrams" could be revived. For psychologists, at any rate, the latter is the more urgent problem: since we can test learning and memory only through performance, we are primarily interested in recall and anything that influences it. There is general agreement that the registration of sense impressions implies a modification of nervous tissue. It also seems that the tissue amenable to such modification is in the so-called association cortex. From many research reports we can infer that the visual association cortex serves the registration of visual memories, the auditory cortex that of auditory memories, and so on. It stands to reason that recall should require a reactivation of the modified cells in the same pattern (spatial and temporal) that occurred during the original registration. In contrast, in imagining something, we reorganize remembered experiences in new spatial and temporal patterns. Consequently, the circuits activating sense impressions in recall must be different from the circuits activating them during imagination.

Since we are looking for the connection from sensory to motor areas, using the clues from our phenomenological analysis, we would expect that the circuit mediating recall would start from the structures mediating appraisal, that is, from the limbic system. Integrated sense experience seems to be registered in sensory association areas and is recalled, I suggest, via a memory circuit that runs from the limbic system via the hippocampal circuit to fornix, midbrain, sensory thalamic nuclei, and back to the sensory association areas (*sensory recall circuit*). An *affective memory circuit* can be found to go from limbic cortex via cingulum, postcommissural fornix, mamillary bodies, and anterior thalamic nuclei back to the limbic system. An *imagination circuit* carrying visual, auditory, and other sensory patterns can be found to run from limbic cortex via amygdala and thalamic association nuclei to the cortical association areas.

Bodily movement seems to be initiated via the *action circuit* from the limbic system via the hippocampal system to fornix, midbrain, cerebellum, and ventral thalamus to the frontal lobe; *motor memory* seems to be registered in the prefrontal area and reactivated during movement via the action circuit. *Motor imagination,* finally, seems to employ relay stations in the amygdala, connecting with the dorsomedial thalamic nuclei and prefrontal area. All appetitive tendencies, including emotions, seem to be mediated via the action circuit and registered in the prefrontal area. They would be experienced when the relay of nerve impulses over the action circuit arrives in the premotor area. Since the action circuit activates not only voluntary muscles but also glands and involuntary muscles, particularly those of the blood vessel walls, the influence of emotion on muscular tension, glandular secretion, blood pressure, and heart rate can easily be accounted for. So can the fact that these emotional effects are cumulative, for they are preserved as dispositional changes in the prefrontal cortex.

With every new emotion, the motor effect of similar past emotions is revived, which accounts, for instance, for the increasing muscular tension in chronic fear.

The (now abandoned) surgical operation of prefrontal lobotomy, which separates the prefrontal cortex from the thalamus and hypothalamus and so interrupts the action circuit, markedly reduced severe anxiety and intractable pain. The patients reported that they were still afraid or in pain, but it did not bother them any longer. I would say that they still felt fear (the premotor area and its connections with the thalamus were largely untouched) but the distressing physiological symptoms of fear were considerably reduced because the new danger no longer revived past fears and their physiological accompaniment. Interestingly enough, when relief from anxiety was insufficient or temporary, and the lobotomy was extended farther back to encroach upon thalamic connections to the premotor area, the patient was permanently relieved of fear but did not feel much impulse to action, either. He might sit for hours doing nothing at all. This would indicate that the premotor area does mediate impulses to action, including emotional response tendencies.

I would like to emphasize that this sketch of various circuits is not just unsupported speculation. It is based on thousands of actual research studies reported in the literature and is extensively documented in Volume 2 of *Emotion and Personality* (Arnold, 1960). The theory may be wrong in some details, but I am convinced that an approach like this is essential if we want to unravel the complex cat's cradle that is the brain.

B. Emotion and Motive

As we have seen, experienced emotions are tendencies to action but do not always lead to action. Accordingly, I would like to define a motive as a "want that leads to action." A want could be described as a goal, or a course of action leading to a goal, appraised as desirable. A want will entice or impel to action, provided there are no contrary wants, no subsequent appraisals that interdict action. Human wants are based on deliberate as well as intuitive appraisals, and lead to voluntary decisions as well as emotional impulses to action. "Decision making" really consists in refusing to reappraise the matter further so that the last appraisal stands and now flows into action.

If motives stem from appraisal, they must be at least partly conscious. A man may want to make a trip and is quite aware of the reasons that speak for it. He may not be too aware at the moment that his deeper reason for the trip is the chance he may see that slick chick he had met there before. The conscious motives do not become spurious because an unconscious motive is also present. In fact, it has been argued that unconscious motives are far less important in well-integrated people than in neurotics (Allport, 1953), who almost by definition are helpless in the face of their emotions. I need hardly say that in my opinion such "unconscious motives" are the affective memories that are touched off at this moment so that we experience desire or anxiety without remembering the original situation that gave rise to such emotions.

C. Conditions of Appraisal

I have said that the first appraisal (that something is good or bad for me here and now) is experienced as liking or dislike and will flow into an action impulse, which is the appetitive tendency. Now the second appraisal, of the action to be taken, will refer to the conditions that determine the emotion. If what we perceive and like is "a bird in the hand," we feel *joy* or *delight*. If what we like is unobtainable, or if it is lost to us, we keep thinking of it, keep wanting it, and feel *sorrow* or *sadness*.

What we like may not be at hand but relatively within reach: our tending toward it is *desire*. If we dislike something and can easily get out of its way, we feel *aversion* or *repulsion*. There will be times when the action to be taken has to be strenuous. Then the simple impulse toward or away from a thing is intensified into an urge that is the mark of *contending* emotions. For instance, something we like may require effort though it is attainable: we *hope* for it. If, however, we are convinced that it is utterly out of reach, we fall into *hopelessness* and *despair*.

If something bad, hence disliked, is on its way to us but we realize that it can be met and overcome, though with some difficulty, we feel an urge to face it *bravely*. But if we appraise it as something to avoid, at whatever cost, we feel the urge to flee because we are *afraid*. On the other hand, if something harmful is upon us but is evaluated as something we can overcome, though with some effort, we feel *anger*. But if we judge that we cannot get away from it at all, no matter how much we want to, we fall into *dejection*.

Accordingly, an intuitive appraisal confronts various conditions on which the resulting emotion depends: the goodness or badness of the object, its attainability or unattainability, whether it is at hand or at a distance; and finally, whether something bad can be overcome or is to be avoided, no matter what the cost. These polarities of appraisal produce the polarities of emotion. Of course, a given situation may be appraised in many different ways, one after another. For this reason, emotions are chameleonlike and change with every new aspect that is evaluated. However, certain appraisals become habitual. The resulting emotions become more intense and are more quickly aroused because of affective and motor memory (see Section II, D). They become emotional attitudes. When emotions are acted out repeatedly, they soon become what could be called emotional habits.

D. Physiological Accompaniment of Emotion

All action tendencies result in the activation of a whole pattern of voluntary and involuntary muscles, of glands of internal and external secretion. But only in the case of emotion is the activation of the autonomic nervous system and the organs it innervates really conspicuous. This pattern of activation depends on the appraisal for action, or on the sequence of appraisals that comes before the final decision to act. We know that some emotions, notably fear, result in sympathetic nervous system excitation with adrenaline secretion, which produces pallor, fatigue, fast and shallow heartbeat, and eventually exhaustion. (The spurt of energy on sudden fright, which makes it possible to escape danger, is the result of the activation of the neural action circuit that occurs before adrenaline has diffused into the blood stream. The longer the fear lasts, the more the exhausting adrenaline effects become noticeable; see Arnold, 1960, Vol. 2.) Anger, on the other hand, is accompanied by sympathetic excitation with noradrenaline secretion, which does not have the enervating effects of adrenaline but favors vasodilatation and a sudden access of muscular energy. Sorrow, hopelessness, and dejection seem to have some of the effects of fear (pallor, shallow heartbeat) but are also characterized by a general slowing of respiration, heartbeat, and metabolic functions, which soon produces a picture of powerlessness as well as hopelessness. In contrast to these enervating emotions, positive emotions like love seem to be accompanied by parasympathetic excitation producing muscular relaxation, soft voice, vasodilatation, wide pupils, moderately rapid respiration and heartbeat, secretion of sex hormones, moist conjunctiva, salivation, and a feeling of warmth (Cobb, 1950). As soon as the action tendency becomes stronger, and love becomes desire (or hope for the presence of the beloved), muscular relaxation is replaced by muscular activation. It is obvious that such positive emotions produce the conditions that are most favorable for organismic well-being, while negative emotions, like fear, sorrow, hopelessness, and dejection, interfere with physical well-being.

These effects are temporary as long as the corresponding emotions are transitory. But when emotions become attitudes and habits, their physiological effects become cumulative and can greatly influence an individual's health. The happy and contented man or woman is usually healthy. The fear-ridden neurotic has innumerable physical complaints that are not imaginary but are the result of physical changes during fear. A person in a deep depression, completely hopeless, can neither work nor do anything to help himself.

IV. The Human Use of Human Functions

Up to this point I have discussed the way in which psychological functions are organized, whether in man or animal. Perception (or rather, its ingredients—preliminary appraisal, recall, appraisal of object, imagination of action and possible consequences, appraisal for action), appetitive tendency, and action: this sequence represents not only a logical analysis but a causal sequence, even though we only experience the full-blown emotional desire, the end product of this sequence, without much insight into its antecedents.

Many complicated sensorimotor sequences are organized at a time in life when the temporal sequence can be observed. For instance, we learn to read a strange word letter by letter, then pronounce it as a whole, and after using it for a while, read it immediately as a unit. The skilled reader reads not only words as units, he reads phrases. In speed-reading, he gradually learns to read whole lines at a speed much faster than the slow reader reads words. Since reading starts with seeing and ends with pronouncing the words, this is a fairly close analogy of the sequence from perception to action. In learning to read, it is easy to remember the slow beginnings so that there never is any doubt that the finished product is the result of a sequence of painfully slow steps finally speeded up a hundredfold. In the progression from sense experience to action, on the other hand, the organization of the sequence is not remembered simply because the processes involved escape inspection. We remember situations but not the process of remembering, and recall at best what is being imagined and not the fact of having imagined something. Still less can we recall estimating the effect of various things on us though we are well aware of the feelings and emotions they have aroused in us. What makes reflection on this sequence even more difficult is the fact that each action may be preceded by many rounds of recalling, imagining, appraising, liking, and wanting before we decide on action.

This inherent organization of psychological functions will determine their temporal sequence so that a new situation will inevitably touch off memory and imagination; and the appraisal of this situation, together with affective memory, will absolutely determine the action tendency it arouses. However, the appraisal that determines action is much more complex in human beings than in animals. The animal can only appraise concrete things as good or bad for its concrete needs. The human being can also appraise something as beautiful, and the corresponding action impulse may be to admire or contemplate rather than to acquire it. Or an object may arouse feelings of awe and reverence with an impulse to worship rather than to admire. But in such cases, the appraisal is never exclusively intuitive, it always includes a value judgment based on conceptual knowledge. To judge something beautiful means going beyond the concrete object and its concrete use and appreciating it for the harmony of line or pattern—concepts not available to the animal. Thus the animal's intuitive appraisal is exclusively in terms of what is good or bad for action here and now, while a man can evaluate things and concepts in a hundred different ways. Since he is a unit, he will be attracted by something he has judged beautiful or important; in other words, his value judgment is often, though not always, accompanied also by an intuitive judgment.

However, once he has intuitively appraised something, this intuitive appraisal will arouse an affective tendency; when strong, this will be felt as emotion. Hence emotions, particularly when intense, are experienced as something that breaks in on us, something outside our deliberate control.

A. EMOTIONS AND THEIR ROLE IN LIFE

On the animal level, there is no doubt that emotions have an important role. As action tendencies, they urge the animal toward things that are good for him and away from things that are harmful. It is only in exceptional circumstances that emotions become harmful to the animal: terrified wild horses stampede and may hurt themselves or their colts. Fear of a snake may paralyze a bird or small animal so that it cannot escape. Two bucks may fight so fiercely that neither of them survives. But on the whole, fear does urge animals to escape danger; anger does give them strength to defend themselves; what they like is good for them. It is only in the psychological laboratory that they develop anxiety neuroses because things change their significance capriciously so that the animal's emotions are no longer a sure guide. So the rat may "freeze" rather than avoid the electric shock, the lamb develop an anxiety state because it cannot find safety with its ewe, and the monkey become morose and antisocial because as an infant he has had neither a natural nor a terrycloth mama to comfort him.

It is different with human beings. Not only is excessive emotion harmful because it prevents effective action, but emotion often interferes when it is not at all excessive because the momentary attraction or repulsion of its objects overrides reflection. The human being lives in a human environment that is even more disconcerting than the psychological laboratory is to a rat. He needs more than intuitive appraisals to know what is good or bad for him in every situation he encounters. Since emotion takes us into action effortlessly, while reflection has to weigh alternatives and often must make an unpalatable course of action at least minimally attractive before action will be undertaken at all, emotion often wins out against a person's better knowledge. A boy may know that his sweetheart is interested only in clothes and parties, but he is in love and cannot be without her. Once he is married, she bores him to tears and he can no longer understand what he could have seen in her. Or a man likes the race track and cannot keep from betting even though he knows he cannot afford to lose. It could almost be said that there is *always* danger that emotions will lead us astray.

Emotions may distract us: The boy who wants to train for a profession cannot afford to spend time on hobbies, however interesting they may be. Emotions may actively hinder us: A boy who is painfully shy will find it difficult to become a public speaker or a concert pianist, no matter how gifted he may be. The sheer physical effect of emotion can turn liking into craving, love into bondage, fear into cowardice, and make reasonable action all but impossible. Reasonable human conduct demands that we reduce the intensity of attractions that distract us from a chosen goal, and overcome the hampering fear and lack of confidence that prevent us from following it effectively.

1. *Emotional Control*

To control emotions does not mean to suppress them. Emotions are response tendencies and we cannot do without them. But they are aroused by intuitive appraisal, which we can educate but not directly control. The gradual education of emotions from childhood to maturity will be discussed in the next section. Here I would merely like to point out that it is possible at any stage in life to reduce the intensity of pleasant emotions when necessary and to overcome the pressure of unpleasant emotions so that neither will influence us unduly.

Since emotions are aroused by appraisal, and appraisal depends on what is experienced, remembered, imagined, we can use imagination to good purpose if we want to influence appraisal. If we dwell on the positive aspects of something we fear or dislike; if we resolutely turn from what we have lost toward what is good to have here and now; if we consider ways and means of overcoming an annoying obstacle instead of indulging in fruitless anger, the emotion will soon change or give way to useful planning. In contrast, the undue attraction of something that arouses love or desire is not helped by using our imagination. The emotion itself, aroused by what is desirable, directs imagination unfailingly into channels that increase the attraction. Consequently, we must find some occupation that will demand all our attention and take imagination captive. But in the long run, the only way to ensure that we have the strength to turn away from something desirable for a good reason is to do without pleasurable things at least for a while, from time to time, so that we learn that it is possible to live without a coveted pleasure. In this way, a habit of reasonable action is acquired that will assert itself when it is needed.

2. *Development of Emotion: The Self-Ideal*

For the animal, emotions are strong appetitive tendencies that together with instinctive appetitive tendencies, lead to the acquisition of what is useful for individual or species survival. In the young child, similar emotional tendencies act in similar ways. While this organization of response tendencies includes all possible action tendencies of the animal so that all his life long the animal is determined by emotional attractions and repulsions, the child slowly develops other action tendencies, based on deliberate evaluation, in addition to the appetitive tendencies that continue to influence him. Conceptual thinking and reflective judgment represent additional realms of knowledge accessible to the child. He begins to see things that are emotionally attractive against the perspective of long-range goals that may demand painful effort but promise continuing interest.

But not only does his vision become clearer as his understanding develops; he also begins to broaden his interests by discovering what other human beings have to offer. First of all, he loves and admires his parents—not only because they provide food, love, and comfort but because they do things he cannot do. Father and mother become models for the child, models he wants to emulate. Love and admiration, like all emotions, are action tendencies and so provide the urge to approach the parents—not physically but intentionally, by lessening the distance that separates the child's actions, opinions, and beliefs from those of his admired parents. He makes their principles his own, not in slavish imitation, not by a symbolic "incorporation" of mother or father, but by realizing that his parents are admirable so that he is willing to accept their opinions as worth having and worth following. While he is very young, the child adopts his parents' opinions because he loves and admires them. In adolescence and afterward, he judges his parents as well as their principles and may decide that both fall short of what could be expected from adults. Adolescent rebellion seems to be a reaction to the established ethical principles and customs because the youngsters believe that the state of the world brought about by adherence to these principles is stagnation, if not regression. It takes more maturity than can be expected from the young to realize that conditions as they exist are not necessarily what their parent generation had aimed for, even though they may be the consequences of their actions.

By evaluation, emulation, and rebellion, the young man or woman forms some idea of the direction he wants to take in life: he gradually forms a self-ideal. This self-ideal is not so much what he wants to become as it is what he wants to do and in doing will become. Every choice of action helps to establish value preferences: going to school rather than goofing off; studying in one's spare time rather than warming the boob tube; suffering the boredom of droning lectures for the sake of the knowledge that lies beyond; sharing other people's concerns and risking rebuff rather than going it alone; working for a worthwhile ideal rather than for the quick buck. To search for "identity" is as much a chase for an illusion as is the search for reality or happiness. Identity is the reward of self-determined action. It cannot be had by laborious introspection or ecstatic experiences. And happiness is the state of a person who has chosen a self-ideal appropriate to his human personality and has steadfastly followed it. As soon as a man's direction in life is chosen, every other choice becomes an integral part of the scheme. His ideal is the capstone in the hierarchy of values he has set himself to achieve; it is not based on a bloodless intellectual judgment but is something he deeply desires and works for in one way or another. This desire for a life goal, whatever it may be, is an intensely human emotion that gives depth and significance to his life. Though he may remain a wayfarer and never reach his goal, the pursuit itself is exhilarating and brings enough satisfaction to encourage him to further effort—that is, if the goal he has chosen is really right for him.

In this attraction toward a dominant goal we see the role played by emotion in its most important aspect. Without the inherent attraction of wisdom for the sage, justice and equity for the socially responsible person, or the love of God for the saint, the pursuit of his life goal would be a dreary uphill plodding that no one could keep up for long. The desire to achieve something worthwhile also illustrates the difference between human and animal emotion. Animal emotions are simple because they tend toward concrete objects under concrete conditions. For human beings, however, the objects that attract them have become not only complicated but abstract. To send a man to the moon is a desire no animal could grasp even if we could communicate the concept. To create a great painting or sculpture, to compose a symphony or a dance is a real emotional desire for the artist. And when the work is finished and found good, he feels a satisfaction that goes beyond mere sensory pleasure. For the human being, anything he can achieve and anything he can make, fashion, or design can become the object of his desire. The work he envisions is highly valued, not only as a matter of reflective judgment, but as a fact of continuing intuitive appraisal, and thus produces the emotional urge to achieve it.

Human judgment is never wholly abstract, never wholly reflective. Accordingly, a deliberate decision to act is accompanied by emotion that is the stronger the more important the goal—though it is not necessarily the most intense emotion. On the other hand, there is hardly any intuitive appraisal without a simultaneous reflective evaluation, so that human emotion at its best takes on the character of reasonableness and intelligence. Even the uncomplicated liking of food, friend, or mate is enriched by the human significance of each. Except in severe starvation, food is not attractive unless it satisfies the eye as well as the palate. A friend is far more than a member of the same species made familiar by propinquity. And human love can outlast sexual desire, withstand separation, and transcend death. Human significance deepens all emotions that tend toward humanly relevant goals. That man is most truly human whose desires reach out for immaterial before material goals because only those aims can draw him out of himself and encourage him to transcend his limitations.

While positive emotions can spur a man on, negative emotions may make him less than human, let him sink back to the level of his meaty carcass. Fear can make a man fail his friends and himself; anger can make him say and do things that make him ashamed afterwards; sorrow locks him to the past, and dejection paralyzes him altogether.

B. EMOTION AND PERSONALITY

Our discussion of the self-ideal forms a natural transition to the role of emotion in personality. With Gasson (1954) I would consider personality as the *patterned totality of human potentialities, activities, and habits, uniquely organized by the person in the active pursuit of his self-ideal, and revealed in his behavior.* Together with deliberate action tendencies, emotions urge the human being to pursue his ideal. The same combination urges him to aim for particular goals. These tendencies have a bimodal way of action: toward acquisition of what he wants and toward actuation of the self by making these possessions really his own. Feelings and emotions together with reflective judgment and self-determined choice are the concrete links between perception and action. But more importantly, they are the means by which the personality is organized, by which the self-ideal is formed and pursued.

Though the self-ideal is chosen at first unwittingly and only much later corrected by reflection, it is not altogether subjective. If his ideal reflects what this man can achieve, given his equipment, his talents and weaknesses, it represents the perfection of his humanity, and as such is objectively valid. When a man's self-ideal sets too low an aim, or a perverted aim, he is in fact neglecting the requirements of his own nature and will reap discontent and disharmony instead of happiness and contentment. In the same way, if the natural working of any human function is perverted or prevented, we experience a peculiar malaise and discontent, whether we try listening to a ball game through a lot of static, try to run when out of breath, or are forced to sit around "resting" when in vigorous health.

Since a valid self-ideal is the perfection of a man's humanity, he will court unhappiness if he chooses a self-ideal that suits merely his own convenience, and will experience conflict whenever he is tempted to act contrary to his proper ideal. This, like every conflict, grows out of a decision that is countermanded as soon as made. Instead of a final appraisal for action coupled with a refusal to consider any other aspect of the situation, the other alternative is still admitted as a possibility even after the decision is made. Thus action is never singleminded but is started for a moment and soon stopped to continue deliberation; and a new appraisal may result in a step in the opposite direction. Conflict is never pleasant because it prolongs deliberation, saps confidence, and interferes with effective action. But conflict in an important matter that touches upon a man's chief aim in life is far worse. And if that conflict centers on the problem as to what self-ideal to choose, it is profound indeed. At this point, a man may be confused about his "identity," for he has not been able to fit himself to any goal. At this point also, he may fall prey to existential anxiety because he is uncommitted and drifts without anchor.

Often such drifting comes from a basic unwillingness to take the trouble of finding something to which a man can commit himself. It is so much easier to live like the birds of the air or the flowers of the field; to have love-ins and happenings and mind-enlarging trips. Man does not live by experience alone, just as he does not live by bread alone. Man is the doer even more than the spectator or the lover. If his society is unsatisfactory, it will not be reformed by those who disdain participation and spurn responsibility.

Emotions, whether mob violence or passive love-ins, seem to have been chosen by many young people as sole guide of their actions. They cede control to raw appetite instead of making an effort at educating emotions and using their power for responsible human conduct. But emotions are harsh masters. They demand more and more satisfaction the more they are indulged, regardless of reason or expediency. Thus emotional indulgence can only lead to social and personal disorganization. This is true not only for antisocial outbreaks like looting and rioting, the brute exploitation of the force of anger for private gain, but also for the passive indulgence in "love" and psychedelic orgies. Such passive experiences of love and counterfeit mysticism bring about neither a new culture nor a better society. Instead of reforming the society they disdain, today's hippies attach themselves to others of their kind, turning away from the straights and squares all the way, and lie in the lap of their emotions waiting for something to come of it. But passive enjoyment of sensory attractions soon palls. Having renounced all action, their joy is bound to end in disappointment. And if they defer it by turning to more potent drugs to prolong the ecstasy, they exchange certain disappointment for total ruin.

The rebel of today seems to have as his chief goal the destruction of what does not belong to him; and the hippie, to love only those who come to belong. Both extremes seem to have no goal beyond the aims dictated by momentary feelings, no aim for excellence, no specific concern for the future. This is the real problem that involves far more than a generation gap. There are more than enough young people who do have a valid self-ideal and do strive after it. But they will have to cope with rival ideologies not too far removed from the anarchism and nihilism of the first decades of the century. Slightly modified and puffed up, these "ideals" have suddenly become respectable, even desirable: an ideal of destruction, and an ideal of passive delight in sensory experience. Between the two poles of violence and passivity, today's young generation will have to hew out their future.

1. *Negative Emotions and the Self-Ideal*

Even if a man has chosen a valid self-ideal, his effort to strive toward it will suffer many setbacks. He may be tempted by pleasure, gain, even love or friendship to do what he knows is less than his best. When he has done something that contradicts his self-ideal, he will experience shame, embarrassment, remorse, regret, or repentance—negative emotions that urge him to make amends.

A man feels shame when he realizes he has fallen short of his own estimate of himself. He feels embarrassment when he is being found out by others for having done something unbecoming to his dignity. In either case, the emotions of shame and embarrassment induce him to set himself right with himself or his neighbors, and the memory of his lapse will make it less likely that he will fall short again.

If his failure is more serious, if he has broken a strict rule of conduct, he will judge himself guilty. This judgment may arouse remorse and repentance, or fear of punishment; but it may also produce an impulse to "rationalize" his conduct, either to argue that the law he has broken is not valid for him, or that it is out of date, or unjust. Guilt is not an emotion but a juridical or moral state based on a man's judgment of his action. But this judgment, while deliberate, is also accompanied by an intuitive appraisal that results in emotion.

There are other negative emotions that can help a man in his progress toward his self-ideal. Some are felt when his hopes for the good things of life are frustrated (e.g., suffering); others, when he is disinclined to pursue a valid self-ideal (e.g., boredom). Negative emotions urge him to change his way of life—but he need not change it constructively. Shame or remorse may lead to despair; suffering may spawn rebellion and finally lead to apathy; boredom may be allayed for a time by a round of distractions. For good or ill, emotions influence a man's actions but cannot force them. To draw positive benefit from his emotions, he must recognize their origin and solve the problem they indicate rather than evade it. Shame, remorse, or boredom will lead to a change for the better if he will resolutely strive toward a valid self-ideal. Suffering can be borne constructively if he can see it as the unique chance to come to terms with his life, his death, and his ultimate end.

2. Some Positive Human Emotions

The desire to know is the first action impulse aroused by anything new that is sensed and appraised. In this form it has been called "spontaneous attention," "curiosity," "orientation reflex," or "exploratory drive," depending on the psychologist's theoretical orientation. It is experienced by man and animal alike and leads to looking, exploring, and manipulating. But human beings can experience also a desire to know that leads first to "voluntary" attention and next to reading, collecting data, experimenting, reasoning, and similar activities possible only to beings who can form concepts and use symbols. "Interest" is the sentiment that develops from the desire to know, and leads to an enduring preoccupation with a given problem. When this interest leads to the well-integrated knowledge of a particular field, it becomes a habit of action. Scientific method is such a habit of thought and action, which finally results in a body of knowledge, a science. When this interest is turned toward the general problems of human life, its conditions, and its purpose, and toward all the facts as they affect the human being, it leads to wisdom, a virtue all but forgotten in our age. The wisdom of the sage, more than the scientist's knowledge, leads to a realization of what is worthwhile in life, and to a better knowledge of a valid self-ideal. For any given individual, the love of wisdom, instead of a thirst for knowledge, can be a powerful spur.

In addition to wisdom, human love is needed to form and pursue a valid self-ideal. An animal can feel an attraction to things and living beings, but man can reflect on the meaning of the world around him and on the personal significance of others like him, and so finds his love illuminated by knowledge. There is admiration in every truly human love. Without admiration, love becomes bondage or addiction. Because he admires his beloved, the lover tries to make himself worthy of being loved. For this reason, love and admiration are the prime movers in a man's progress toward a valid self-ideal. As with any other emotion, love also can be misused so that it comes to serve a narrow egotism instead of enlarging the lover's heart. If it is excessive, it may occupy his mind to the exclusion of everything else.

3. *The Joy of Doing and Making*

Pleasure in activity is a basic psychological reaction, experienced by animals and small children as easily as by adults. Gradually, activity becomes more complex. The child discovers the joy of patterned and rhythmic motion, of swimming and skiing, singing and dancing. Gradually also he discovers that he can master the things he finds around him—not by destroying them, as the small child does, but by imposing a new pattern upon them, by drawing, working with clay, building, or making something. Thus the human being improves on what was there before, and gives expression to his ideas. The joy of creative endeavor is for man alone, whether his efforts result in a poem, painting, philosophical system, piece of machinery, social enterprise, or just a gadget.

When a man's effort is aimed not at making something useful but at making something beautiful, he experiences the greater joy of artistic creation, a self-expression of an entirely different kind. The satisfaction he feels is the joy in the realization of his intention rather than the simple pleasure of doing or making. Indeed, he learns to put up with the travails and frustrations that any creative endeavor entails and keeps on despite repeated failure or partial success until his idea is realized in full.

The singleness of purpose and the discipline necessary for such creative effort is the same as that necessary for the pursuit of the self-ideal. Indeed, the self-ideal is often intimately bound up with the vision a man tries to realize in his creative endeavor. It is true that a great artist may not have much wisdom in the conduct of his life. But it is also true that he would be a better man if his artistic ideal were robust enough to make of his life a work of art.

All these emotions: interest, love, the joy of doing and making, and that of artistic creation; can help the human being in the pursuit of his self-ideal, provided he gives them the right direction. It takes a deliberate decision and quiet persistence to follow the self-ideal that is fitting and feasible. Without such direction, the desire to know may become avidity for gossip rather than an interest in knowledge; love may become egotism *à deux;* admiration may go to the strong and brutal rather than the powerful and gentle; esthetic emotion may become so sophisticated that it serves as a substitute for the desire for truth and the love of goodness.

The religious man would insist that emotions tend to excess or toward egotistic ends by their very nature unless they are moderated and balanced by a more steadfast emotion, the love of God. He would also argue that this is the human response to the experience of the absolutely good, true, and beautiful, and thus the only emotion that will promote a valid self-ideal. Whatever be the rights of this notion, history has verified that such love leads to action, and often produces prodigious achievements even in the practical realm, as for instance those of Paul of Tarsus, Francis Xavier, Albert Schweitzer, Damian of Molokai, and a host of others.

V. Conclusion

Our discussion has covered most of the topics relevant to a psychology of personality. What is left is to spell out how the various aspects are integrated. I have suggested that *perception* includes not only sensory experience of objects but conceptual knowledge, memory, imagination, appraisal; and that appraisal (intuitive and reflective) produces affective and deliberate action tendencies that lead to action as soon as attention is turned away from other alternatives; that is, as soon as a *decision* is reached. Thus appraisal is the link between receptor and effector functions; and affect is the first effector function in this sequence, which flows into action if no contrary tendency intervenes. This analysis is supported by a review of neurophysiological findings, which make it possible to describe the structures active in appraisal, and to identify memory, imagination, and action circuits.

According to this scheme, *formal learning* (improvement of performance) would be the setting of a new goal appraised as good. On the basis of recall and imagination, action is initiated and performance improved until appraised as successful. In addition, there is *incidental learning* (acquisition of knowledge), which is the memory of anything appraised as good to know. *Latent learning* would be the acquisition of knowledge not as yet translated into recorded performance.

A motive is a want that leads to action, that is, a goal appraised as good for action without further deliberation; it includes affective and deliberate action tendencies. *Imagination* is the reorganization of available memories in the light of a particular goal. It can be called creativity in the sense that every such reorganization is original with the individual.

Finally, *personality* is the totality of human potentialities, activities, and habits organized by the person in the active pursuit of his self-ideal. While the self-ideal is formed by his deliberate decisions for action, positive human emotions help to establish and pursue this ideal, and negative emotions help to avoid deviations from the ideal or help to correct them, provided the human being uses them in a constructive way.

REFERENCES

Allport, G. W. The trend in motivational theory. *American Journal of Orthopsychiatry,* 1953, **23,** 107–119.

Arnold, M. B. *Emotion and personality.* New York: Columbia Univer. Press, 1960. 2 vols.

Beattie, D. M. The effect of imaginary practice on the acquisition of a motor skill. Unpublished master's thesis, Univer. of Toronto, 1949.

Cobb, S. *Emotions and clinical medicine.* New York: Norton, 1950.

Gasson, J. A. Personality theory: A formulation of general principles. In M. B. Arnold and J. A. Gasson (Eds.), *The human person.* New York: Ronald Press, 1954.

Gasson, J. A. Personal communication. 1967.

Lazarus, R. S. *Psychological stress and the coping process.* New York: McGraw-Hill, 1966.

Leeper, R. The motivational theory of emotion. In C. L. Stacey and M. F. De-

Martino (Eds.), *Understanding human motivation.* Cleveland, Ohio: Howard Allen, 1963.

Olds, J. Physiological mechanisms of reward. In M. R. Jones (Ed.), *Nebraska symposium on motivation.* Lincoln, Neb.: Univer. of Nebraska Press, 1955.

Olds, J. A preliminary mapping of electrical reinforcing effects in the rat brain. *Journal of Comparative and Physiological Psychology,* 1956, **49,** 281–285.

Watson, J. B. *Psychology from the standpoint of a behaviorist.* (3rd ed.) Philadelphia, Penn.: Lippincott, 1929.

Young, P. T. *Motivation and emotion.* New York: Wiley, 1961.

THE CONCEPTUAL DIMENSIONS OF EMOTIONS

ABRAHAM I. MELDEN

I. Introduction

My purpose in this essay is to bring into clear view some of the complex conceptual dimensions of emotion. This task is important if we are to make satisfactory progress, not only in psychology, but also in philosophy itself, where too often discussions proceed apace without due recognition of the conceptual ramifications of this notion. The field of human emotion, however, is much too broad and too varied to be treated adequately within the brief compass of an essay. Nonetheless it will serve our purpose of providing the necessary cautions for psychologists and philosophers alike, to consider what often has been taken to be a relatively simple class of cases, and if, as it turns out, conceptual complexities emerge upon closer scrutiny of such prima facie uncomplicated items, we shall be forewarned against taking too simple a view of patently much richer instances of human emotion.

The emotion or emotions with which in the main I shall deal come under the general heading of anger. I shall offer no single and no simple conceptual theory; that would be, in my opinion, a mistake. Rather, I shall examine cases and views (actual or possible), bringing them into juxtaposition with each other, and in so doing provide reminders of conceptual features and complexities—the dimensions of emotions—of what all of us commonly recognize but quickly forget in our zeal to advance and defend the doctrines to which we are committed.

II. The Emotion of Anger

Consider the view, certainly tempting, that the emotion of anger is a feeling, a kind of internal disturbance generally but not necessarily exhibited by, and hence connected in some purely contingent way with, its usual bodily manifestations: reddening of the face; tightening of the muscles of the neck; slight protuberance of the eyes, in addition to perhaps other changes in the physiognomy of the face (all that is suggested by our common talk about angry looks and bearing); a raised tone of voice, along with characteristic extravagances of speech (consider our common talk about angry voices, tones of voice, and angry words); an aggressive or threatening posture or action directed toward those with whom one is angry (we do talk about angry acts, about acts done in anger); and so on. An individual can avoid displaying, venting, or showing his anger in any or all of these ways. And that he is angry if such concealment occurs, unusual as this may be, only the person who feels the anger can say; no one else can tell. And if this be true, it would appear that the anger is something purely internal of which we are directly aware and connected in purely contingent ways with any or all of the ways in which it may be exhibited to anyone else.

But this is only the beginning for the view that the emotion is an internal mental entity or content of consciousness. For what shall we say of the connection of the emotion with that which provokes it—its cause? And with that at which it is directed—its object? How, if at all, *must* the emotion be connected either with its cause or object?

For Hume, whose treatment of emotion as impressions of reflection is the clearest classical example of the view under discussion, the connection between an emotion and both that which provokes it (its cause) and that at which it is directed (its object) would appear to be purely contingent, explicable in terms of the *de facto* constitution of the human mind. "A passion," he tells us, "is an original existence, or, if you will, modification of existence, and contains not any representative quality, which renders it a copy of any other existence or modification" (Hume, 1739, Bk. II, Pt. iii, Sect. 3.). That is to say, unlike my idea of red, which can function as such an idea only by being a copy of an anetecedent impression, there is no essential reference in the emotion of anger to that which provokes it or to that at which one is angry. Hume could not possibly be more explicit on this point. For he tells us that "when I am angry, I am actually possessed with the passion, and in that emotion have no more reference to any other object, than when I am thirsty, or sick, or more than five feet high" (Hume, 1739). The fact that when one is angry one is angry at or with so-and-so is thus no matter of logical necessity at all but dependent on *de facto* principles of association: "the uniting principles among our internal perceptions," as he calls them, which are matters of psychological fact and hence are "not known to us in any other way than by experience" (Hume, 1739, Bk. I, Pt. iii, Sect. 14.). On this way of looking at the matter there would be nothing self-contradicting in being proud of the achievements of a total stranger or in being proud of the festering sore on the arm of the unknown passerby. For the idea of pride does not, as such, involve the idea of self but is connected with it only by an association of ideas. In the same way, the fact that there is something that provokes or causes anger is a matter of empirical fact, dependent on causal connections that are purely contingent. For as an emotion, anger is "an original existent," distinct from that of its cause, and hence thinkably separable from any and all other existents, however connected as a matter of brute fact it may be with them. There could be nothing self-contradictory, therefore, in the idea of being angry, but not over or with anything at all.

Whatever one might say about Hume's view concerning pride, and recent writers have commented on the absurdity of the view to which Hume is led,* the notion that thinkably anger can be free floating with respect to both cause and object may not appear to be transparently incoherent. Generally there is something that provokes one's anger, whether this be the mere sight or act of another or even the frustrating circumstances in which one is involved (as in the case of the irascible man who loses his temper because of the heavy traffic that delays him on his way to keep an engagement). But are there not, as a matter of fact and not mere logical possibility, free-floating cases of fear? And why not therefore of anger? No doubt there appear to be cases of unprovoked anger that turn out on closer examination to have their provocation in something that the subject himself may be unwilling or unable to recognize; but it would be unreasonable to insist that in every case the subject, of logical necessity, must be angered *by* someone or something. Let it be that in such cases, unusual as they may be, there are disturbances in the nervous system that

* See Kenny (1963, p. 24) and, earlier, Philippa Foote (1958–1959, pp. 86–87).

explain in some relevant sense the flashes of anger that occur; but these are not the causes of anger in the relevant sense at issue here. For whatever the bodily mechanisms or events involved in the occurrence of anger may be, it would be nonsensical to say that an angry person is angered by these bodily factors; and it is causes, in the sense of what caused the person to be angry, where this is equivalent to what it is *by which* the person was angered, that is at issue here. And if, as it seems likely, there are on occasion cases of anger in which there are not causes in this sense, then the connection between anger and its causes, in this same sense, would appear to be contingent. And given that this can happen, why not take the further step and maintain that, conceivably at least, there need *never* be any causes of anger at all; that in no case of the question "By what is X angered?" could anything be cited as its cause.

So one might be inclined to argue about the object of the emotion. There were, of course, the angry young men of another generation, but these will hardly do as cases of free-floating anger with respect to their objects. For here, like the case of the woman angry with her husband, whose infidelity she has just discovered, the case of the angry young men does involve objects—things with which they were indeed angry; the difference is merely that the objects of their anger were larger in scope: society, the state of the world, or whatever. But there are peculiar cases of self-deception in addition to simple cases of mistake with respect to the identity of the thing with which one is angry. I may, of course, be angry at or with the wrong person where, mistakenly, I attribute Y's misdeed to X. But there are cases of self-deception that go further in the kind of error that takes places with respect to the very object of the emotion itself. If, for example, I act indecently in order to secure my advancement in the office hierarchy, I might well, later on, be filled with self-disgust, be angry with myself. And if the deed is sufficiently heinous, I might well be loathe to admit it to myself, and vent my anger upon my wife when she fails to have my dinner waiting on the table for me upon my return home that evening, persuading myself that my wife, now the victim of my anger, is really the one with whom I am angry, even disgusted. And if the anger is one thing—some content of consciousness, a mental disturbance or feeling—and my ideas and beliefs are something else, perhaps even a more radical type of error would appear to be possible. For perhaps even in the so-called normal case error occurs with respect to the object of anger simply because, for reasons too obscure for us to fathom, one connects the emotion with the wrong idea, so that one is not really angry with the one with whom one takes oneself to be angry. And why not go further and conceive of the emotion disengaged from any idea of any object: a free-floating anger that, like certain

actual cases of fear, is directed at no object at all. "Are you angry?"
"Very." "With whom?" "No one." "You mean that you are not angry?"
"On the contrary, I am furious." And since what is thinkably the case
sometimes would seem to be thinkably the case always, who can deny that,
thinkably, at least, all cases of anger should be without any object at all?
Why not, indeed, if we identify anger with some feeling, some internal impression, from which everything else, being distinguishable, is, thinkably at
least, completely separable?

But what are my feelings when I am angry? Without attempting a historical survey of the topic, it is well worth noting certain of the views
entertained by previous philosophers. Hobbes likened the passions to sense
in that both are, in the body, only motions. The appearances of the motions that are produced by the actions of external objects on our sense
organs are colors, smells, sounds, and so forth, of the various sorts familiar
to us in sensation. In the case of our emotions, these movements within our
bodies, which he calls endeavors, either toward or away from the exciting
objects, are felt by us (or appear to us), respectively, as delight or pleasure, and "trouble of mind," pain or displeasure (Hobbes, 1651, Pt. I,
Chapt. 6). The differences between the various emotions, under which
Hobbes collects desire, aversion, courage, anger, and so on, are then accounted for by reference to a number of different factors. Anger, for example, is explained as sudden courage, courage as fear with the hope of
avoiding hurt, fear as an aversion with the opinion of hurt from the object;
and aversion, finally, while it is, in our bodies, a movement away from the
object, is felt by us as "displeasure," "trouble of the mind," "pain," "uneasiness." Some of the anticipations of later psychological theory are, of
course, apparent: the talk quite recently about emotion as the "felt tendency towards or away from an object" (Arnold, 1960, Vol. I, Chapt. 9),
no less than the view of James and Lange that emotions are felt changes
within the body involved in its avoidance of or approach to factors in the
environment. But what is of interest at this point is the view that anger as
feeling is an uneasiness, pain, or "trouble of the mind." The same view is
to be found in Locke, divorced, however, from the Hobbesian suggestion
much later revived by proponents of the James–Lange theory that such
feelings are appearances of bodily changes. But clearly Hume is on sound
grounds in avoiding pinpointing the feeling involved in anger to anything as
specific and special as uneasiness. An emotion, for Hume, is an impression
of reflection derived from impressions of sensation either with or without
the assistance of intervening ideas. Such impressions of reflections may be
pleasant or painful. Pride is an example of the first, humility of the second.
In itself, however, it may be associated with pleasure or pain; each is a

simple impression, concerning which he tells us that "it is impossible we can ever, by a multitude of words, give a just definition of them, or indeed of any of the passions. But as these words, *pride* and *humility,* are of general use, and the impressions they represent the most common of any, everyone, of himself, will be able to form a just idea of them, without any danger of mistake" (Hume, 1739, Bk. II, Pt. i, Sect. 2).

Fond hope, indeed, as Wittgenstein has argued, that "everyone, of himself, will be able to form a just idea "of anger," if nothing can be said about it but that one has it—whatever it may be, if indeed it is anything at all! And that is precisely the difficulty I want to emphasize. For surely it is a mistake to say that whenever anyone is angry, he feels "trouble of the mind," mental pain, or displeasure. For our anger is anger whether it depresses or exhilarates us, whether we find it annoying and distasteful or positively relish and enjoy it. Anger can be many things in the life of the same person. And people do vary in temperament: just as some enjoy a good cry and look forward to nothing so much as a proper funeral, so there are those who nurse their anger and indulge themselves in bursts of temper. Indeed, if we look to the feelings people do have when they are angry, but nevertheless insist that anger is a felt content of consciousness, Hume's resort to unanalyzable simples would appear to be the only philosophically open move in the face of the actual facts in the case. And if this same move is brought into conjunction with the conceptual divorce of the emotion from all of its normal manifestations, and even from its object and its cause, the emotion turns out to be a most elusive will-o'-the-wisp. Philosophical prepossessions must surely have misled us if they lead us to view the most obvious and familiar of the occurrences in our lives as such shadowy, even problematic, entities.

III. The Concomitants of Anger

What kinds of feelings do we have when we are angry? It would be a twofold mistake to answer "anger." A man can be angry without recognizing the fact; but he cannot feel anger without being aware of it. But, further, the reply provides no answer. It is true, of course, that emotions vary in intensity just as feelings, such as those of hot and cold, do. And a man's anger, like other feelings, is an episode in his life. Sometimes, or characteristically, he may be either slow or quick to anger; it may mount as in a "slow burn," or it may flare up explosively. And sooner or later, after it reaches its peak, it does subside and disappear. Further, unlike the case in which we speak of a man's feeling that a given candidate for office will not be elected, "anger" designates something that can be felt, whereas the "that clause" with which one expresses one's beliefs does not, even though a sinking feeling might well go with its utterance. For while we speak of a feeling of anger or of feeling anger just as we speak of a feeling of pain or feeling pain, we do not speak of *having* an anger as we do of having a pain, a sensation of heat or cold, or a sinking feeling in one's heart. It is in fact at least a very queer way of speaking to say that one has a feeling of anger, unless this is taken to mean either that one does have some one of the feelings that, characteristically, one has when one is angry or, simply, that one is angry. The point is that, unlike the case in which, when one feels pain, the pain is the feeling that one has when one feels it, there is no simple or single feeling one has such that feeling anger consists in having it and nothing else.

What sorts of feelings, then, do we have when we are angry? Here no doubt we are likely to think of bodily feelings. And these vary greatly if for no other reason than that anger shades off imperceptibly from irritation and annoyance to fury and rage. It would be a mistake to identify such feelings, as did James and Lange, with feelings (i.e., perceptions) of visceral or vasomotor changes. Such changes do in fact occur, whether during or after the anger is felt, but if they do, this is a matter that can be established only empirically and experimentally, and this fact can hardly be conjoined with the identification of the emotion itself with the feeling or perception of such changes. For if the fact is to be established experimentally, it can be done only by correlating such changes with the occurrence of the emotion of anger; and if this is so, the emotion must be intelligible independently of the notion of such changes; that is, it cannot involve in its description any reference to such bodily changes. Besides, we do not feel such changes in the way in which we feel the smoothness of an object or the accumulation of saliva in our mouths; we need not have the least idea that such changes are taking place when we are angry. The bodily feelings we do have, when we are angry, are of quite a different sort from these suggested by James and Lange. These may be a felt tightening or set of the jaw and neck, a feeling of dryness in the mouth and throat, perhaps a felt trembling of the hands, and so on. But none of these is necessary and none of these, in any combination, is sufficient. A man may grow cold, or hot, with anger, and the bodily feelings he may have may be much too diffuse even to be noticed by him at the time he does feel angry. In any case, such bodily feelings may occur not only when he is angry, but also when he is gripped by fear or filled with indignation, disgust, remorse, or shame. If we look to bodily feelings—add to them as we wish—we shall hardly assure ourselves that these are the items that constitute the emotion of anger.

No doubt, too, there may be felt discomfort or "trouble of the mind," as when I am disappointed in and angry with a misbehaving friend. But if I detest one who behaves badly, if indeed I wish him ill, my anger is one I might well relish as I vent it upon him.

These are by no means the only feelings that are relevant in some way or other to the phenomenon of anger. There may be agitations, but there need not be any undue disturbance of mind. The anger may be intense and uncontrolled, and like a raging storm bring our thoughts and feelings into total disarray. But it may also be just and sure, for not every case of anger is one in which one is agitated, overcome, or deprived of one's senses.

Earlier I remarked that one reason for the manner in which feelings vary from case to case is that anger shades imperceptibly into annoyance and irritation, as well as fury and uncontrolled rage. But this, while true, is hardly of decisive importance; it shows merely that anger has its penumbra of vagueness and in itself would leave unexplained the fact that in clear-cut cases of anger the feelings that occur when one is angry can vary as greatly as they do. And this may puzzle us. Should we not expect there to be standard or central cases of anger such that, notwithstanding minor variations, feelings tend characteristically to cluster together?

Certainly we should, if we think of the anger as constituted by the occurrence of feelings, where these are taken to be mental occurrences conceptually cut off, as it were, from all reference to the body, no less than from the circumstances in which the person is placed. When we ask ourselves whether someone is angry, our question is not whether such and such events are transpiring in the hidden chamber of his mind; nor do we, when we feel angry, turn our attention inward from the things that provoke us, the persons with whom we are angry, and the circumstances in which we show, display and vent our anger. This fact might suggest, as it has to some, the irrelevance of feelings to the emotion. Errol Bedford, for example, properly skeptical of this identification of emotions with feelings, goes so far as to deny that statements about emotion are used in any of their important functions to communicate information about matters of psychological fact. The principal functions of such statements, he holds, are "judicial," not "informative"; they serve to convey appraisals and assessments and, far from being statements about the inner feelings of those who feel anger, are not even statements about what they do (Bedford, 1956–1957, pp. 281–304). No doubt a man seeking reelection to political office who declares that he is proud of his record in office is concerned not to inform his hearers of the feelings he has, but to claim that his performance in office has come up to high standards. And as in the case of the other examples cited by Bedford—utterances in which terms like "jealousy," "envy," "shame," "disgust," "disappointment," or their derivatives occur —there is no doubt that emotion words can and often are used to serve a variety of purposes: to impute responsibility and to blame, to question or to affirm the wisdom of choices, to condemn or to praise, indeed, even to convey information about the social status or relations of the persons involved. But the examples cited by Bedford would appear to be special instances of the use of emotion terms (Peters, 1961–1962, pp. 118–119).

In any case it would be fallacious to argue that being proud, ashamed, or jealous does not involve feelings on the ground that statements in which these terms occur are used to provide information about, respectively, the recognition by someone of his own excellence, culpability, or social relation to another. One might as well argue that pain is not a sensation or feeling on the ground that "The pain is in my foot" can be used to inform others of where the damage to one's body has occurred. Besides, the account given does not seem plausible, on its very face, in the case of certain conspicuous uses of the terms "fear," "anxiety," and "anger." It may well be that we need more than the occurrence of certain feelings as a warrant for the application of these concepts, but to be devoid of any feelings of the variety of sorts that go with the occurrence of these emotions would emphatically count against their application. For there are *feelings of anger* no less than *the feeling that* one has received sufficient provocation, feelings *of* hostility and feelings *about* those with whom one is angry, no less than the feeling *that* one has been dealt with shabbily or with hostility, and what the present account of emotion leaves quite inexplicable is this central and essential connection between emotion and feeling.*

Defective as Bedford's account may be, there is good point to the negative part of his thesis, namely, the repudiation of the traditional identification of an emotion with some sort of internal impression—a content of consciousness—that is conceptually unrelated to, however causally connected it may be with, its surroundings, including not only the bodily conditions of the person but even his situation.

Consider for a moment the bodily feelings that often go with anger: the felt set of the jaw, the dry feeling in the mouth and throat, or the felt trembling of the hands. When, for example, I feel my jaw set, it is not the case that I have a feeling of a certain kind X that experience has taught me

---

* See M. Perkins (1966, pp. 139–160). It is this central importance of feeling that R. S. Peters rightly emphasizes and connects with wish in his important essay, "Emotion and the Category of Passivity" (1961–1962).

to connect with the forward position of the jaw, any more than when I feel a pain in my foot I have learned to associate that peculiar kind of pain with the damage that has been done to my foot. There is no local sign—an intrinsic character, as it were, of the feeling—by means of which I am able to tell on the basis of past experience that the description "feeling the jaw set" applies to the bodily feeling in the way in which I have learned that this feeling, so described, is connected with the contraction of a certain particular muscle in the jaw. It is essential to the description of the feeling that it refer to the jaw, just as it is essential to the pain that one feels it to be located in the foot. And if we strip the reference of the feeling, in either case, from the relevant part of the body and attempt to discover some characteristic by which this connection with the body can be established, we are captives once more of the traditional picture of feelings as contents of consciousness concerning whose qualities we shall be forced to say, as Hume was in the case of pride, that they are indefinable. The trouble, however, is that there are no such discoverable qualities, and the claim that there are, indeed, that there must be such, is merely a philosophical requirement masquerading as an empirical claim.

Surely, therefore, we ought to reconsider and to question the consequences to which earlier we were led, that when one feels anger, there is some one or more felt impressions—internal mental occurrences—that constitute the emotion of anger, whose connection with both its cause and its object and with all of its surroundings: not only with the ways in which it is manifested in the behavior of the person who feels the emotion, but also with the situations in which it occurs, including perhaps the social and even moral circumstances of the person; is purely contingent.

I do not wish to suggest the view often held by philosophers and psychologists that bodily feelings are the only ones involved in emotions. One can feel, in addition to the localized feelings mentioned previously, a lump in one's throat, not only when it is obstructed or constricted by the presence of a foreign object, but also when distressed by the plight of another person. One can feel chilled to the bone in very cold weather, but one can also feel the chill in one's heart on receiving dreadful news. One can feel heavy and logy when sated with food as one rises from the table, but one can also go about one's business with a heavy heart when dulled by the burden of an awful happening or disappointment. These are some of the ways in which the feelings of those in the throes of emotion are described and expressed. No doubt such expressions are used derivately. They are similes, but it would be implausible to hold that they are metaphors, capable of being cashed in the way in which, for example, this is transparently the case in "the captain of the ship of state." As similes they tell us something of the way in which the persons to whom they apply see, view, and respond to the events that befall them. A man with a heavy heart does indeed move sluggishly, hardly with the quick movements of one exhilarated by happy tidings. His movements and reflexes may well be like those of a man who has overeaten. But it is not with the ways in which he moves his body that we are concerned, but with his feelings of indifference, dullness of mind, and even inattention to the events to which normally he is alert, as his troubles weigh upon him. To apply "a heavy heart" to someone is thus to intimate far more than a characterization of bodily movements; it is rather to intimate something of the special character of his feelings and experiences as he goes about affairs in which, normally, these feelings do not occur at all (see Benson, 1967, p. 351).

Our vocabulary of feeling words is quite poor; hence, the use of similes. But poets, dramatists, and novelists employ other devices in order to convey to us the full force of the feelings of their characters. Unlike the vocabulary used by philosophers (limited as it is to a few simple summary names: pleasure, pain, distress, anger, etc.), that of poets and novelists is constantly in the making as they seek by means of new techniques and devices to do justice to the endlessly varied and complex nature of our feelings and emotions. They may use similes, but there are also the rhythms of speech and the images and allusions that these afford. And there are other devices: when Laeretes cries out in *Hamlet*

> That drop of blood that's calm proclaims me bastard,
> Cries cuckold to my father, brands the harlot
> Even here, between the chaste unsmirched brows
> Of my true mother

he does indeed convey to us the full measure of his feelings of horror, shock, and turmoil in terms of the state of mind of one who receives the suggestion that the mother he worships is not only faithless but a harlot as well. The cry succeeds in its intent only because we share with the speaker this kind of profound attachment to another human being; and the poet, by asking us in effect to imagine what it is like to hear that the person we worship is most vile, succeeds in telling us what the feelings of Laertes are on learning of the death of his father. But to be told in this way what such feelings are like is to be told much more than that there are agitations in the recesses of the mind. It is to be told something of the way in which one views and responds with horror to a situation in one's life, and in a life of a certain kind at that. Nothing could be more foreign to the poet's account than the idea that feelings are internal entities, conceptually sundered from the circumstances, the situations of the character who is in the throes of his passion.

The whole subject of feeling has been very badly mismanaged in philosophy. And it is scandalous that those who write in moral philosophy and in the philosophy of taste take little or no pain to get clear about what for them is a matter of fundamental importance.

IV. Conceptual Reconstruction of the Emotion Anger

Earlier we considered the suggestion, fostered by the philosophical view that an emotion is a felt impression or content of consciousness, that no reference to anything in which it is manifested, or to anything that is its *de facto* cause or object, is essential to the concept of emotion. But thus stripped clean, nothing is left to be said about emotions, for nothing is left at all. In the preceding discussion of the role of feeling in emotion, the bankruptcy of this philosophical view has become obvious: no account of feeling does justice to the facts except by reference not only to bodily states but also to the ways in which, in thought and in action, those who feel emotions deal with the matters that confront them. We need, therefore, an analytical reconstruction of the concept of an emotion in order to exhibit its conceptual connections.

It is a matter of fact that on a particular occasion a person shows, displays, or vents his anger in given ways: he flushes, stutters, trembles, snarls, juts out his jaw, or lashes out aggressively at the person who provokes him. Or, on another occasion, it is a matter of fact that he remains calm and quiet and gives no inkling of the anger he feels; yet he *is* angry, so there must be something going on. And what on earth can this be? Here we are likely to have recourse to bodily events, to felt aggressions or hostilities, or to dispositions of one sort or another. No doubt there are bodily events that take place when one is angry, but just what events these are that are present whenever and *only* whenever one is angry, no one knows. No doubt, too, there may be felt aggressions and hostilities: the desire to damage or hurt the person who provokes one. But this is either too special or, if sufficiently general, altogether unilluminating. If I am angry with my child because of her misbehavior, must I want to lash out and hurt or damage her? Certainly I may want to rebuke her, to bring shame to her cheeks when she realizes how badly she has behaved, and if I display my anger, the display need consist only of impressing upon her the severity of my disapproval. And if we are to say that this is a display of aggression or hostility, surely these words are now so broadened in their meaning that they cease to enjoy their familiar function; to say in this way that anger is felt aggression or hostility is altogether unilluminating. No doubt, too, a man who is angry wants to, or is disposed to—what? He may desire or be disposed to offend, hurt, embarrass, rebuke, and so on, with or without *being* angry. To be sure, the man who *is* angry wants to do something about it; but no general specification of what he wants to do will serve, short of the altogether unilluminating "whatever it is that this particular angry man in this particular situation desires or is disposed to do."

A. Behavioral Implications of Emotion

It is worth noting that these attempts to elucidate the concept of "anger," defective as they are, do provide for some conceptual connection of the emotion with behavior. Aggression and hostility are behavioral in their conceptual implications, and so, by the same token, are feelings of aggression and feelings of hostility. Dispositions and desire carry similar implications. This is not to deny that a man may have a certain disposition or desire without exhibiting it on a particular occasion, and that whether he does or does not is a matter of fact that is determined by the *de facto* circumstances in the case. Nor is it to deny that the translation into action, on a particular occasion, of feelings of aggression or hostility is similarly a matter of empirical fact; and so, too, with those cases in which inhibition or restraint prevail. It is rather to deny that the concepts of "felt aggression," "felt hostility," "desire," and "disposition" can be elucidated in complete independence of the concept of action.

Further, it is also to bring into question the maxim earlier enunciated in connection with the view that an emotion is a purely internal mental occurrence that is conceptually divorced from actions and from its cause and its object, namely, that whatever is thinkably the case sometimes is thinkably the case always. A man may, of course, desire the woman next door without ever succumbing to the temptation, but does it make sense to think of a man never doing anything about any desire whatsoever? Our concept of desire is one that is conceptually related to the concept of action precisely because desires are, at least sometimes if not generally, acted upon. And were this not the case, whatever, if anything clear at all, we should then mean by "human being" or "person," we simply would not employ the concept of desire that we do have.

B. Emotion as a Disposition

Granted the empirical status of the proposition that a person acts on a particular occasion on any felt disposition to harm or to hurt, granted even the empirical status of the proposition that this, that, or any human being ever feels hostile or aggressive toward anyone else, it simply does not follow that it is a matter of brute fact that anyone ever acts on dispositions of any sort. For what then would we mean by a person, and by a disposition, such that persons would have dispositions, none of which on any occasion whatsoever would be displayed in any way whatever, in look, posture, word, or deed? Once more we should be returned to the essential incoherence of purely internal occurrences, conceptually divorced from all relation to conduct of any sort in the picture we should then have of a disposition. And so too with emotions, their manifestations, causes, and objects. Indeed, we should go ever further and look askance at the supposition that because some emotions—dread, anxiety—are thinkably, at least, free floating (whatever the status of the truth claims of Freudians on this matter may be), that therefore all emotions, including anger, pity, jealousy, and so on, are, thinkably at least, similarly undirected or objectless. That makes no sense. Thinkably, if not as a matter of empirical fact, one might feel fear, but of what one does not know. And thinkably, if not in point of actual fact, a man may have feelings of dread, but of nothing that either he or anyone else could cite. But even if it does make sense to say that a man could feel anger, pathological as this case would be, without being angered by anything, it would not make sense to say that he could feel angry but not at anything of which he was aware or at anything at all. The following dialogue, except as a feeble attempt at humor, is simply a model of incoherence: "I am angry." "At what or with whom?" "Nothing at all." "You mean you are not angry?" "On the contrary, I am furious."

Still, the difficulties cited earlier in the attempts to identify the emotion of anger with felt tendencies or dispositions of aggression, or hostility with the felt desire to harm, hurt, or to avoid the unpleasantness, evil, or harm created by others, are likely to elicit the response that the trouble lies in the essential vagueness of our ordinary talk about anger. The counterexamples cited, it will be argued, merely demonstrate the essential looseness or muddle in a commonsense notion that psychological theory must erase if it is to get on with its business.

C. Circumstances and the Sources of Emotion

But the demand for conceptual reconstruction would have some antecedent cogency only if, at least in some preliminary way, incoherences or muddles in the commonsense notion were explored; and it is certainly no argument for the existence of such defects in our everyday notion that the identification of anger with any of the factors we have considered is objectionable. Besides, the identification of the emotion is one thing; its alleged source in psychological factors is something else. And psychologists who purport to discover the roots of anger in certain factors (whether the readiness to strike, aggression, hostility, or certain allegedly basic needs or drives), of whatever sorts these may be, cannot, without logical incoherence, identify the emotion with such factors. Indeed, both the formulation of their theories and the adducing of empirical evidence in support of them presuppose not only that the concept of anger cannot be elucidated in terms of these factors but also that this concept, in its everyday employment, is sufficiently clear and coherent to serve as a basis for empirical investigation (cf. Arnold, 1960, Vol. I, pp. 152–155). Conceptual reconstruction can always be purchased at the cost of irrelevance to our subject matter; and where it is necessary, that fact must be established.

The trouble with the sampling of moves we have considered in this section lies elsewhere than in some imagined defect of our common usage. It lies in the attempt to find the essence of anger—the necessary and sufficient conditions for its presence—in some internal factor, in total abstraction from the situation in which the emotion occurs. Granted that this factor, whether it be a felt disposition, tendency, instinct, or drive, is conceptually linked with the concept of behavior or response, there is nonetheless a neglect of certain situational dimensions of the concept. In our remarks concerning the feelings of anger, we have seen that attention needs to be paid to the way in which the person in the grip of the emotion feels about the relevant circumstances of the situation in which he is placed, and that it is by reference to these circumstances that his feelings are often described. This should suggest that no account of anger is adequate unless it recognizes the pertinence of the situation. And if we follow this lead, we shall discover that the emotion is many pronged. An angry man may tremble and snarl and act aggressively. Or, he may feel disposed to acts of aggression without giving any indication of his hostility. But aggression, evinced or not, is by no means the only thing that counts in favor of his feeling the emotion. Nor, indeed, need it occur at all: we shall see, if we explore the situational dimensions of the concept, that there is no single paradigm of anger; but cases and cases, varying broadly as these dimensions, differing as they do from instance to instance, are brought into play.

V. The Situational Dimensions of Emotion

It may be useful to begin by considering instances of emotion in which the circumstances, being relatively uncomplicated, provide only a minimal set of the emotion's situational dimensions. We can contrast such conceptually truncated instances of emotion with more full-blooded instances in which the requisite complicating circumstances are present.

Animals tremble and cower or flee in terror; and they growl, snarl, or lash out in anger. These are the natural expressions of these emotions, expressions that are clear to anyone familiar with the habits of these creatures. Here there are few of the complications that are evident in the case of human beings. The provocations—frustrations, dangers, irritations, or other disturbing circumstances—that arouse the emotions are, in general, direct and immediate. The angry bear is not provoked by traps to which it expects it will fall victim the next day, but by the trap that now bites into its leg or, if it is sufficiently cunning and has learned from recent painful experience, by the trap it now sees in its path. Here the distinction between the thing that provokes its anger—the cause of the emotion—and the thing at which it is angry—the object of the emotion—tends to disappear. It is the trap that pains it and it is at the trap that it is enraged. Cunning and intelligence of a relatively high order for the lower animals is required in order for the bear to recognize the man as the being responsible for its plight, so that it may direct its anger at the man, however provoked it may be by the trap that bites into its leg. And if it is enraged or frightened by some noise-making device at a campsite, which it takes to be a clear and present threat, its fright or its rage may lack foundation, but it is hardly unreasonable. The latter term implies that there is a norm with respect to which there is some failure of the agent; but no such norm of good bearish emotion, action, or belief is in order here.

Given the limited needs and interests of animals, the manner in which these are connected with their immediate environment and the resulting circumscribed character of the intelligence that operates in such relatively simple lives, it is understandable that the emotional life of animals is limited in both character and range.

1. An animal may be disturbed, even annoyed, when feeding, yet not lash out. It may fear an approaching hostile intruder, but, if sufficiently hungry, it may continue to eat, while keeping a wary eye on the intruder. The fact that flight and aggression are, respectively, natural expressions of fear and anger does not mean that they always occur, or that there are no other ways in which an animal expresses these emotions. The animal's stiff posture, as if ready to take flight, and the wary way in which it continues to take notice of the danger, do serve, when flight is inhibited by severe hunger, as expressions of its fear. So, too, with anger. There are natural expressions of anger other than that of aggressive or hostile action, and how an animal shows its anger will depend on which of its needs and

interests is brought into play. But these needs and interests are relatively restricted, and there is, therefore, a relatively restricted set of alternative ways in which it expresses its emotions in its behavior.

2. Except in a relatively high order of animal life, the needs and interests of animals are brought into play by occurrences in the creature's immediate environment. It makes no sense in such cases to apply certain emotion terms that require for their intelligible application a history and a pattern that extends over a relatively long and complex set of events during a period of one's life. A man may now be in love, or now feel grief, just as he may now be playing chess, but it would make no sense to suppose that his love or his grief or his playing chess are complete and entire in a relatively brief moment in the way in which this is true of his pain or even of his fear or his anger (cf. Wittgenstein, 1953, II, i). Not even joy or sorrow could be significantly ascribed to an animal, whose life is limited to its responses to what is given to it immediately and directly. Nor would it make sense, as Wittgenstein has remarked, to ascribe sorrow or joy to a being, whatever his bodily expressions might be, if these experiences alternated rhythmically with the ticking of a clock (Wittgenstein, 1953). If dogs do grieve over the death of their masters, much more than their unhappiness is involved; they must, if this way of speaking is to be taken seriously and literally, have some sense or understanding of the death of their masters, including the realization that the latter will never reappear; and they must show their unhappiness over an extended period of time as a blight in their lives and in various ways, depending on circumstances. In short, the concept of an emotion involves not only its expression, which serves as criterion of its occurrence, but in some cases, a history and a pattern in a life of the requisite degree of understanding and intelligence.

3. If there are social aspects of the lives of animals, these are relatively simple and rudimentary. A pet dog may enter into the life of the family, and it may be trained, as are children, not to scatter its food on the carpeted floor. But the terms "shame," "guilt," and "remorse" do not apply to the offending pet caught in the act. For the possibility of applying these terms requires the recognition by the offender of some norm or standard of proper behavior, and the understanding that violations of the rule are wrong and not merely unpleasant if discovered. No matter how "fastidiously" a dog may eat from its dish, it is not well mannered in the sense in which persons are when, for example, they observe the familiar rules of etiquette. No matter how much a dog may cringe with its tail between its legs when caught in the act of dragging its bone across the family's prize oriental rug, it does not feel guilt or shame. And no matter how endearingly it then proceeds to lick the hands of its master, it is not

feeling remorse or asking to be forgiven for a shameful performance. Neither can it be indignant, that is, angry at the contemptible behavior of others or outraged by their inconsiderateness or indecencies. There are, in short, emotion terms that require for their intelligible application participation in and understanding of the social and moral features of the lives of human beings; hence their use in sentences in order to impute responsibility, to praise or blame, or to assess the moral quality of an agent or his conduct.

4. By the same token, some of the conceptual dimensions of our concept of anger are missing when we apply it to animals who lack certain rational abilities displayed by humans. The dog's anger and hostility provoked by the appearance on the scene of the man it does not recognize, who happens, however, to be the master's business associate, may be, from any reasonable human point of view, misdirected. But it cannot be called unreasonable, since this would carry the implication that it could have been aware of the association and, hence, of the propriety of the man's presence. Other appraisal terms like "just" and "unjust" similarly apply to anger in human beings, but hardly in any literal and straightforward sense to the anger of animals. For not all cases of anger are the undesirable disturbances that interfere, as Plato suggested, with the proper functions of reason. Anger may be misdirected, excessive, or unfounded, and the man who is too quick to anger may be prevented by his ready bias from taking proper account of the relevant facts. But the man who is never angry is unfeeling and indifferent; and the man who falls short, who is never indignant or outraged or angry, with either himself or others, is, as Aristotle once put it, "a sort of boor" (1941, II, 6). Emotions, no less than beliefs, actions, and desires, are subject to appraisal as reasonable or unreasonable, justified or unjustified. And, as Aristotle put it, to feel them "at the right times, with reference to the right objects, towards the right people, with the right motive, and in the right way" is no easy matter (Aristotle, 1941). It is essential to our concept of anger, the concept *we* employ with respect to human beings, that it be appraisable in these ways just as it is to our concept of belief and action. Whatever else anger may be, it cannot be an internal feeling or state conceptually unrelated to the functions of intelligence in the social circumstances in which it occurs. One might paraphrase a remark made by Wittgenstein about fear:

> To someone who tells me 'I can't think of the man who told us that our employment was terminated without being angry at him,' I might well reply 'That's no reason for being angry. The company was being dissolved, and it was his job to inform the employees that there would be no more work for them.' And this is one way of dismissing anger (cf. Wittgenstein, 1967, p. 501). For one can reason a man out of his anger, but not out of his pain, itch, twitch, or nausea.

5. An animal, whose needs and interests are very restricted, expresses its anger unmistakably and in a limited number of ways, in aggressive action with the intention of doing damage, in growling and snarling as if ready to spring upon the offending object, and so on. Here the anger is, so to speak, wholly on the surface. Except for those who are either obtuse or quite unfamiliar with the species, the action, posture, and sounds emitted by the animal are manifestly hostile. There is no need to cite the animal's anger in order to explain its conduct: the very descriptions of the animal's conduct usually embody a reference to the anger that moves the animal to act. To see that a dog is snarling, circling, and tearing away at the arms and legs of a man is to see a dog in its full fury. What one sees here is not *evidence* that the dog is angry, as if the anger were something hidden from what one sees. *This,* the fang-baring, snarling, and attacking animal that one sees, *is* an angry dog.

There are, of course, playful performances, that need to be distinguished from these cases. It may be, too, that these are borderline cases, and even that that which begins as play sometimes develops into the genuine article as it proceeds. But there are criteria we do employ in order to distinguish these cases, and these relate to the character of the bodily performances of the animal during the course of the incident. In the case of human beings, however, the criteria employed are much more varied and complex, and these introduce complications of a sort not encountered in the behavior of animals.

What, for example, counts as the angry act of a human being? Consider the act of slapping someone, a generally unpleasant experience for the recipient. But even here we need to know the circumstances in which the act is performed in order to understand it. A slap may be administered by a husband to his hysterical wife in order to bring her to her senses. A slap may be administered to someone who has fainted in order to bring that person back to consciousness. A slap may be administered by an actor during a play. A slap may be administered by a parent to a misbehaving child, and although this may be done in anger, it need not be so. Thinkably, a slap may be administered by a physician during the course of a physical examination. And a slap may be administered in anger. A tunnel-vision inspection of the act of slapping will not establish what in fact is being done or whether the person has acted in anger. We need to know the circumstances, including even the social relations of the persons involved, in order to make these determinations. Only a moment's reflection is needed to convince us that it is *not* the case, in very many instances at least, that the anger of a human act lies, so to speak, on the surface.

6. Because of the enormously complicated and varied circumstances of human life, there is no single paradigm of angry action. Sometimes anger

is manifested in overt aggressive behavior in which bodily injury or physical pain is inflicted upon the object of the emotion. But there are quite different ways in which a husband, for example, may show his anger toward his wife: rudeness, inconsiderateness that may take many forms, an icy silence, or even a degree of excessive politeness that would pass as altogether proper for a casual acquaintance. Again, a subordinate need not display his anger at his superior by knocking him down or telling him off; it may be done quite effectively by quitting his job or even by an unaccustomed insistence upon leaving the office promptly at quitting time despite the unfinished business on his desk. What counts for angry behavior in one case need not in another. We need to know a good deal about the people involved, their social relations with one another, their habits, and their practices, to which rules of behavior of various sorts are relevant, in order to ascertain whether in any given situation we have a case of anger. And it is because of this background understanding we do have of human beings that learning that a person is angry sometimes does enable us to interpret his actions—to see more clearly the patterns of anger in what might otherwise appear to be altogether innocent or puzzling conduct.

7. Certainly an angry man desires, tends, is disposed, or inclined to do something. The conceptual connection between the emotion and desire or disposition is clear enough, whether or not the agent acts on his desire or does what he is disposed to do. But any attempt to provide a general specification of the desire, disposition, or tendency that applies equally well to every case of anger, regardless of the endlessly variable situations of human life, and regardless, too, of the quite variable habits, personalities, and cultural backgrounds of human beings, breaks down. Hence it is that either the attempt to define the emotion in terms of a specific disposition, tendency, or desire fails to stand the test of instances, or there is recourse to such expanded uses of terms, like "aggression" and "hostility," that can be used in the specification of the desires or dispositions, that the formulas advanced are empty. An angry man wants or tends to do—what? Anything that *that* man in *that* situation wants or tends to do.

In the same way, dissatisfaction may be felt with the commonplace observations that an angry man, in attending to things, sees, feels, and thinks about things in distinctive ways. A man angry with his wife for spending the afternoon at the beauty parlor rather than shopping and in the kitchen preparing the evening meal is not likely to give her new hairdo more than a passing glance. Nor is he likely, when his attention is directed to it, to enjoy looking at it, take pride in his wife's appearance, approve of her choice of hairdo, or, while his anger continues, regard or treat her with his customary affection. But the commonplace observation is no mere summary formula that is intelligible independently of the background knowledge we do have of human beings. One might as well argue that the moral remark that we should treat members of the human race as persons is utterly empty. The moral dictum is a reminder and a caution of what we are likely to ignore under the pressure of events. It is *not* a formula and it is not a recipe that even a moral idiot could understand or employ. Neither is the observation that angry men see, think, and feel about things in distinctive ways a general formula. It, too, serves as a reminder, because of the background understanding we do have, of how in quite varied ways the thoughts, perceptions, and feelings of human beings are colored by this emotion. And knowing as we do the character, circumstances, and situations of persons who feel this or that emotion, we are able without difficulty to specify what it is that they want, what it is that they are disposed to do, and how it is that they view, feel, and respond to the things about them.

8. It should be clear by now that there is no simple paradigm case of anger. We have, instead, typical cases that vary with situations and circumstances. Even allowing for the familiar penumbral effect—for anger does shade off into irritation and annoyance at one end and, at the other, into uncontrollable rage and fury—there are, in addition, very considerable variations among clear-cut cases of anger. The factors that count for something being a case of anger—the criteria of anger—are multidimensional; these pertain not only to a person's conduct but also to his feelings, thoughts, desires, and wishes: his state of mind. But anger is a cluster concept; and a man may be angry without showing it in what he does or even without being agitated or disturbed. But if he is behaving in anger, the behavior may take a wide variety of forms, depending on the situation in which he is involved no less than on his ordinary habits of behavior in that situation, his social and even moral relations with the person or persons at whom he is angry, with respect to which a variety of rules are relevant. Doubtless his anger, whether or not he shows it in word or deed, makes a difference to the way in which he thinks, speaks, sees, and attends to things, but any general account that ignores the details of circumstances and situation may mislead. The indifference with which one person views the distress of another may mark callousness or boorishness; but if the person in distress is no mere stranger or casual acquaintance, but one with whom there have been close ties of affection, the indifference can and indeed sometimes does serve as a measure of the anger that is felt. And what in one set of circumstances counts for anger, in another way will count for malice or jealousy.

There are, of course, dictionary definitions of anger. If these could not even be attempted, anger would be not a cluster concept, but an unrelated cluster of concepts. Here, what provides unity to the cluster concept, as Peters has observed, is the concept of feeling and wish. But even a dictionary definition is open ended; and by offering examples of provocation and of the ways in which the angry man feels toward the object of his emotion, a good dictionary does give fair warning that there is no single paradigm, but typical cases, varying from circumstances to circumstances and from situation to situation.

VI. Conclusion

I began this essay by exploring relatively familiar, even traditional, views concerning the nature of emotion. I argued that, persuasive as they may appear to be, these views, in one way or another, are incoherent. The remedy proposed was an analytical reconstruction of the dimensions of the concept of emotion. I undertook to indicate how this might be done by contrasting the essentially truncated way in which such an emotion word as "anger" is applied to the relatively uncomplicated incidents in the lives of animals, with the full-blooded and conceptually rich manner in which the term is applied to episodes in our own lives. The result, if the program has been successful, is to show the essential complexity of the conceptual dimensions, not only of anger, but of other emotions as well.

Such a conceptual reconstruction is in my opinion a necessary but important preliminary to the further questions that need to be explored: In what sense does an emotion serve as a motive for action? How does the anger a man feels explain what he does *in* anger? And what can we reasonably expect to be the general character of the ultimate causal laws, if such there be, that explain (in whatever sense is here relevant) the occurrence of emotions in our lives and the manner in which these are channeled and manifested in thought and in action?

But, although I have attempted no sally into this area of discussion, the complex character of the conceptual features of the concept of emotion should warn us against too easy, too simpleminded, a set of answers. We should be forewarned against any attempt to apply Humean models of causality to the relation between an emotion and the behavior in which it is exhibited, as if the emotions could be understood simply as some internal event and its manifestation in behavior as a bodily movement produced by it. Such a conception does violence not only to the conceptual dimensions of emotion but also to the conception of a human action. It is as human beings who are reasonable or unreasonable in the situations in which we go about our business that we feel emotions and act as we do because of them. Here nothing less than our status as rational and social beings in situations of enormously varying degrees of complexity—as the whole human beings that we are—must be invoked in order to provide any reasonably adequate account of the role of emotions in our lives. It is for this reason that various attempts to formulate explanations in terms of drives or tendencies of one sort or another do not appear to me to be auspicious steps in the search for fundamental laws relevant to human behavior. My own hunch, ill-informed as it is, is that the ultimate "mechanisms" or causal laws, if such there be, that are relevant to emotions are neurophysiological in character, but of a nature and degree of complexity we have not yet begun to fathom. But how such "mechanisms" are related to emotions, as we on a common-sense level understand them, is still another matter that lies outside the scope of this discussion.

REFERENCES

Aristotle. Nicomachean ethics. In R. McKeon (Ed.), *Basic works of Aristotle*. New York: Random House, 1941.

Arnold, M. B. *Emotion and personality*. New York: Columbia Univer. Press, 1960. 2 vols.

Bedford, E. Emotions. *Proceedings of the Aristotelian Society*, 1956–1957, **57**, 281–304.

Benson, J. Emotion and expression. *Philosophical Review*, 1967, **76**, 335–337.

Foote, P. R. Moral beliefs. *Proceedings of the Aristotelian Society*, 1958–1959, **59**, 83–104.

Hobbes, T. Leviathan (1651). In W. Molesworth (Ed.), *English works*. Vol. III. London: John Bohn, 1839.

Hume, D. *Treatise of human nature*. 1739. L. A. Selby-Bigge (Ed.) London and New York: Oxford Univer. Press (Clarendon), 1888.

Kenny, A. *Action, emotion and will*. New York: Humanities Press, 1963.

Perkins, M. Emotion and feeling. *Philosophical Review*, 1966, **75**, 139–160.

Peters, R. S. Emotion and the category of passivity. *Proceedings of the Aristotelian Society*, 1961–1962, **62**, 117–134.

Wittgenstein, L. *Philosophical investigations*. Oxford: Blackwell, 1953.

Wittgenstein, L. *Zettel*. Oxford: Blackwell, 1967.

COMPLEX BEHAVIOR IN NATURAL SETTINGS

PETER MADISON

I. Introduction

In recent years I have been studying college students with the purpose of formulating a theory of personality development in college. My efforts to understand the young person in his campus context have led me to reflect both upon certain shortcomings of psychology when applied to the study of such complex behavior in natural settings and upon the limitations of the student's commonsense attempts to comprehend his own situation. Neither seem sufficient to the task and one of my purposes will be to indicate ways in which improvements can be made. A second purpose will be to use what I have found in order to examine the relationships between psychology and

223

the commonsense framework, stressed by the philosophers participating in this conference, and to propose a unified view.

First, a word about my observational base. During the past decade, psychologists have discovered the college student, a topic that Henry A. Murray (1938) and his associates at the Harvard Clinic and Theodore M. Newcomb (1943) had tried to interest us in as early as 1935. After a slow development, this work came to have a significant professional impact when Nevitt Sanford (1956) and his associates made an effective case for research on college student personality through the Vassar College study (begun in 1952). Research groups for the study of personality in college are now widespread and exciting work is in progress.

Research on personality in college has taken two forms. The primary effort has been the use of tests, either existing or new ones, to investigate whether personality development takes place in college and how much. The results of such studies have been difficult to interpret because of the uncertainties attached to the meanings of personality test score data. Along with this main thrust has gone a descriptive and theoretical effort based upon conjectures made from interview data. Nevitt Sanford (1962) has made the most ambitious attempts of this kind.

Since 1952 I have been making detailed qualitative studies of college students, using autobiographies, repeat interviews, student journals (periodic diarylike descriptions of daily life on campus), and personality tests. My effort (much like that of Henry A. Murray, 1938, and his group, or the studies reported in Robert W. White, 1952) has been to achieve an understanding of the individual student in depth. The student is studied early in his college career and followed year by year to graduation and sometimes for as long as five to ten years after. In some cases the extensiveness and depth of study is comparable to the understanding that would be achieved over several years of intensive psychotherapy of an individual.

My purposes in making such studies have been to understand my observations in terms of contemporary psychological theory and to formulate this understanding in ways that would communicate effectively to college students. These two purposes have led me, on the one hand, to examine certain aspects of psychological theory and, on the other, to look at the student's own scheme for self-understanding, and to think about the relationship between the student's "conceptual scheme of common sense" (see Peters in this volume) and psychological theory.

As a result, I am proposing some new theoretical emphases, new ways of putting together ideas from areas of psychology that have been kept separate, and some new concepts (see Madison, 1969). In this paper I want to examine the problem of how to conceive the role of past experience in present functioning. I will first consider this topic from the standpoint of how the influences of past experience upon personality are understood by the student in terms of his own commonsense scheme and will point out some limitations of the everyday view. Next, I will do the same with several of the concepts in terms of which professional psychologists understand the influence of past experience. I will then show how the perspective provided by my studies suggests points at which theoretical additions and modifications of both commonsense and psychological concepts are needed. Finally, I will use the foregoing analysis to reflect upon the existing relationship between psychology and common sense, and will propose a unification of the two in line with what I see as the position of the philosophers in this conference.

II. The Influence of the Past

Neither the undergraduate nor the psychologist seems to be sufficiently aware of the extent to which the student's response to college is dominated by his past nor well prepared to comprehend this fact in either common-sense or theoretical terms. Consider a student like Trixie, who was first studied in her sophomore year and followed through repeated interviews until two years after graduation.

A. TRIXIE

Trixie developed a distinctive childhood-adolescent personality, partly because her parents differed so sharply from one another and she was influenced by both. As a child, Trixie perceived her father as intelligent, attractive, selfish, teasing, active, authoritarian, stubborn, defensive about masculinity, unresponsive to her interest in him, and religiously dogmatic. She saw him as a father who did not show his feelings for her and as rather retiring socially except in his professional role. Trixie perceived her mother as passive, accepting, loving, and conciliatory. As a child, Trixie both modeled herself after father and furiously rebelled against him, while perceiving mother and femininity as weak and beneath consideration. A younger sister, Lucy, exaggerated these trends by taking on a passive, model-child role with infuriating success, driving Trixie into an even more extensive rebellious independence to differentiate herself from Lucy, whom she both opposed and wanted as a friend. (The quotations that follow are taken from the preliminary edition of my book *Personality in College*. Reading, Mass.: Addison-Wesley, 1966.)

I find myself at a complete loss when it comes to describing Lucy as a person. She is a *sister,* which entails reactions and counter-reactions well outside the normal sphere of friendly relations. Lucy is like Daddy, yet more so, in that I have resented her and rebelled against her to such an extent that to me she is more a frustrating barrier to my own personality than a person in her own right.

Lucy and I have taken opposite paths for as long as I can remember. She early gained recognition by helping mother with the housework and cooking. I professed my scorn for them both, earned pin money washing the car, helping put up storm windows, mowing the lawn. I always had a mad passion for dogs and horses. Lucy developed a love of cats, which has gradually dwindled and is now nonexistent—it was the first act of differentiation. Lucy has lately become interested in wild and gaudy prints, as opposed to my preference for soft pastels and solid colors. Our rooms are perhaps the best and most striking example of our divergent personalities. Lucy's is pink with a rose rug; maple furniture—a rocker, frilly dressing table, an old-fashioned desk, and knick-knack shelves. It is warm, completely feminine. My room is blue with no rug; modern furniture; a Van Gogh on the wall. It is, I'd say, cool and more invigorating. I feel almost smothered when I walk into Lucy's 'boudoir' (Madison, 1966, Chapt. 2, pp. 24–25).

When Trixie came to college she was advised to major in English by her high school teachers, who felt she had gifts along such lines, and was wooed by the college English department for the same reasons, but she chose to major in astronomy "for some wacky reason," as she said, and scorned English as "weak." She hoped to be the first woman to land on the moon. Several failures in mathematics (she had done well in high school mathematics) led her to shift to psychology, which she saw as "pioneering" and "adventurous." Despite an apparent unsuitability for psychology (except for a truly unusual capacity for self-analysis), Trixie persisted in it and took more than usual interest in the "hard" side of the subject (physiological and experimental psychology) as well as in personality study ("soft"). Late in her senior year, Trixie acknowledged that English was really her field and that she had been stubbornly ignoring this plain fact all along. Her basic response to the problem of choosing majors was governed by whether they were "masculine" or "feminine" (or father–mother, more specifically).

In her response to roommates, Trixie found herself attracted to Lucy-like girls (feminine or model student types) but then ended up treating them in ways that came to resemble her childhood rivalry with Lucy. Thus, when she and her junior year roommate, Helen, spent a summer camping, Trixie found herself caught up in a very Lucy-like relation to Helen.

One interesting thing I noticed during the summer was that I kept wanting to take on the masculine tasks. For instance, I soon found out that Helen couldn't put up a tent or unpack and pack the car as easily as I could. So gradually we fell into the habit of my putting up the tent and she preparing the dinner. But after a while she got so that she wanted to put up the tent too. I may not have been very tolerant of that. We were usually so tired when we stopped, and I felt she was more of a hindrance than a help.

Also, we had problems with the driving, because—well, she is what I call an extremely feminine person—much more feminine than any girl I've known. Consequently her reaction to a car is, I feel, a very feminine reaction. She is sort of scared of it. She never drives as if she really has the control of the car. This made me nervous whenever she was driving.

We got along fine until we were driving over a dangerous mountain road. My mother had explicitly warned us about this road, so I started out driving over it— I didn't know where the worst part of it was. After stopping for lunch, she wanted to drive. I really couldn't say anything about it. It turned out that going down the other side is really the worst part, because of a horrible cliff. The gearshift was worn and one had to hold it up in second while going down around those hairpin turns and drive with just one hand. She was swinging out on every turn, with others yelling, 'Hold your lane!' Finally, I said, 'Why don't you let me hold the gearshift in second?' But she is stubborn too. I finally reached over and held it up. But she held it too; she wouldn't drive with both hands. We went down all the way like that. I really got mad at her; I thought she was putting us both in unnecessary danger by doing that.

We are still good friends, though I think we have sort of drifted apart at the end of this year. We are such opposites really. This 'tomboyishness' of mine is really thrown into relief by my living with her—she is so exactly opposite, so very feminine (Madison, 1966, Chapt. 2, pp. 33–35).

Maura, Trixie's senior year roommate, seemed to Trixie to epitomize the other aspect of the childhood struggle: Lucy's infuriatingly successful model-child role in the family. Maura's initial attractiveness as a friend and roommate increasingly gave way to irritation over her "perfectness" and Trixie found herself fighting Maura by refusing to study (Maura was being critical of Trixie's neglect of studies) to the point of near failure.

Maura went with me on this waitressing job last summer. I had known Maura from my freshman and sophomore years—we lived in the same hall. We roomed together at the resort where we worked and it all proved to be very interesting. We were intending to be senior-year roommates but had not known each other well before last summer, so this was the ideal opportunity to get acquainted. . . .

My experiences at the resort were not too pleasant as far as the work went. I started out waitressing, which was what I was hired for, and I just wasn't a good waitress. I had never been concerned with the finery in life, finery in manner, dress or anything—I just can't concern myself about the exact position of knives and forks, and bringing finger bowls and doing everything just right and in a proper fashion— so I was a sloppy waitress as far as they were concerned.

Maura became wrapped up in her waitressing—she wanted to be a perfect waitress, and she was. She was best of us all and I don't know whether this had an effect on me or not, whether it even pushed me a little in the other direction, but she was such a good waitress, and I always had the brunt of the criticism from the manager, and this might have had some effect. Anyway I got moved out to the snack bar and became a soda jerk. . . .

Maura has an aloof demeanor, an appearance of looking down from a pedestal, that makes practically everyone feel uneasy around Maura. She never displays any weaknesses she may have; she is to all appearances as serene and as condescending (i.e. aware of her superiority) as a goddess. On the surface she is like polished silver, without a flaw to be found. The only clue to her real feelings is in her almost compulsive need to tell you how good she is. She makes remarks about her own virtues and accomplishments very naturally—so naturally that at first it seems like a modest self knowledge. But after a while it becomes depressing. For one thing, her self-eulogizing remarks are always stated in a contrast to an off-hand description of something one has done or felt himself, and in a way which makes one feel as low as earth, or as if he's still wetting his bed. To follow up this sterling exterior, Maura has super-human (what seems to me at times *in*human) self-control. She is annoyingly *perfect*. . . .

As far as my senior year at college goes it's become more and more disturbing because I think I have found that I just can't handle everything that I've gotten myself into. And also relationships have become strained with Maura. Maura became very critical of me when she found out that I wasn't doing everything that she thought I could be doing. She was taking it upon herself to act as my conscience or something, and this of course just doesn't work, me being the way I am. . . .

I sort of made a decision to not let academic discipline worry me too much, that I would give first priority to the things that I thought were important for my own development, and do the best I could in my courses, but this decision had always bothered me and I think that Maura really did make me miserable for a while because she was always reprimanding me, criticizing me, and saying I wasn't as perfect as she thought I should be. . . .

I have been in a state of mental and emotional decline. My three weeks of strenuous work on activities were a heavy burden but also an escape from Maura's critical eye and her sudden intention to concentrate on studying for exams (which meant she gave up *every* outside diversion to study). Her example, her over-disgust for my having fallen behind in my studies and for my study habits in general, and my own anxiety over my situation, preyed heavily on my conscience. I seriously debated leaving school. When I finally had time to catch up, I couldn't utilize my time efficiently—I couldn't understand why. A good part of my time was spent worrying, or concealing the amount of work I had done from Maura. . . .

Up to this past week my reactions to the situation have been irrational and even pathetic. I can see now (especially after having written this), that I have been reacting to Maura almost exactly as I reacted to my sister. Yesterday Maura accused me of having a 'disgustingly defeatist' attitude toward my studies. This is exactly the case. In fact, I was conscious of it almost the very moment I adopted it. This was also the case with respect to my behavior toward the family years ago. After a time I gave up competing with Lucy in that way, indeed, I leaned over backward in the opposite direction. I just gave up trying to be 'good.' Now I enjoy telling Maura that I haven't finished my paper or done my reading. If it keeps up I will smugly flunk out of college. (Madison, 1966, Chapt. 2, 35–38)

Trixie responded to boys (particularly Robert) in whom she perceived certain father qualities: selfishness, teasingness, being hard to get, and "defensive about masculinity." Her strongly rebellious and angry reaction to a summer resort manager and, later, a landlady reminds one of her fights with father over her insistence on being independent of his surveillance, particularly with respect to her early adolescent relations to boys whom he objected to. Her strong feelings about drinking, smoking, and sex on campus were exaggerations of parental values, on which, even as a child, she outdid her strict parents, toward whom she came to feel superior when father took up smoking and when she once discovered them sipping a liqueur.

B. Problems with the Representation of Past Experience Influences in Everyday Life

Neither the overall course of Trixie's undergraduate career nor her daily experience of herself and her surroundings could be understood without taking into account her precollege past. In everyday life such influence is recognized in the concept of "memory" and student autobiographies are testimony to the richness with which what has been learned or experienced on past occasions can be reproduced and consciously identified. The problem with memory is that so much past influence appears in perception and behavior without being spontaneously connected with the person's store of memories. Thus, from the observer's standpoint, Trixie's response to the summer resort manager seems to bear transparent relationships to her feelings, actions, and perceptions of her father. But Trixie did not spontaneously perceive this resemblance; she reacted as if the properties she perceived in him existed entirely in his person and that she was simply responding in appropriate ways.

Even out in the snack bar where I was away from them and wasn't under their watchful eye all the time, I would find the manager peeking around, and this was all very disturbing. Towards the end of the summer after Al and I had been working out there together, and after it became obvious that we were very good friends, the manager decided that we had become romantically involved. This was absolutely taboo for an employee, something they discouraged very much. There's a funny incident: Al and I both wanted a Monday off (usually employees had Monday off), but the snack bar stayed open on Mondays, so that one of us had to stay on, but both of us wanted Monday off. I was going out with Maura and another girl, and Al was going to see his family. We both asked for the day off and the manager decided we were going to go some place together, and he thought that this was just terrible, we were both being disloyal to the club—deserters, traitors. We tried to explain that we weren't going to the same place at all, but he would not believe us. We finally started kidding him, and we said that we were going to the same place, and as a matter of fact that we were engaged, and we were planning on getting married next Monday. And he believed it all, and dragged the owner of the resort into it, who of course believed us when we did explain what had happened—it was very funny. We started speaking of the 'snack bar law' after that to indicate our animal status—the idea that if you put male and female together something is bound to happen. It was all very disgusting.

I almost quit one time. We had to sign in and out so that they could clear our hours, and at one point after I was particularly aware of the management's suspicions concerning me, I noticed one day when I left in the afternoon and signed out that the manager checked up on me—he thought I hadn't signed out and that I was sneaking off. This made me so mad I could barely control myself. I got into such an emotional state that I couldn't think. . . . I swore I was going to quit then, and Maura persuaded me not to, and then after a while I calmed down. But the fact that they thought I was being dishonest got me because I had never really been dishonest with them. I had been impertinent, and everything else, but not dishonest (Madison, 1966, Chapt. 2, pp. 39–40).

There is no doubt that, objectively, the manager possessed many of the qualities that Trixie attributed to him, but consider how parallel her experience of the episodes just recounted are to the following experiences with father.

Mother and Daddy tried to stop me from going with Alfred as much as they could, mostly by talking to me. They knew that if they tried to separate us forcibly we would revert to subversive means of seeing each other, and although they were greatly tempted to do it, they refrained from it. But I remember Mother telling me one day that she wished Alfred wouldn't put his arm around me when we were standing around on the street. On another occasion Daddy revealed his strong feelings on the subject. One night Alfred and I had gone across the street to a friend's house for a while, then up the hill, and subsequently back to my house. We were standing there talking when my father came storming out and wanted to know where we'd been; he said he'd been calling me all evening. I told him that we had been at a friend's and had walked up to the hill for about fifteen minutes, but that was all. He immediately said that I was telling a lie; that he had been calling and calling and had even sent my sister out to find me. I don't know how I could have missed hearing them, but I hadn't—I was completely ignorant of the fact that they wanted me home. But Daddy couldn't talk rationally; Alfred and I said we were sorry, that we hadn't known, but Daddy just got madder and madder the more we insisted that we hadn't known, and hadn't heard him, because he thought we weren't telling the truth. Finally he grabbed me by the scruff of the neck and the seat of the pants and carried me bodily in the house. This in front of the whole neighborhood! It embarrassed me and hurt my pride; the minute I got in I went into a rage and stormed up to my room, where I burst into tears. This was getting to be a frequent action on my part; I would usually stay up there for hours, even skipping supper. Mother would finally come up and try to talk reasonably with me, and say that Daddy didn't really mean what he did, that actually they did love me. I would ultimately be reconciled, but these instances made me very bitter toward my parents —sometimes I thought I hated them (Madison, 1966, Chapt. 2, pp. 18–19).

There is little doubt that the reactivated traces of past episodes like the foregoing one with father (there were many) were participating in Trixie's perception of, and response to, the manager, and were both exaggerating these qualities and distorting them in directions that would tend to make the manager appear more fatherlike in his suspicious surveillance of her. This failure of past influence to be represented as such in awareness is all the more striking in Trixie's case because she was an extremely sensitive self-observer who was not reluctant to perceive such relationships. As the reader can see, the camping trip relations to Helen were spontaneously described by Trixie as involving a masculinity–femininity aspect, which she was aware were traceable to the aftermath of her relations to father and mother and to her sister Lucy. As we also saw, in the spring of her senior year, in the midst of writing about the matter, Trixie spontaneously made such a connection between her response to her other roommate Maura's criticisms of her and similar reactions she had had to sister Lucy. She observed that she had been refusing to study to the point of failure as a reaction against Maura and that this was a continuance of her childhood resentments of Lucy. Thus, interconnections between memories and perceptions or actions sometimes spontaneously develop, and very likely more so for highly verbal, introspective students who volunteer as research subjects than among most. But clearly, such occasional interconnections cover only a minor portion of perception and action. In the usual case the person experiences residues of past significant emotional experiences as qualities of the present external world. This fact has not gone unrecognized in everyday life and has been repeatedly described by poets, dramatists, and writers, but somehow the conceptual scheme of common sense persistently underrepresents this influence in its concepts and language.

On the action level, past experience effects are most clearly represented in the concept of "habit," but the recognition is a limited one applying to the conspicuous instance of stereotyped repetitions of well-practiced motor actions. As with perception, behavior tends to be experienced by the viewer as a sensible response to external realities that obviously and sensibly require the actions he is taking.

In other function modalities, like emotion and motive, the everyday view tends even more seriously to underrepresent the contribution of the past, possibly because, phenomenally, both emotion and motive present strongly organized conscious qualities that do not easily suggest any involvement of the person's past. Again, the writer has always portrayed such past influences upon his characters, but the commonsense frame of reference has behaved as though it were willing to acknowledge such influence in a particular life history of a fictional or biographical character, but unable to recognize it as a common aspect of daily life in the same way that "memory" and "habit" recognize the influence of the past on consciousness and repetitive actions.

The undergraduate's self-understanding suffers from these shortcomings of his commonsense conceptual scheme. Thus even Trixie, whose self-insight was keen, had a very incomplete picture of the extent to which her response to college was a carryover from the past. She did not see, until her senior year, how irrationally she had chosen her majors, and she found English and a potential career in writing too late to work seriously toward these objectives as an undergraduate. Simply having concepts in which to perceive herself and terms in which to formulate her experience would not, in themselves, have given her better control of her life, but they would have influenced her experience. For instance, once she perceived that she was responding to Maura as to her sister, being angry at Maura could not mean the same thing, and when a different experience registers, the person begins to change.

C. PSYCHOLOGY AND PAST EXPERIENCE

If we look at the way psychologists currently conceptualize the influence of past experience against data provided by complex behavior in natural settings, we shall see that theoretical improvements are also needed. Such an examination does not suggest new ideas so much as a better use of some insights from the past that have been left aside in the essentially political jousting for a place that characterizes young fields of inquiry that have not yet developed more effective means of deciding among concepts: it also suggests a better integration of current ideas from different areas of inquiry that have made little contact with one another, for the same political reasons. Generalization and perception are instances in point.

1. *Generalization*

Pavlov demonstrated that the laws of association of ideas could be applied to animal behavior, and American psychology since Watson has enriched the concept in many ways. Carl Hovland's (1937) study has served as a paradigm of the generalization phenomenon widely quoted in psychology and learning texts. Hovland conditioned his human subjects to expect to be shocked after a tone of a given pitch was sounded and investigated the extent to which the resulting anticipatory fear of shock generalized to tones of varying frequency. He measured the fear response indirectly through variations in the amount of palmar sweating as measured by changes in resistance to passage of an electrical current (GSR). The sweating is a physiological reaction that accompanies the pain of the electric shock, or the later fearful anticipation of it when the tone also is sounded. Plots of his electrical resistance data show a regular curve of decreasing fear reaction to tones as their pitch becomes less like the original tone to which the shock had been given.

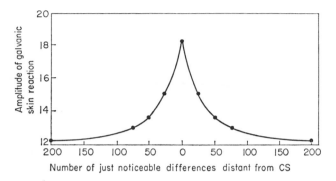

FIG. 1. A plot of Hovland's (1937) data, reproduced in Gregory A. Kimble and Norman Garmezy, *Principles of General Psychology,* Second Edition, p. 144. Copyright © 1963 The Ronald Press Company, New York.

"Generalization" is usually defined by psychologists as follows:

The effects of learning in one situation transfer to other situations; the less similar the situation, the less transfer occurs. Stated more exactly, reinforcement for making a specific response to a given pattern of cues strengthens not only the tendency for that pattern of cues to elicit that response but also the tendency for other similar patterns of cues to elicit the same response. The innate tendency for transfer to occur is called innate stimulus generalization. The less similar the cue or pattern of cues, the less the generalization. This variation in the transfer is referred to as a *gradient of generalization* (From *Personality and Psychotherapy* by John Dollard and Neal E. Miller. Copyright 1950, McGraw-Hill. Used with permission of McGraw-Hill Book Company.)

Although smooth generalization gradients like Hovland's are derived from overtly visible responses (e.g., the palmar sweating reaction), generalization has come to be used as though it applied to all function modalities in the same way. Thus, Dollard and Miller (1950) apply it to thinking.

But data from everyday life situations involving perceptual identification do not seem to follow such even gradients. Perceptual identification of a contemporary person as being like someone known earlier may not occur at all, even though, on a behavioral response level, one can see generalization effects. Thus, in Trixie's case, the resort manager was treated (emotionally and behaviorally) like father when the situation is examined from the external observer's viewpoint; Trixie was sure he was watching her and suspecting her conduct with boys as father did in her adolescence, and she became angry at the manager much as she had done toward father. But looked at from an internal frame of reference, Trixie did not consciously experience the manager as "like father." There is no generalization gradient in the sense of Trixie's thinking: "This manager is like father to such and such extent." The same is true for a difficult landlady with whom Trixie refought her furious battle of wills with father, while consciously seeing no connection.

On the other hand, with Maura there was at first no recognition of a relation to sister Lucy's perfectness and model-child character but later, when she wrote her senior year account, Trixie did perceive such a resemblance. Such recognition of similarities also came about spontaneously in the case of Trixie's perceiving likenesses between her father and her boy friends.

Perceptual identification seems to take place in an all-or-none fashion rather than following a gradient. Resemblances are either seen or not. Once perceived, they may become gradientlike in that degrees of resemblance become apparent upon deliberate search. In other words, the dimension of perceptual recognition cannot be treated as a generalization gradient. Then, too, one has the interesting situation that behavioral generalization may be occurring without there being a corresponding perceptual recognition gradient at one moment, and the next moment such a perceptual generalization can suddenly develop. Behavior theory has tended to assume that concepts developed on the behavioral dimension must be automatically applicable to any other modality of psychological functioning. Perhaps this is not so. Behaviorists pay little attention to work in perception, where the all-or-none character of certain perceptual phenomena is well known, as in investigations of binocular rivalry, figure-ground perception, or Necker Cube reversals.

2. *Perception*

In psychology's recent past, perception was pretty much left to the Gestalt psychologists, who always formally recognized the influences of past experience upon perception (it was one of Wertheimer's original "gestalt laws"), but mostly ignored it in their research and writing. In his *Place of Value in a World of Fact,* Wolfgang Köhler complained that "in psychology we have no adequate term for this influence of the past which is akin to memory, although it is not memory in the usual sense" (1938, p. 233). At Swarthmore College, Köhler and my other departmental colleagues had to use a localism for such influence: they called it "the Höffding function." Köhler did not deny the influence of past experience on perception, but insisted that it could only enter into the temporal development of a percept after "more fundamental" processes of organization had taken place (figure-ground, grouping, etc.). Thus, past experience could lead one to perceive a hammer as imbued with a quality of "something-to-pound-with," but only after contour perception and figure-ground organization had taken place and the shape of a hammer came into being as a stimulus necessary to locate and activate past experience traces of earlier hammer activity, which, once aroused, would then contribute to the already formed hammer figure the further perceptual quality of looking like "something to pound with."

Karl Duncker (1939), in one of the most informative studies of this issue, challenged his own school's assumption that the influences of past experience on perception were, in some sense, secondary. He chose color perception and had subjects match a green leaf and a gray donkey to a color wheel in which the subject was to make a color mixure equivalent to the perceived color of the leaf or the donkey. Unknown to the subject, the leaf and donkey were of the same color but the greenness was reduced to a gray-green by using red illumination. He found that subjects used 100% more green in the color-wheel mixture they matched to the green leaf than they did to the one they matched to the donkey. This difference disappeared if the color wheel and the leaf or donkey could be seen simultaneously. To get the effect, the subject had to look at the leaf, then turn so that he could not see it and adjust the color wheel from memory of the just-seen leaf. Lacking a theoretical term for the demonstrated effect, Duncker used Hering's 1920 term "memory color."

Aside from pointing up Köhler's problem of a missing terminology for an obviously important finding, Duncker's study provides a model for the perception of personal qualities in everyday life. Thus, when the resort manager was perceived as suspicious and distrustful of Trixie's relationship to Al, we can suppose that the traces of her father's suspicions were aroused and entered into her perception of the manager analogously to the memory color of the green leaf entering into the perception of the matching shade of green on the color wheel. In both cases the subject remains entirely ignorant that past experience traces have been aroused and that they have added something to what is "objectively there." The addition appears as a simple objective quality inhering in the external object.

The study of complex behavior in natural settings brings out Köhler's problem that psychology, like everyday language, has no terminology for the mechanism of trace finding, arousal, and interaction; no terms that identify the past experience component of perceived object qualities. "Projection" will not do, since it does not recognize the subtle *intermixture* of what is objectively present and what is subjectively contributed; moreover,

Freud gave that term a defensive connotation that would be inappropriate in the Duncker type of situation, which provides the best model for everyday life.

III. Reintegration and Objectification in Perception

A. OBJECTIFICATION

Psychology cannot begin to deal effectively with everyday life without a term referring to the influence of past experience on perceived object qualities, and Sir William Hamilton's 1836 concept of "redintegration" has struck me as highly suitable. In 1941 Robert Leeper introduced me to this concept, used by Hamilton (1882) in his *Lectures on Metaphysics and Logic*. Hamilton offered the "Law of Redintegration" as his attempt at reducing Aristotle's several laws of association to a single more general principle:

> Those thoughts suggest each other which had previously constituted parts of the same or total act of cognition. Now to the same entire or total act belong, as integral or constituent parts, in the first place, those thoughts which arose at the same time, or in immediate consecution; and in the second, those thoughts which are bound up into one by their mutual affinity . . . by this one law the whole phenomena of Association may easily be explained (Hamilton, 1882, Vol. II, p. 238).

Leeper and I have preferred the alternative spelling, "reintegration." The concept emphasizes the tendency of past experience to enter into the present so as to restore a former state of affairs.

Drawing on Köhler's (1938) own analysis, I would add "objectification" to refer specifically to that part of the percept that is determined by past experience. Some perceptual qualities, like contour, shape, figure–ground, and certain grouping phenomena, appear to be native. Köhler's "something-to-pound-with" quality of a hammer would be a reintegrated and objectified quality in this proposed terminology. So would Trixie's perception of Maura as "critical," or her perception of Robert or her boy friends as being "defensive-about-masculinity." In the research study of which Trixie was a part, over 30 independent descriptions of Robert were gathered; not one mentioned "defensiveness about masculinity." So Trixie must have contributed much of this quality. Since Robert, too, was a research subject, it is possible to give an informed clinical judgment that he was, indeed, somewhat sensitive on this point, although not sufficiently so for this attitude to strike his friends as a quality to be included in a description of Robert. His sensitivity was, however, great enough, the reintegration–objectification concepts would suggest, to touch off Trixie's father traces. Once aroused (reintegrated), these interact with the present stimulus features of Robert and are objectified as perceptual qualities inhering in his voice, manner, and actions as perceived by Trixie.

B. THE VARIABLE TEXTURE OF STIMULUS CONSTRAINTS IN PERCEPTION

Thus far, it has been proposed that Köhler's and Duncker's analyses of the influence of past experience upon perception be explicitly acknowledged in theory by using Hamilton's name (reintegration) for the processes by which incoming sense data locate corresponding traces of past experience in like situations, arouse them, and interact with them to produce the percept conceived as a joint product of the present stimulus situation and aroused traces. It was proposed, further, that the trace contribution to perception be called "objectification" (following Köhler's general analysis but without necessarily accepting his view of past experience as in some sense "secondary" to "more fundamental" influences).

Objectification is the past-experience-determined portion of perception experienced by the viewer as intrinsic properties of the objects, qualities, or relations being conveyed by the sense organs. Objectification contributes one portion of the percept. The "present situation" or "the structure of the situation" (in Kurt Lewin's sense of the psychological environment), or "stimulus influences," can be used to refer to those aspects of the percept that are not determined by past learning.

The study of complex behavior in natural settings calls attention to another theoretically known aspect of perception, but one that is not emphasized in treatments of perception that take their cues from what is impressive in the laboratory, namely, that the relative extent of past experience influence varies with the strength and clarity of the stimulus influence. This well-known principle was systematically demonstrated once more in the 1950s in studies of the influence of motivational attitudes upon perception. To show the influence, it is necessary to introduce ambiguity in the stimulus by techniques such as reducing illumination, allowing only brief exposures of the stimulus, or presenting only stimulus fragments.

Perception in everyday life differs from usual laboratory analogues in the wildly variable extent to which objectified past experience influence enters in from moment to moment. We know from systematic studies that there is

great variability even within the perceptual field of a person staring fixedly
at a point in his visual surroundings, in that objects projected upon the
center of the fovea are much more stimulus constrained than those in the
margins of the visual field. The latter seem to be almost as much "hallucinated" as they are perceived. Such variability of sensory constraint borders
on the chaotic when one considers a simple situation like the 10-second
interval during which Maura comes into the room where Trixie is sitting at
her desk and the two of them exchange a few words. Thus, Trixie's perception of the fact of Maura's entry is tightly stimulus controlled; the color of
Maura's dress might be a bit less so (recalling Duncker's findings on
"memory color"). Maura's facial "expression" as perceived by Trixie
could be "frowning disapproval" when in fact Maura is just feeling a little
grim after having come from a hard examination. Maura, noticing Trixie's
position at her desk, tries to be sociable but is too preoccupied with her
recent examination to put much spirit into her effort and comes out with
"Studying hard?" Trixie hears this as "criticism" (she had been alternately
reading a drugstore magazine and staring into space for some minutes
before Maura came in, the adventure story having revived a 10-year-old
fantasy of being Tarzan). Then Maura, too self-engrossed to have noticed
what Trixie was reading, says something unintelligible from the depths of
her clothes closet as she rummages for a change of clothes (she actually
said "I wish I could just lie down") and Trixie hears, "I wish you weren't
so lazy." Furious, Trixie refuses to talk and sits in stony silence while
Maura, exhausted, takes a nap.

From Trixie's standpoint, the problem about understanding past experience influences is twofold. First, she is only dimly, if at all, aware that the
degree of stimulus control in the perceived color of Maura's dress differs
radically from that of such control in the perception of Maura's "frown of
disapproval." The perception of Maura as being in her clothes closet is a
tightly constrained stimulus fact but, from an internal viewpoint, it has no
more reality status than Maura's misheard words. Second, Trixie is unaware of the extreme variation of stimulus control within the structure of
the episode. Subjectively, there is only a homogeneously perceived reality.
Objectively, the mixture of "real" and "objectified" may have changed
from "very real" to "almost hallucinated" and back to "real" a dozen times
in the 10-second sequence. The analysis suggests the general concept of the
stimulus situation as having a variable texture of constraint. It also suggests introducing the following terms to refer to at least a few degrees of
admixture between situational and reintegrative influence upon perception.

1. *Stimulus-constrained perception* denotes perception under strong sen-

sory control, such as looking steadily at a coin at reading distance under clear illumination.

2. *Reintegrative fill-in* denotes perception in which the general framework of the percept is stimulus determined but details are supplied reintegratively without the subject's being aware of such past experience influence. B. F. Skinner (1956) has demonstrated the principle in his "verbal summator" technique, in which vowel sounds are repeated in various combinations on a record played at such low intensity that the subject is easily led to believe that he hears meaningful words. That the "heard" words proved to be highly correlated with their frequency of occurrence in everyday life when Skinner analyzed a thousand responses shows that the vowel sounds act as a framework that reintegrates past experiences with words. The vowel sounds are the stimulus portion of the percept. They act as a framework into which the reintegrated meanings are fitted and "heard" as words.

3. *Hallucinatory reintegration* denotes extremely convincing imagery strongly determined by past learnings but experienced by the subject as a perception. Ellson (1941) produced hallucinations of hearing in 32 of 40 subjects by sounding a very low tone 60 times (the experiment was presented as a hearing test) at the same time that a light was turned on, and then presenting the light alone, whereupon most of his subjects reported hearing the tone.

IV. Reintegration and Other Modalities of Psychological Functioning

The same logic of fractionating perception into stimulus and past experience determinants can and should be applied to "behavior," "emotion," and "motive," all of which have a similar status in everyday psychology in that the contribution of the past is just as hidden from the viewer, and the extent of this contribution can be just as highly variable as in perception. As with perception, motive, emotion, and behavior are terms that psychologists have taken from everyday language and tried to improve, just as philosophers did before them. In each case the poet, writer, and dramatist long preceded the philosopher and social scientist in recognizing, at least to some extent, the role of the past in these modalities. Yet, as in perception, the everyday person does not often seem to let such artistic insights overcome his natural mode of experiencing in his own life. Psychology has contributed much documentation to the principle that behavior and motive are strongly determined by the past. Judging from college students, their parents, and such adults as admissions officers, however, we find that simply growing up in our society and learning the distinctions made by common sense and in ordinary language do not leave these individuals with an effective knowledge of the principles that they use for understanding such things as study motivation or scientific interest. In this sense, a sufficient understanding of the past experience determination of these aspects of living is not yet an effective part of the conceptual scheme of common sense.

1. *Motive*

Consider study motivation. The cases of Phil and Sidney illustrate the relation between past experience and motivation and how little this relation is understood by students, parents, and deans. Both Phil and Sidney were equally high-aptitude students (in terms of college board scores) who had outstanding high school records and very similar levels of parental education. They attended the same highly selective college and were regarded as fine applicants by the admissions office, which gave Phil a bit of an edge over Sidney as being "well rounded." Yet Phil was failing at the end of his junior year, while Sidney went on to claim every scholastic honor the college could bestow:

> In terms of fellowships and academic honors, I got everything I wanted. I was elected to a Woodrow Wilson Fellowship and awarded a graduate fellowship by the National Science Foundation. I graduated summa cum laude, was elected to Phi Beta Kappa, and received a coveted award from the college. I was admitted to all of the graduate schools to which I applied and have been given a large scholarship by the university I will attend (Madison, 1966, Chapt. 5, pp. 1–2).

Phil, speaking in April of his junior year, at the end of which he was required to withdraw for scholastic deficiencies, had this to say:

> I have been given an ultimatum that either I bring my grades up or withdraw from the university. . . .
> When I have assigned work to do, it is hard for me to sit down and do it. I don't know—it's almost as though I'm waiting for someone to come along and ask me to play cards, or something like that. This is not always the case, but I sometimes have this feeling that I have studying to do, and I know I have to do it, but, somehow, I don't want to walk over to my desk and sit down and do it. It usually gets done, but in many cases I've done it because I haven't found anything else to do (Madison, 1966, Chapt. 5, p. 2).

The difference between Sidney and Phil lay in the childhood and high school emotional experiences of these two young men. Sidney's parents were programmed by their own values to reinforce him (very likely unknowingly) strongly whenever he did anything verbal or scholarly. Here is a typical passage from his childhood autobiography.

At the age of two in a bakery with my mother, I pointed to some cookies and said, 'Delicious, nutritious, they make me feel ambitious,' parroting some current advertisement. This caused general amazement and admiration. Much of the precociousness for which I was highly regarded centered around my vocabulary. At age four, our housekeeper asked me how I wanted my egg-salad sandwich cut. 'Diagonally,' I said. Jane then asked my mother, 'What does diagonally mean?' (Madison, 1966, Chapt. 5, p. 7).

Phil's childhood memories offer a contrast:

Beginning in the first grade I realized my liking for sports. I remember how mad I used to get when our first grade teacher would make us miss play period to write, 'I will not talk in class,' one hundred times. We never missed play period entirely but it would always cut off some time from our baseball game which we played the year round. I think it was the neighborhood in which I grew up as much as my personal make-up that was responsible for the devotion I have for athletics. There was always some game going on regardless of the time of day. As I grew older, I began to play baseball in school patrol leagues and also on summer playgrounds. I would also follow baseball in the papers and on television. The collection of baseball trading cards was a favorite neighborhood pastime.

In the meantime my school work was coming along well. I was making good grades and doing my work but I did not have the dedication here that I had in my sports. I can hear my father saying to me as he did often, 'Do a little more than the teachers ask.' It was seldom that I heeded his advice.

In Junior High School, basketball became a favorite. I also became quite active in student government. I was pretty shy during this time though and had to be coaxed into running for office because it meant making a speech in front of the student body and faculty. I finally did and was elected president of the student council.

The period of my life that I enjoyed the most was high school. I played three years of basketball and baseball, and in my senior year played on the varsity football team. In addition, I was active in student government, being a member of the student council for two years and president of the senior class. The reason that I enjoyed high school so much was not because of the recognition I received. This period in one's life is carefree and happy. The atmosphere of high school adds to this feeling because the work load is not heavy enough to cause a lot of worry among the students. Consequently, everyone is cheerful and fun-loving.

My interest in baseball began one day when my father bought me a glove and ball and started tossing a ball with me. I remember picnics—the men would go and play softball. I would go tearing off and chase it, happy as a lark. I guess television helped generate the interest.

There was a group of boys in the area and we always played from sunrise to sunset—take time out for dinner and that's all. Being together, the relationships to those boys, really cemented my interest. My success kept my liking for it going.

When I was a boy, I would take that sport page and really study it. I could quote batting averages, pitchers, players for all teams, who got how many hits each day. I studied these all the time and I could quote them any day of the week.

My high school was a large school of two thousand students. The atmosphere was one that placed a heavy emphasis on activities: student government, activities of many kinds. Studies were there too, you had to work. But there were a lot of diversions—athletics was naturally popular and my participation in athletics helped me a lot. Not only the fun I had in athletics, but they helped me in these other activities. I carried a lot of positions—they seemed important then.

I was pretty popular in high school. I held offices and I was well known. My parents were obviously proud of me. I would make them feel real good. Often, someone would come up to Mother and say, 'Oh, you're Mrs. C., Phil's mother.' This happened quite often to her when she used to go shopping and it would make her feel real proud.

High school turned out so well for me because of my success in athletics. I was always playing on teams that were older than I and I got to know a lot of people that were well known in high school and so I came, as a tenth grader, to be better known than most students in the school. The fact that I made the varsity basketball team at the start made me even better known. And from then on I was always kind of in the light. Everything came easy. I was asked to two dances by senior girls and things like that. The reason I was so successful was because of athletics. That is why high school turned out so well.

My good grades were not because I was regarded as a teacher's pet. I worked hard enough when I had to. When I was given an assignment I would do it and I would make sure it was correct before I would turn it in. I took my books home every night and I never went out on week nights—my parents would have disapproved of that. I studied, and watched television. There was never any desire on my part not to get my work done. I knew it wouldn't take me real long and that I wouldn't have to dig, so I just did it.

In high school I knew what I had to do in my assignments and I had the feeling that I could do them right, a feeling of confidence that I was going to get an 'A.'

I think I can be said to be conscientious in my studies, but only to a point. It's not that I don't want to work, or don't care about it. But it's that I . . . I *do* care. I realize, I'm aware of what I have to do. It's just a matter of thinking over what I have to do and then getting up and going to the movies. And then when I get back to my room and start to get ready, I won't . . . that thought will kind of leave me and I'll say, 'Yeah, well, I'll start that in a minute,' and will play a record and, at the end of that time, if nothing else has happened, I'll probably get up, go into my room, sit down . . . stare at the book for two or three minutes . . . look around my room again . . . and . . . there's a certain point where this original thought will come back to me and I finally realize what I have to do and I'll sit down and do it. . . . It's like I'm not concentrating on what I have to do (Madison, 1966, Chapt. 5, pp. 23–25, 32).

The interesting thing about Phil, his father, and the college deans is that none of them could understand why he was failing. Phil, in fact, spent more time at his desk than did Sidney. His father wrote a moving letter to the dean telling of the long hours he knew his son spent with his books, reviewing his outstanding high school record and high aptitude test scores, and concluding that it must be the college that had failed since he could see no other explanation for his son's poor performance. The deans were equally puzzled. They admitted they could not see why Phil was failing. Phil could feel his disinterest in his studies, but had no explanation for it. He knew something was missing: "I have the ability. If there was something that would stir that ability to action, I believe that would solve the problem."

Phil was stirred in college, but on another front:

In my freshman year, I went out for basketball. I had played in high school for three years, and for a while, when I started out here in college, I was the last man on the team. There were sixteen of us and the coach is a peculiar fellow. He has trouble learning names, but eventually he had learned everyone else's name but mine, so things weren't going too well. But I knew that I was better than that, and I wasn't going to spend the season on the last team. So I worked real hard and, after the first game, I started every game after that. Basketball was a success as far as I am concerned. I enjoyed it very much, and I always have, and that was a real success. But to achieve it, I put out more work than I ever did for anything in my life. I looked at whom he had chosen as his starting team and I honestly felt I was a better player than some he had started and I was determined I was going to start. So I set out with that in mind. It took a while. But I started after a while. I made it through aggressive play. I picked the best man to guard in scrimmage and would do my best to keep him from scoring. It was on defense that I made it. I bottled up the first team so many times it made him realize he better move me up and he did—I got on the varsity (Madison, 1966, Chapt. 5, pp. 36–37).

Unlike Phil, Sidney had a conceptual grasp of motivation that he could apply when asked to explain his interest in studies (he had read widely in personality theory even in high school), but his immediate experience was in the same terms as Phil's: he felt directly interested or disinterested in aspects of his environment. The interest is experienced as an objectified quality inhering in the activity; it does not spontaneously link itself to a consciously remembered past. As Sidney said: "I do a lot of thinking about my reading because I'm really interested in what I am doing. . . . When I was taking literature, I really loved literature, I was interested."

2. Motives as Reintegrative Resonator Systems

It would seem that Phil, his father, the deans, and perhaps psychologists need to supplement the ordinary ways in which we think of motives, or formulate existing concepts in a way that is easier to link up with both the individual's past history and the subjective aspects of motives as experienced in living. Since the entry of past experience trace systems into motivated action as this takes place in everyday life is not represented in awareness, this fact must be represented conceptually. On the other hand, what is represented in subjective experience must be related to the theoretically conceived portion, the whole being made up of an integrated relationship of theoretically conceived and subjectively experienced events.

One way to represent past experience influences upon motivated action is to use an analogy of a resonating system like the sound chamber of a musical instrument or the echo chamber of a cavern. An incoming stimulus like the coach's forgetting Phil's name can be conceived as analogous to a whisper entering a cavern full of echo chambers. Some chambers are shaped just right for a wave of this particular amplitude and their resonating effect strongly amplifies the incoming sound. Amplifications from several sympathetically resonating chambers combine and their effect is such that what entered as a whisper comes out as a roar.

The "roar" in the case of Phil and the coach appears subjectively to Phil as a great internal welling of energy on the one hand, an experienced "interest" in getting into the scrimmage, and a goal of bottling up the best player. His total experience is one of "feeling motivated." In a "reintegrative resonator" conception, the past experience component of motives is located and aroused by the incoming stimulus and enters in to "energize" the person and to give interest to objects in the environment and meaning to goals. In Phil's case, when his mother told him of instances when strangers in the community exclaimed, "Oh, you're Phil's mother!" or when he was elected to student office because of his athletic prominence, or received dance invitations from girls on the same basis, or made the varsity in competition with older teammates, each of these stirring experiences left in its wake another "room" in his echo chamber resonating systems. The energizing property of motives comes from the sympathetic resonating of these echo chambers to the present situation. Motivational "energy" comes from their power to amplify incoming stimuli quickly and strongly. This is conceived as a reawakening (reintegration) of the aftermath of the original experience, assumed to continue within the person as a trace system. Reintegration changes a motivational trace system from a state of latency to one of active arousal (energy is released). Once aroused, the motivational traces interact with influences from the person's contemporary life situation and this interactive product then appears in consciousness as an interest in, valuation of, or emotional responsiveness to the resonating aspects of the current situation.

Of course, none of these intervening sequences are represented in consciousness. Only the end product is there: the emotional interest in some aspect of the present. Even when a person can recall some of the past experiences that resulted in the formation of inner resonating chambers, and even when he is theoretically sophisticated (as Sidney was) about their effects upon him, the past experiences still do not appear to the person as the *reason* for his interest. Rather, certain immediately present things around him simply look interesting.

When Sidney participates in a class discussion, this view suggests that, in some sense, he is once more the two-year-old astounding everyone by reciting the jingle in the bakery shop; the four-year-old discovering that he knew "diagonal" whereas an adult did not. The scheme explains Phil's response to the interviewer's question what single thing in his life as a college junior gave him the strongest emotional charge: "Reading batting averages."

Motives, of course, are not just reintegrative resonator systems left over from past significant emotional experience. There is, first, a cognitive appraisal of the current situation; second, this appraisal arouses the appropriate resonator systems, whose entry into the motive process gives meaning to the perceived situation. Third, the aroused resonator systems link up with the perceived current situation in such a way as to give rise to an intention to attain some objective appropriate to the perceived meaning. Fourth, there is ensuing motivated action guided by the interaction of the intention to attain the goal and the structure of the current situation.

3. *Emotion*

Emotions, too, need some purely theoretical constructs to supplement the quality of phenomenal experience by which we identify them in everyday life. As other contributors to this volume have suggested (see particularly Arnold and Peters), there is an appraisal aspect to emotion, but I want to point out that the appraisal, or cognitive, aspect of emotion is poorly reflected in awareness. (This point was stressed by Leeper in personal discussion in 1954 and is represented in Leeper and Madison, 1959, Chapter 7.) In fact, the cognitive aspect of emotion is so sketchily present in awareness and so unnoticed alongside the dominating feel qualities that we need to represent its presence conceptually, and must relate it to the felt emotional quality along a dimension extending from consciousness into incompletely conscious and unconscious states. Köhler likened such partly conscious, partly unconscious processes to amphibians who live partly in water and partly in air and referred to them as "transphenomenal" processes (1938, Chapter 4).

Emotion, then, seems to need two conceptual additions linked to the conscious feel qualities that so dominate the experience: (1) a not-very-conscious appraisal aspect and (2) a reintegrative resonator aspect. In the latter sense, emotions do not differ from motives: both involve the arousal of reintegrative resonator systems by the person's appraisal of the current situation. But emotions go no further. Consciousness is flooded with the aftermath of such resonator arousal and we are "seized" by sadness, or joy. If this aroused state links up with the present situation in a way that gives rise to an intention to attain a goal appropriate to the aroused state, a motive develops. When no such linkage occurs, emotions are experienced. Some states occur so regularly in both forms (anger, fear) that we class them as both emotions and motives.

The resonator view of emotions helps explain why, as Peters stresses in his contribution to this volume, emotions have a quality of "seizing" us, and why the person experiences emotions passively. The "seizure" feeling comes from the effect of having a relatively slight current stimulus touching off some "very big " trace systems that come into play and overwhelm us. We are passive because no action linkage to the current situation is possible; we just feel, or suffer.

4. Behavior

The obvious determination of visible behavior by past learning presents difficulties on a theoretical level when one tries to bring complex behavior under the leading concept of generalization. Generalization, as usually defined by psychologists, fits well enough in traditional laboratory arrangements like the one used in Hovland's classic study. But if one attempts to apply generalization to complex behavior, such as Helen and Trixie making camp, one discovers that generalization is occurring on at least three levels that differ so much in their meanings that one cannot apply a single term to them without blurring fundamental distinctions. Each level considered in isolation fits the generalization model implied in Hovland's laboratory analogue, but in complex behavior several levels of generalization can be taking place within a single episode. In the interest of research control, the laboratory analogue allows only a single generalization gradient to be recorded at one time. To construct a laboratory analogue for even a simple episode like making camp one must have a minimum of three generalization gradients operating simultaneously and interacting with one another. If, in addition, each level has quite different meanings for the human situation, a conceptual differentiation of the generalization term is called for. I propose that we recognize three levels: (1) personal construct generalization; (2) situational structure generalization; and (3) response generalization. Let us consider each as it applies to the episode of making camp.

1. At the level of analysis to which the term "personality" refers, the significant fact about making camp is that Trixie chooses the "masculine" tasks and that her choice is transparently related to her similar childhood preferences for father-associated tasks like putting up storm screens, washing the car, or mowing the lawn, while sister Lucy helped mother with "feminine" activities.

2. An activity like putting up a tent involves sequential patterns of actions: pounding a tent peg is followed by stringing ropes and this by raising the canvas structure with a center pole, and so on. Moreover, putting up the tent, in turn, is just one complex pattern of responses that are a part of a whole related series that constitute making camp. Thus, the whole campsite is first examined from such standpoints as drainage in case of rain, choosing as level a spot as possible for sleeping comfort, orienting the tent so that the opening is pointed away from a neighboring tent for privacy, locating it in the right relation to a built-in fireplace, and so on. To be sure, one can say that the execution of each set of response patterns is an instance of "generalization." Thus, for Trixie, paying attention to drainage may be a generalization from a previous occasion when she overlooked this and her tent was flooded. And orienting the tent for privacy may be a generalization from still another specific experience at a very different time and place; and so on. But her response to this particular campsite represents a unique combination of such patterns, each of which is, in itself, complex. One needs a term like "situational structure" to refer to the particular combinations of instrumental act patterns that must be carried out to accomplish a given task in relation to a particular environmental setting.

3. At the molecular level of individual movements, an act like pounding a tent peg may be considered as a generalization from like preceding occasions of pounding. In behavior theory, "response" at first referred to such visible movements, or to glandular secretions, and such a molecular term is essential to a refined analysis at levels of action such as tent-peg pounding.

Having distinguished and labeled three levels of analysis, we can return to a consideration of why such distinctions are necessary. Suppose we say that our task as scientists is "to understand the episode of Helen and Trixie making camp in terms of theoretical concepts." A sufficient theoretical explanation would require us to account for all that an observer might have seen had he been present. The explanation would be still more satisfactory if we could bring this one episode into relation with other episodes in the life of each participant. What is the relation of Trixie's performance here to what she did in selecting a college major, reacting to her roommate, or responding to boys?

If we begin at the level of response generalization, note that applying the concept to tent-peg pounding does not allow us to describe the whole act of putting up a tent since the latter involves patterns of responses. Nor does recognizing such patterns suffice. These patterns are interrelated in ways that are governed by the structure of the campsite as an environment, and we must add a concept like "structure of the situation," else we have no way of explaining the particular response patterns that generalize to this setting and combine into the unique overall behavioral sequence that we observe. "Situational structure generalization" helps at this molar level. Note that we can explain much of the episode without invoking a "masculinity construct" for Trixie. This level of generalization enters in most clearly at selective points like task choosing. We cannot account for why Trixie chooses to put up the tent and encourages Helen to cook if we restrict ourselves to the first two levels. The task of making camp can be accomplished by either of two persons taking on either role. On the other hand, we cannot ascribe the division to chance because observing other episodes of camp making by these two would reveal a systematic preference. But note, also, that if we restrict ourselves only to the personal construct level, we cannot account for very much visible behavior. The individual movements are simple response generalizations that can be explained without invoking "masculinity." The moment-to-moment steering of action is entirely controlled by the requirements of the situation. "Masculinity" does not direct orientation of the tent for privacy, paying attention to slope and drainage, and so on. It can enter in to give a certain style (e.g., pounding vigorously) to the way the acts are carried out, but the patterns of behavior an observer would see need not be ascribed to the workings of a "masculinity construct."

If we broaden our perspective and consider Trixie's life as a whole, the masculinity construct becomes primary. We need it to account for choosing father over mother, astronomy over English, preferring jeans to skirts, and insisting on driving the car on the camping trip. At such molar levels, theoretical categories like situational structure, or response defined at a level of individual movements, become irrelevant. But the moment we focus on particular episodes and fine movement sequences they become essential. Since each level of generalization has significant meanings that differ from one another, we need a differentiated terminology. We cannot restrict ourselves to using "generalization" for all three without losing distinctions essential to understanding complex behavior.

The analysis reveals the insufficiency of the laboratory analogues we use to study generalization. We need much more complicated models involving simultaneous interactions of a number of generalization gradients at different levels. The study of complex behavior in natural settings suggests that when experimentalists develop such models and seek to comprehend the resulting phenomena in theoretical terms, they will need a more differentiated conception of "generalization" along the lines suggested above.

V. A Field Theory View and the Reintegrative Dimension

The foregoing analysis of the interrelation between personality and situational structure reveals that understanding behavior is facilitated by the same type of interactional scheme used in perception. In perception, stimulus structure can be stronger or weaker and reintegrative fill-in occurs at weaker points just as it does in behavior at points where situational structure is less determinant. In both, a past experience aspect interacts with a present situation aspect and a subtle blend occurs that is experienced subjectively as a unitary whole and is also observed from the outside as a single act. Theoretical understanding requires the blended whole to be fractionated into two broad components: person and situation; and these must be conceived as interacting to produce the subjectively and objectively perceived unity of percept or behavior. Lewin (1951), of course, called such an analysis a "field" conception and the study of complex behavior shows that such a person–situation interactional view is inescapable in theorizing about real life activities. It has not been so compellingly necessary in laboratory analogues of generalization because, as in Hovland's study, the situation becomes unimportant since, in the interest of maintaining research control, it is not allowed to vary. But in everyday life, situations vary wildly and their influence must be conceived and entered into the theoretical formula.

The discussion so far has shown that past experience enters into all functional modalities—that motives, emotions, perceptions, and so on are interactional products involving the present situation as well as reintegrations of the past—and that the influence of past experience has some unique features peculiar to each modality. From the standpoint of personality, we need to acknowledge both of these facts in theory. We need, first, to recognize "a reintegrative dimension" in psychological functioning that disregards the modality in which the past experience influence may appear. The need for such a general dimension becomes clear when we look at a complex episode like Helen and Trixie descending the steep mountain grade. In any real life situation such as this, past experience is entering into all modalities simultaneously. Trixie's masculine attitude leads to her perceiving Helen as not having control, to making her feel irritated, to making her take hold of the gear shift, and so on. From the standpoint of trying to understand what is going on in an everyday frame of reference, it does not matter which modality is affected. Typically all are, and simultaneously. So, from this standpoint, what is needed is theoretical acknowledgment of a general past experience, or reintegrative, dimension.

But recognizing a reintegrative dimension does not do away with the necessity of retaining a past experience analysis on the levels of the different modalities because if we dismiss these, the person has no way of understanding himself since these modalities are basic phenomenal categories in terms of which he experiences himself and others. A reintegrative dimension cannot be directly experienced. Its influence can only appear as effects upon emotion, motive, behavior, perception, thinking, and so on. Yet, as the foregoing analyses show, the forms that the reintegrative dimension takes have sufficient uniqueness in each modality so that a person who wants to understand himself, or others, must learn to recognize these different forms of past experience. He has no trouble when it appears as "memory," but understanding memory does not label for him the past experience component of emotion, and having understood emotion, he has to start all over in perception. Clearly, both a reintegrative dimension and specific modality level theoretical formulations are needed.

VI. Freud's Theory of the Influence of Past Experience

Having examined the laboratory psychologist's contributions to the understanding of how past experience enters into the present, we can look at the clinician's attempt to formulate the same problem. Since Freud's theory made childhood influence upon adult personality the cornerstone of almost all later theories in the psychotherapeutic frame of reference, it can be used as the prototypic case for our inquiry. The determining influence of childhood on later personality is explained by Freud in two ways: the repression-defense theory and the concept of "repetition-compulsion tendency."

A. THE REPRESSION-DEFENSE THEORY *

From the first 1892 paper on hysteria (with Breuer) that marked the beginning of psychoanalysis, Freud considered repression to be the princi-

* A more detailed discussion of Freud's views on this matter can be found in Madison, 1960.

pal reason why pathological systems of ideas and feelings persisted so strongly without losing their original freshness. Repression brought about persistence by cutting off painful memories from the rest of the mind. The segregated systems were not subject to the influences that Freud believed would normally dissipate the emotions that had been produced by traumatic childhood experience, and as long as ideas had a powerful emotional charge they remained fresh and strong. Repressed childhood material had its influence upon adult personality through its disguised entry into everyday life. The specific defenses, like reaction formation, projection, turning round on the self, isolation, undoing, and conversion, were particular forms that the disguise took in clinical cases, while dreams, jokes, and slips of the tongue represented such disguised entry of repressed material in everyday life.

Freud's concept of segregated psychic systems as a way of accounting for the strange phenomena of psychopathology was not novel: Pierre Janet and others before him had come that far. What Freud supplied was a new reason for the segregation. Instead of the Charcot–Janet explanation of some sort of hereditary brain defect to explain dissociation, he said that it was emotional resistance that kept the psychic systems segregated. The ideas and affects were too painful to recognize consciously. Resistance was the cornerstone of the repression-defense theory and became the mainstay of the theory of transference in psychotherapy. Although Freud never made his assumptions on the point explicit, the direct implication of the concept of resistance, as it came to be formulated in relation to repression and defense, was this: if there were no emotional resistance, there would be no repression and no transference. The assumption was that, in the absence of resistance, the segregated systems would come into contact with the rest of the mind and its interaction with the pathological material would restore normalcy. Similarly, without resistance, patients in therapy would simply remember their past rather than reliving it in the disguised form of transference feelings toward the therapist.

The clinical validity of repression and other defenses is widely accepted by psychotherapists. But college student data are not greatly illuminated by the concept. Instances of repression defense are to be found in everyday student histories, but the assumption that we will remember the past when there is no emotional resistance to doing so, or that recalling the past will prevent transference, is not supported by a case like Trixie's. Thus, Trixie's resistance to recognizing the aftermath of the Lucy relation in her perception of Maura must have been very slight, since she spontaneously made the connection by simply writing an account of it. But a lack of resistance did not keep her, for a whole summer and most of the following academic year during which the two were roommates, from being unaware that her attitude toward Maura was connected to her past. Then, too, she was quite conscious that she was attracted to boys like her father, but being conscious of it did not prevent her from transferring father feelings to them.

In other words, insofar as resistance plays a role in states of unconsciousness in everyday perception of persons and relations to them, it must act as an added, complicating influence rather than a basic one. Basically, the influence of the reintegrated past upon perception, behavior, emotion, and motive is unconscious simply because awareness is naturally a limited function that represents only a small part of what is going on. The state of an idea or emotion being unconscious has nothing to do with resistance in the ordinary case, even though a certain amount of repression can be seen in everyday life and the phenomenon tends to have a good applicability in clinical cases. Repression defense, therefore, cannot be used to explain the massive persistence of the past that characterizes everyday life as well as psychopathology.

B. The Repetition-Compulsion Tendency

As Freud's theory matured, the repetition-compulsion tendency came to occupy the central place as his explanation of persistence. He was driven to postulate a tendency to repeat in psychic life, in part, by facts somewhat like those reviewed above, namely, that after the traumatic events were made conscious by the therapist's interpretations, they did not cease their repetition. The patient seemed to return day after day with new instances of the childhood conflict showing itself in living. Freud called this long period in psychotherapy "working through" and its presence posed a problem for the repression theory of persistence. He finally decided that the repetition that necessitated "working through" must be due to a compulsion to repeat in psychic life, and speculatively linked it up with a variety of phenomena, such as the tendency of battle dreams to recur, of children to play repetitive games, and of everyday relations like friendships to repeat similar patterns. In his 1920 *Beyond the Pleasure Principle* (1955, Vol. XVIII) Freud decided that such tendencies to repeat were due to an underlying instinctive tendency in psychic life to reinstitute the past. The idea led to the concept of a "death instinct" through the further speculative step that the earliest state toward which this regressive tendency led must be an inorganic one, on the supposition that it preceded organic life and, being earlier, would therefore be the ultimate objective of the tendency to reinstitute the past.

Freud, of course, was speaking of what is here called the reintegrative tendency, which indeed must be acknowledged to be innate. But innate is not instinctive. The knee jerk is innate but it is not instinctive in the drive sense of "instinct." The latter connotes a need to achieve a certain end state (death, in Freud's theory). Reintegration is Freud's repetition tendency shorn of its speculative status as a drive, and his implicit recognition of the principle indicates how inevitably some such conception arises in any area of psychology that looks closely at personality over time.

VII. Personality and Common Sense

We have examined common sense, psychology, and Freud's theory with respect to their accounts of how past experience is carried over and enters into the present, noting their effectiveness or shortcomings in comprehending everyday behavior as seen in the lives of students. In each case the analysis shows that improvements are possible and these have been offered in terms of the reintegration theory and its associated concepts. Now it is time to ask why common sense and psychology as represented by the laboratory and the clinic have been so separate, and to consider what their proper relationship to one another should be. On this question I find myself on the side of the philosophers at this symposium. I had not expected to do so, and at first found this disconcerting, but have come to see that we are arguing from a similar point of view because I too am judging psychology from the standpoint of what Peters calls "the conceptual scheme of common sense." What I understand the philosophers to be saying (among other things) is that distinctions made in our everyday language are far richer and more complex than those made in psychological theory today, and that, consequently, common sense is not to be dismissed as lightly as psychology tends to do. In fact, it should be regarded as our principal source of theoretical knowledge about man, to which psychology has only added in modest ways as yet.

What are the psychologists' beliefs about the relation between his science and common sense? To put it bluntly, psychology has assumed that its ultimate objective is to replace common sense. It has assumed that its goal is to get rid of the everyday frame of reference and to substitute for it a scientific conception of man constructed from ideas developed and tested in its research laboratories.* This view of psychology's ultimate purpose is directly implied by authors who begin their books by decrying the fallibility and inconsistency of "common sense" as contrasted with the scientific

* Sellars' discussion (1962, Chapt. 2) has helped me to see the matter in this way.

views to which the reader is about to be introduced. Having thus dismissed man's rich heritage of thought and language, the psychologist proceeds with his reports of research findings and concepts that they illustrate. But, on this view, what is to become of the everyday language and the common sense it embodies? Is there to come a day when people will give up the everyday terms they use in making distinctions about persons for a different conceptual language taken over from psychology? The point is never discussed. Common sense and the everyday language are simply labeled "bad," while a presumed substitute, called "science," is labeled "good" and the matter left there.

As Peters points out in this volume, such disparagements of common sense ignore and oversimplify the richness and complexity of understanding that it contains. The proper aim of psychology is not to replace common sense and the everyday language, but to refine and add to it as do poets, writers, physicists, social scientists, and the man on the street. The impact of all these influences will gradually transform the everyday language at points where it is now insufficient. In time the whole may look very different, more "scientific," than it does today, but the process is one of evolution from something very good to something better; not a replacement of something bad with something good.

A. THE EVERYDAY FRAME OF REFERENCE AS BASIC TO PSYCHOLOGY

The dismissal of common sense is part of a more general attitude toward the everyday frame of reference as contrasted to a "scientific" one. It has to do with the psychologist's attitude toward the research settings in which he works and the relationships of his concepts to such settings, as contrasted to their relationship to the everyday frame of reference. The events observed in the laboratory setting are assumed to have some kind of fundamental superiority, as not only establishing the original meaning of the concepts with which the psychologist works, but as continuing to be the "real" or "scientific" base for the concept. As far as any transfer of the concept from its originating context to events in everyday life is concerned, such transfers are seen as "applied" psychology and by definition inferior to "scientific" psychology.

But there is another way of looking at the matter. One can, instead, take everyday experience as the "real" phenomena to which our concepts and knowledge are to be related. On this view of social science, the psychologist's role is to take ideas and observations from everyday experience and language into controlled research settings for testing. When he finds they have some merit, he can ask whether the everyday view is comprehensive enough, explore its limitations, refine and extend the idea, and explore the relation of the phenomena to events with which everyday thought would not have connected it. Once this part of his work is through, the psychologist must reintroduce the modified idea to the everyday framework of observation and language from which he borrowed it in the first place. Professionals in psychology dismiss this step as merely "applied" work, with the implication that "application" is a menial task to be turned over to others. Underlying this attitude is the assumption that the "real" meaning of psychological concepts is to be found in their relation to specified laboratory observations. One direct consequence of the attitude is the present gulf between psychology and everyday experience.

The problem lies in psychology's premature adoption of physics as its model of science. The physicist need not relate his concepts regarding a meson or a neutrino to his personal life or to the everyday language. But social sciences are not physics. They are about man, and man has built up a complex system of ideas that becomes a part of each new generation. In learning to behave like human beings, we at the same time acquire this complex structure of concepts and language without which we could make no sense of human life. It is everyday situations construcd in terms of this frame of reference, not laboratory phenomena, that are psychology's basic datum; they are the "real" events to which psychology's concepts must be linked. The laboratory's role in a social science is purely one of providing a controlled situation for improving observations and for stimulating the theorist to refine concepts upon the basis of such improved observations.

B. COMPLEX BEHAVIOR IN NATURAL SETTINGS

While it is to be expected that controlled research will be extended to increasingly complex behavior, today, the most complex behavior that can be brought under effective research control is still so remote from real life complexity that one cannot pretend that the laboratory has refined concepts through research studies of complex behavior. What we have available are some terms taken from everyday language and refined through study in highly restricted settings or through applications to clinical problems. The refinements they have undergone have fitted them better to these specialized settings but to what extent these refinements have improved their usefulness in understanding complex behavior in natural settings has not been considered. Since the laboratory settings may differ critically from life

settings, there is no reason to assume without examination that the refinements, however ingenious, will not have taken the concept off in some quite
irrelevant direction. Until our laboratory models become much more sophisticated, such a deterioration of usefulness is as likely as is improvement.

What is to be done in the meanwhile? I believe that the present situation
in psychology calls for a scientific strategy of proceeding simultaneously on
two fronts. On the one hand, we should proceed in the way that we now
do; that is, by beginning with a reproducible phenomenon in a controlled
setting, like Pavlov's dog salivating to a tone. The observation that the
conditioned response of salivation, established to a given stimulus, such as a
tone of a particular frequency, will also be elicited by other similar stimuli,
such as a tone of related frequency, gives rise to the concept of generalization. Once the phenomena to which the concept refers are shown to be
reproducible, the strategy is to modify gradually the observational situation, for example, by trying out perceptual gradations of stimuli. Since each
modification requires developing appropriate techniques and creating new
research designs that maintain adequate control, the process of extending
the observational base on which the concept is founded is a slow one.

The foregoing strategy of enlarging the observational base in the laboratory context is basic and indispensable. It will always be the workhorse of
science. But an exclusive reliance upon this strategy has its dangers. The
risk is that the empirical dimensions present in the laboratory context will
be less important in wider contexts. Dimensions important in complex
situations of everyday life may not be represented at all in the research
context, or they may be held so constant by the experimenter's need for
control as to be excluded from theoretical consideration. Such an impover-
ished observational base can lead to a large expenditure of effort on developing concepts that fit laboratory contexts increasingly well, but have
modest value when tried in a wider setting.

I therefore believe that this standard research strategy, basic as it is, can
never be sufficient. It is essential to add to it the study of complex behavior
in natural settings. There are three reasons for this. One is that such studies
are the way to discover empirical dimensions being overlooked in laboratory studies and to add these to what is already being systematically studied. Such tests would help prevent psychology from being preoccupied with
concepts having only limited applications. Of course, tests of laboratory or
clinically originated ideas in real life settings must be carried out qualitatively, that is, by naturalistic observation in which the investigator looks at
what he sees in terms of contemporary concepts drawn from these more
restricted settings, and asks how well they fit, and what is left unexplained.

But the matter is not left there. Having located gaps or poorly fitting concepts, the theorist must exhaustively study the phenomena that have eluded conceptual understanding until he achieves the intuitive understanding that will allow him to hypothesize the missing ideas or propose corrections of existing ones. Nor can he rest with this step. To have a science he must then devise an observational situation that will allow research control and submit his ideas to correction by unbiased facts. The surviving modifications are then ready to be tried out qualitatively in natural settings once more, and the whole cycle is endlessly repeated.

A second reason for moving back and forth between real life and laboratory research is to improve the laboratory models in which ideas are refined. In psychology's recent past, problems of gaining adequate research control have been so difficult that the relevance of the model to life could not be considered primary. Almost any controllable situation was seized upon for study, and theoretical development was attempted with whatever data the controlled setting happened to make available. Relevance was a luxury that the investigator could not afford. Thus, as Peters points out, psychologists investigated such questions as the recognizability from photographs of the facial expressions of emotion, without concern for the relevance of their research model to life. Using photographs of emotional expression (often posed) allowed research control, and objectivity was still so new in psychology and so prized that questions of relevance were not seriously raised. The fact that emotions involve a cognitive appraisal by the individual, and that such appraisals involve the perceived significance of complex contemporary situations in terms of even more complex and individually unique past life histories, was never made a point of inquiry. Since psychology developed research control but not relevance, it has no theory of emotion other than some physiological speculations and what existed in the everyday language and philosophical analyses before psychology developed.

In his paper, Toulmin points out that in the study of language the effort to control rules out the investigation of the most essential aspect of language, namely, its contextual meanings. The investigator whose method involves a cyclic alternation between laboratory and life will surely develop relevant research models more quickly, and psychology can move ahead on both the fronts of relevance and control without sacrificing one to the other.

The suggestion that concepts tested in the laboratory should be examined by qualitative application to complex behavior in natural settings will arouse suspicion among methodologists, and perhaps justifiably so, in view of psychology's past history. The scientifically naive have been in the habit of making such abrupt shifts from research to applied contexts without noticing that they have lost the meanings of their laboratory-grounded concepts in the transition. Furthermore, there has been a long history of armchair systems in psychology and the social sciences, developed by individuals who did not accept the need for systematic study under conditions of research control. But neither of these courses is being proposed here. Rather, it is proposed that in a social science both strategies are essential and must proceed side by side, not as antagonistic methods by "hard" experimentalists on the one hand and "soft" personality theorists on the other, but as two complementary procedures.

The last and most basic reason for making continuous applications of research-derived ideas to complex behavior in natural settings is that such an effort is the quickest way to move to psychology's objective, which, as I see it, is to correct and fill out the image of man developed over the long course of history and embedded in the distinctions made in everyday language. In Wilfrid Sellars' terms, the destiny of the scientific image of man is to be continually absorbed into the manifest image, which it constantly transforms through its influence. But the everyday image of man is, and will always be, the basic image in a social science as distinguished from the natural sciences.

Concepts like perception, habit, emotion, motive, generalization, memory, and thinking originated in common sense and, as we have noted, psychology has improved and refined these concepts. Now psychology's task is to introduce such findings effectively into the everyday language. But we have not taken this part of our work seriously, and as a result there is a large gap between the science of psychology and the everyday frame of reference.

In teaching students about personality in college, I face daily the consequences of this estrangement of psychology and common sense, and I believe that the college student is particularly relevant if we are to bridge this gap. For he is immersed in his own experience just at the moment when we are trying to teach him about psychological concepts. This fact provides us, as teachers, with a unique opportunity for using the teaching situation as a laboratory in which a first effective reorganization of psychology, in the direction it must ultimately take, can be made.

References

Dollard, J. & Miller, N. E. *Personality and psychotherapy.* New York: McGraw-Hill, 1950.

Duncker, K. The influence of past experience upon perceptual properties. *American Journal of Psychology,* 1939, **52,** 255–265.

Ellson, D. G. Hallucinations produced by sensory conditioning. *Journal of Experimental and Social Psychology,* 1941, **28,** 1–20.

Freud, S. *Standard edition of the complete psychological works.* Vol. XVIII. London: Hogarth Press, 1955.

Hamilton, Sir W. *Lectures on metaphysics and logic.* Edinburgh & London: Blackwood, 1882. 2 vols.

Hovland, C. I. The generalization of conditioned responses: I. The sensory generalization of conditioned responses with varying frequencies of tone. *Journal of General Psychology,* 1937, **17,** 125–148.

Kimble, G. A., & Garmezy, N. *Principles of general psychology.* (2nd ed.) New York: Ronald Press, 1963.

Köhler, W. *Place of value in a world of fact.* New York: Liveright, 1938.

Leeper, R. W., & Madison, P. *Toward understanding human personalities.* New York: Appleton-Century-Crofts, 1959.

Lewin, K. *Field theory in social science.* New York: Harper & Row, 1951.

Madison, P. *Freud's concept of repression and defense, its theoretical and observational language.* Minneapolis, Minn.: Univer. of Minnesota Press, 1960.

Madison, P. *Personality in college.* Preliminary Edition. Reading, Mass.: Addison-Wesley, 1966.

Madison, P. *Personality development in college.* Reading, Mass.: Addison-Wesley, 1969, in press.

Murray, H. A. *Explorations in personality.* London & New York: Oxford Univer. Press, 1938.

Newcomb, T. M. *Personality and social change.* New York: Dryden Press, 1943.

Sanford, N. (Ed.) *Personality development during the college years. Journal of Social Issues,* 1956, **12,** 1–71.

Sanford, N. The developmental status of the entering freshman. In N. Sanford (Ed.), *The American college.* New York: Wiley, 1962.

Sellars, W. Philosophy and the scientific image of man. In R. G. Colodny (Ed.), *Frontiers of science and philosophy.* Pittsburgh, Penn.: Univer. of Pittsburgh Press, 1962.

Skinner, B. F. The verbal summator as a method for studying latent speech. *Journal of Psychology,* 1956, **2,** 71–107.

White, R. W. *Lives in progress.* New York: Dryden Press, 1952.

EPILOGUE

THEODORE MISCHEL

I. Introduction

Since the preceding papers were revised by their authors after our discussions in Chicago, they already reflect the influence of these discussions. For many reasons it was deemed advisable not to publish a record of what was said by various people in the course of discussing these papers. But it does seem important to convey a sense of the issues that arose in our discussions, and this is the aim of this epilogue. It is very far from being an edited transcript of parts of the discussion. Instead, I have written an account of what I see as the underlying issues that arose, in a variety of ways, during five days of intensive discussion of different topics. I have written this account in a way that, I hope, reflects some of the basic points made by all of the participants. Since I have drawn heavily on what they said, my discussion of the issues is clearly and obviously indebted to them. But since it is structured, colored, and extended through my interpretation, I must take sole responsibility for any errors or shortcomings.

II. Psychological Concepts

"Emotion" and "motivation" figure in accounts that we give when we try to make the behavior of human beings intelligible. But just what role do they play in these accounts? One way of conceptualizing their role is to suggest that they refer to events or processes that occur between the stimulus and the response. This approach appeals to some psychologists because, so conceived, emotions and motives would simply be clockable states that occur somewhere between the sensory input and the organism's motor output; the study of emotion and motivation would thus be a straightforward empirical investigation of how these phenomena are related to others that precede and follow them. Of course, emotion and motivation might be introduced, not at the operational level, but as hypothetical constructs in a theory designed to explain what happens between the perception of a stimulus and the response; and such theoretical concepts might, ultimately, be identified with various neurophysiological structures or processes. But we would still be concerned with the empirical investigation of elements in a causal process. Seen in this way, the sensory input will have to be purely sensory; it will be the initial stage in the process, stripped of all conceptual and evaluative elements, and the latter will be regarded as something added on at later stages. Some of these later stages (e.g., phenomenological ones like an "appraisal" leading to action, or quasi-physiological ones like an "arousal" that "energizes" behavior) might then be identified with, or be treated as empirical indicators for, a state of emotion, or motivation, in the organism.

But while an investigation of the sequence of events between sensory input and motor output may yield empirical results of great interest and importance, it cannot tell us what emotions, or motives, are. And philosophers who seek to explicate the meanings of "emotion" and "motive," through an analysis of the way these concepts function in our discourse, point out that these concepts are not normally used to refer to isolable processes that occur at some point in time between perception and action. For whatever be the chain of events at the neural level, our experience is of objects and situations loaded with meaning and value; it is not a mere input, but a conceptual response. Thus our concept of perception, for example, seeing a cup, or a man, already involves classification and memory; and our concept of action, for example, drinking from a cup, or asking a man for directions, already has connections with objects that have been classified as usable in certain ways. What is seen is something that can be properly responded to in certain ways, and what is done is an intelligent response to a situation perceived as being of a certain sort. Since cognitive and evaluative elements are thus built into perception and action, it is hard to see how our concept of emotion can be linked to some isolable stage, for example, of appraisal, that occurrs at some point in time between perception and action. No doubt there are cases in which one can trace a temporal sequence from perception, through appraisal, to action. But there need be no such sequence. A man may see a juicy steak and eat it without emotion; he may recognize a situation as dangerous without being emotionally affected.

In their ordinary use, "fear," "jealousy," and so on, sometimes signify motives that explain actions. And where there is no obstacle to action, there often seems to be no emotion in the normal sense: the man who acts out of jealousy may "keep his cool" and neither show nor feel emotion. To say, in such cases, that jealousy was the man's motive is to say something about how he appraised the situation in relation to some of his past experiences in a social context; it is not to say anything about the physiological arousal that energized his behavior, nor is it to say that he was in an emotional state. On the other hand, a man shows his fear in his trembling demeanor; and we often use "fear," "jealousy," and so on, not to explain actions, but to signify emotional states that explain a failure to act appropriately (when, e.g., someone is overcome by fear). In still other contexts, "fear" or "jealousy" may be used to excuse, justify, or mitigate responsibility for what someone did, or failed to do. And since a man's fears may be childish, his jealousy unjustified or excusable, and so on, fear, jealousy, and the like, not only involve appraisals but are themselves subject to further appraisal. If we pursue such analyses of the way our ordinary concepts of "fear," "jealousy," "anger," and so forth work, we are reminded that these are families of cluster concepts whose application involves extremely complex, context-dependent criteria that have to do, not with what events occurred in the organism between S and R, but with how to characterize molar behavior in relation to wider patterns and constellations of social life.

It may, however, be suggested that whatever be the ordinary meaning of "emotion" or "motive," psychology is free to introduce these concepts as technical terms in empirical theories designed to explain and predict human behavior. But if psychological theories are designed to account for human behavior, then the link with our ordinary ways of talking about emotions and motives cannot be severed. For if we simply ignore the common sense account, then we are in danger of losing contact with what is central to emotions and motives as ordinarily understood; we may then focus instead on, for example, physiological states, and end up with a theory about physiological activations that seems to have nothing to do with emotions or motives. But a psychologist interested in developing a theory of the emotions wants to illustrate his thesis with examples of what we would ordinarily call emotions; he may also want his theory to have implications for the control of the emotions, or to illuminate the relation of the emotions to one's self ideal, and so on. And it is hard to see how this is possible if "emotion" is a technical term whose meaning is stipulated by his theory, a term that has no links to "emotion" in the ordinary sense. Again, at least one of the things a psychological theory of motivation must help to explain is motivated human behavior. But a theory about physiological activations, which serve as directionless energizers of behavior, does not seem useful for illuminating what is at issue when we ask questions about the motives people have for what they do. So if a theory of motivation is to be relevant to its subject matter, then it cannot arbitrarily stipulate the meaning of "motive" but must, in part, be concerned with the conceptual analysis of motivated behavior. The value of analyzing the ways "emotion," or "motive," are ordinarily used is precisely that this serves to remind us of the subject matter with which theories of emotion, or motivation, must deal. Of course, it may still be useful for psychology to introduce technical concepts (e.g., affect, valence, expectancy, a reintegrative dimension, etc.); but such concepts must be designed to clarify, extend, or make more coherent and precise, distinctions implicit in our ordinary talk about motives and emotions, rather than to dismiss these distinctions by breaking the link with ordinary language.

Psychologists can readily agree that the clarification of key concepts must be part of the business of theory construction in psychology; after all, this has always been part of theory construction in physics (e.g., quite a bit of Newton's *Principia* is conceptual analysis). But, so at least some philosophers argue, there is this difference between the sort of analytic job Newton had to do and the task of the psychological theorist: many of the key concepts that the latter has to clarify, in order to develop empirical theories about human behavior, have a social dimension. "Motive," "emotion," and the like are used not only in explanatory but also in justificatory contexts, and even their use in explanatory contexts is frequently connected with a framework of social conventions and rules. When a man is angry he is vexed, but the form that his vexation will take depends, to a considerable degree, on who he is and whom it is he is angry with; that is, on the complex of social practices in which he participates with others. We can use "anger" to make a great variety of human actions intelligible, but can these uses be understood apart from the forms of our social life? Again, people act, for the most part, not under the compulsion of forces or even threats, but because they see compelling reasons for doing something in a certain social or political situation, or because it is morally right to do it, or because it is required by law, or by social convention, or by the rules of the game they are playing, and so on. And behaviors of this sort cannot be understood without taking into account the relevant social or moral practices.

The enormous complexity of the parameters that influence behavior at this level has led some psychologists to suggest that it would be advisable for psychology to start its conceptualization at the animal level. Since psychological theories have to stand the tough test of fact, there is an obvious advantage in starting with relatively simple cases that can be analyzed and tested with greater ease. And we do speak of fear, anger, desire, and so on in connection with animals, so that it may seem plausible to suggest that we have here simpler instances of the sort of psychological phenomena that appear in complex form at the human level. Behaviorists hoped that by starting with fear, and similar states, at the animal level they would, ultimately, be able to build up an account of these phenomena at the human level. Now the behavior of animals confronted by some object or situation can usually be classified as approach or avoidance, and one might think of this as connected with a positive or negative appraisal. One can also specify such measures of response as latency, persistence, vigor, or intensity. Along such lines, conceptual schemes that are very useful for dealing with some of the responses animals make to objects have been developed. But is the extension of such schemes to the human level adequate for dealing with behavior that is typically human? After all, we appraise things not merely as good or bad, but as, for example, puzzling or sublime. To what extent are our responses to objects really analogous to those of animals? Approach or avoidance tell us very little about human behavior until we specify what it is that is being approached or avoided: approaching a town and a woman are very different behaviors. Even to say that someone is approaching a woman he has appraised positively tells us practically nothing about what he is doing. Nor is it clear that all human behavior can be classified in terms of approach or avoidance—for example, what one does, not in going or not going to an art gallery, but when one gets there. Again, one can understand what is meant by saying that when a thirsty rat drinks, its activity has greater intensity than when it is sated; but just what would be meant by the intensity with which someone plays chess? The limited applicability to human behavior of conceptual schemes derived from animal studies has been obscured by the fact that behaviorists have tended to investigate processes that are tangential to the normal capacities of human beings (and, perhaps, even of higher animals), and have done their best to eliminate, or minimize, the role of instructions in experiments with humans. Their experiments have simply ignored the fact that verbal instructions can do very quickly what is "learned" laboriously in laboratory conditioning. Once these arbitrary restrictions are removed, it becomes clear that there is no easy way of extending these schemes in order to illuminate the very large and central range of human behaviors that are language mediated.

The appeal of starting with the analysis of animal behavior is that it seems to be following the method that was so fruitful in the hands of Galileo. Did not Galileo begin with the simple case—the ball rolling down an incline under conditions that have been idealized so as to hold the number of operative variables to a minimum—and then complicate the picture by introducing additional parameters until all sorts of motions under natural conditions (of friction, air resistance, etc.) could be taken care of? But Galileo's method worked because the complex motions of projectiles, or billiard balls, can be dealt with in terms of the same conceptual framework as the simple motion of the ball down the incline. And it is far from clear that psychological phenomena at the human level are simply more complex cases of the same sort as are found at the animal level; that is, that they can be encompassed within the same conceptual framework. For example, one cannot (logically) feel remorse or guilt unless one has an elaborate set of concepts pertaining to complex social and moral relationships. The analogical extension that allows us to speak of fear, or anger, in connection with animals thus breaks down when it comes to remorse, guilt, or even grief. It is simply a fact that many human emotions cannot be intelligibly ascribed to animals. And such emotions cannot be adequately conceptualized in terms of categories derived from a study of fear, or anger, in lower animals. Again, a great deal of human behavior is, manifestly, rule conforming; such behavior is monitored by rules that presupposed a community of language users. Only beings who are brought up in such a community, and thus learn to participate in its forms of life, are capable of behaving in these ways, so that such behaviors are not simply more complex cases of the same sort as are found with animals. They are more complex in the sense of requiring explanation in terms of a more complex conceptual framework, one that can accommodate rational, rule-following, language-structured human behavior.

These are facts, hard data with which psychology must come to terms, even if the attempt to avoid anthropomorphism has sometimes led behavioristic psychologists to deny them. Yet surely the one thing that can safely be said about a psychology adequate to human behavior is that it will be anthropomorphic. Of course, there is an evolutionary continuity between animal and human; language-mediated human behaviors are, in some sense, a development from the sort of "purposive" quasi-intentional behavior found in higher animals. And this has reinforced the belief that the complex (human) case must be understood by beginning with the simple (animal) case and then complicating it. But if psychology is to develop a conceptual framework adequate for dealing with the characteristic features of adult human behavior, then there is much to be said for starting at the human level, and paring our conceptual scheme down in order to take care of animal studies, as opposed to proceeding in the opposite direction.

III. Common Sense, Psychological Theory, and Rule-Following Behavior

If we are to start at the human level, what have we to start with? By being brought up in common forms of life, all of us gain some understanding of ourselves and other people. Without studying psychology, we thus come to have some knowledge of human behavior. Psychologists are often skeptical of this "knowledge." For what we have learned in this way is to use, for example, "anger" in connection with cases that seem observationally very different: "the boss is angry" might be said when he lashes out unreasonably against one of his employees, or when he simply reports feeling angry, or when he does neither. What theory underlies these uses and justifies us in speaking of anger in all of these different cases? Philosophers who seek to explicate the relation of anger to wants, wishes, beliefs, actions, reactions, and so on do not always agree, and there seem to be no empirical criteria for settling such discussions. No doubt, "anger" is a cluster concept; but if we had an adequate theory of what is involved, should it not enable us to predict the precise conditions under which the angry boss will lash out, or report that he feels angry, or do neither? Yet common sense does not seem able to do this.

Perhaps, then, common sense merely provides us with rough and ready categories, based on observations of frequent "co-symptomicity," but without making explicit the conjectures that underlie such classifications. The principles concerning emotion and motivation on which these classifications are based may, or may not, be valid; like the proverbs, they may even be incompatible with each other. And there is no way of finding out unless we spell out the implications of commonsense views, thus making precise and explicit what is vague and implicit in common sense. To do this, to make explicit the implications of our ordinary talk about emotions, motives, and so on, so that they can be tested empirically and modified in light of the facts, is, so it can be argued, the task of the psychologist interested in human behavior. In other words, common sense sees through a glass darkly. It lists psychological variables (e.g., wants, beliefs, emotions) that have something to do with action, and it enshrines vague theories about them that are based on common observation, much as ordinary talk about earth, air, fire, and water implied prescientific physical theories. But it fails to give a coherent account of how these variables combine to determine actions and so, far from providing an adequate explanation, common sense is itself a challenge for explanatory psychology. Psychological theory can begin with the traditional view of behavior and proceed to articulate it through the formulation of hypotheses, which may have to be couched in unambiguous technical terms in order to be empirically testable. And it can attempt to develop mathematical models that make explicit the way in which factors that may, or may not, be present in consciousness combine to determine action, with a view to deciding empirically whether, for example, the strength of the belief that an act will have certain consequences ("expectancy"), and the degree to which one wants these consequences (i.e., their attractiveness, or "valence"), combine additively or multiplicatively to influence one's actions. This, so it can be argued, is the only way we can hope to develop a scientific theory of human action; moreover, empirical research along these lines has already taught us much about human behavior that escaped the conventional wisdom for twenty-five hundred years.

It should, however, be noted that those philosophers who stress the centrality of commonsense concepts have no stake in defending the traditional wisdom. For one thing, commonsense beliefs are not static; our grasp of human behavior is continually deepened and widened through the development of our common life and the absorption of new insights. Could a classical Greek have understood the novels of Dostoevski or Proust? Again, to say that certain reactions persist from childhood so that we sometimes still see and respond to the world as children, is, today, almost common sense; it is the way we now ordinarily explain behaviors that, in the nineteenth century, might have been attributed to the foibles of human nature.

Second, but much more important, what is at issue is not the sanctity of any commonsense beliefs or theories. What has been stressed by some philosophers is not the importance of *propositions* implicit in common sense, but the centrality of the sort of *concepts* and *distinctions* that it draws. No doubt we learn all sorts of generalizations in being brought up in society, and these can, of course, be falsified by empirical research. But we also acquire an enormously ramified network of distinctions that leads us to mark off different modes of behavior in subtle and complex ways. And the question is whether these distinctions can be washed out by psychological theories. To insist on the centrality of these distinctions is very different from insisting on the wisdom of the ages, since brand-new, specifically twentieth-century propositions about behavior can be expressed in terms of these distinctions. From this point of view, psychological theories based on empirical research with human subjects might be regarded as important additions to our knowledge of human behavior that do not depart fundamentally from common sense, even if they are sometimes expressed in the language of "forces," "resonators," and so on—at least, as long as the physical analogies and mathematical formulations are not taken too literally.

How literally should they be taken? Though even commonsense locutions sometimes involve analogies between psychological and physical processes (e.g., we speak of people as "in tune" with others, or as being "highly strung," etc.), philosophers tend to be suspicious of mechanical analogies because talk about "forces" and the like may obscure the differences between, for example, being physically forced to do something, acting compulsively, or acting for compelling reasons. The use of Newtonian metaphors may make such cases look more alike than they really are. But psychologists, at least those who participated in our discussions, have no intention of overplaying these physical analogies. When they speak of "forces" they mean psychological forces connected with cognitive structures, and this may not be too different from talking about considerations that can carry weight, or have force for us.

What leads many psychologists to favor a technical language (of forces, etc.) over our ordinary language is that it seems to provide greater opportunity for formulating the factors that influence action (factors that may be implicit in common sense) in terms of mathematical models that make the interrelations between these factors explicit, so that they can be tested empirically. However, at least at the present time, the dimensions in terms of which such psychological variables are to be measured do not seem capable of being specified with enough precision to allow one to decide empirically whether they combine, for example, additively or multiplicatively. For the use of such mathematical operations presupposes a metrically ordered domain, and measures for psychological variables, especially when we are dealing with human subjects who are asked to respond intuitively to some scale, are generally such as to allow only an ordering of degree, of more or less. Even in the domain of animal learning, which is both more amenable to such treatment and far richer in empirical investigations, debate continues about whether drive (D) and incentive (K) combine multiplicatively, as suggested by Hull, or additively, as suggested by Spence. Of course, this does not show that measures of psychological variables that allow metrical ordering, and clear-cut decisions between alternative formulations on the basis of the data, can never be found. The physics of Bradwardine, or Oresme, provided mathematical schematisms for analyzing conceptual relations between variables, without specifying adequately measures of physical magnitudes that could be substituted for these variables. But this step was finally achieved and these schematisms developed into Galilean physics. Still, at the present time it seems clear that such psychological models function primarily as guides for thinking about problems of human behavior, and that they are expected to yield, not quantitative predictions, but qualitative conclusions and predictions of more or less, stronger or weaker. In other words, they are, at least at this stage, primarily tools of conceptual analysis, ways of exploring the implications of conceptual postulates about human actions and heuristic guides for empirical research.

The question then is whether this approach, or the conceptual scheme of common sense, is likely to be more adequate as a guide for our present efforts to understand human behavior. Do postulates formulated in terms of mathematics and technical concepts allow us to do justice to what is there to be described in more detail, or more adequately and exactly, than do the conceptual distinctions made in our ordinary language? Psychologists tend to answer this question affirmatively, not only because they are suspicious of our ordinary "mentalistic" concepts, but also because they believe that the use of such models makes for greater explicitness, coherence, and testability than does the use of ordinary language.

Philosophers, on the other hand, tend to prefer ordinary language because it seems capable of distinguishing more subtly between different kinds of behavior and does justice to the rule-following, social aspects of human action. How, for example, could talk about interactions between psychological forces allow us to characterize the difference between the ways in which a discussion may be brought to a halt by the chairman's reminder that the time agreed on is up, or by someone rushing in and shouting "Stop!," or by a participant saying "Perhaps we should stop now"? It may be suggested that conventions, orders, and other social constraints can be treated as social forces that influence psychological processes, on analogy to the way physical constraints can influence the operation of physical forces. But this seems to neglect the prescriptive character of social constraints. What tempts psychologists to use the concept of force like an accordion that can be stretched to cover not only the considerations that may have force for a man, but also the effect of food placed in the mouth of one of Pavlov's dogs, or the effect of social constraints on human actions, and so forth, is the hope of "homogenizing" their subject matter. The idea is that this may lead to a system of constructs that can deal with all of these different cases in terms of the same basic elements. But philosophers are more inclined to see the differences between these cases as crucial, and to insist that any adequate conceptual scheme must articulate these differences clearly. In their view, the use of "force" as a generalized notion for degree of attractiveness, or repulsiveness, may obscure important differences without adding significantly to our knowledge. For such a generalized variable of strength does not seem to tell us much about human action, unless we specify the goals toward which a person is attracted and the operative social context, thus replicating the distinctions we ordinarily make in talking about the different considerations that can move us to action.

Further, from an analytic point of view, it is by no means clear that what underlies our commonsense distinctions (e.g., the principle that informs our ordinary use of "anger") is a vague "theory," in the same sense as that in which there are theories in the physical sciences. For pragmatic and judgmental uses may be more central to our ordinary concepts than descriptive and theoretical ones: to recognize that a man is angry is to recognize that he needs to be appeased. We do, indeed, make the behaviors of our fellows intelligible by appealing to their emotions, motives, beliefs, intentions, and so on, but the sort of explanations we thus give do not seem to fit the model of scientific explanations in terms of generalizations or covering laws. In other words, the cluster of ways in which we learn to use "anger," "jealousy," "sorrow," and the like is not only explanatory but also diagnostic, appraising, judgmental, pragmatic. And the latter uses may be crucial for grasping the conceptual distinctions in terms of which we ordinarily think about human behavior; they may be central for understanding the rationale that underlies the ways in which words like "anger" are ordinarily used. Our commonsense understanding of human behavior may thus involve, not so much the development of rough generalizations on the basis of common observations, as participation in common forms of life.

Indeed, there may even be reason to reexamine the common presumption that human actions can properly be treated as "phenomena" that are on all fours with other phenomena, and that can be explained in terms of an overall pattern of laws and forces that is analogous to the pattern of explanation characteristic of the natural sciences. For much human behavior is rule-following and such behavior differs in important ways from the behaviors that are brought under laws by the natural scientist. Of course, this does not mean that people are constantly following rules in what they do. It does mean that the elements of our learned behavioral repertoire, insofar as it is language mediated, can only be understood on the rule-following model; this makes most human behavior very different from, and intrinsically more complex than, lawful behaviors that are not under the subject's control (e.g., reflexes). No doubt there is a story to be

told about the neurophysiological processes that facilitate such human behaviors, a story that will be compatible with the laws of the natural sciences. But whatever that story may turn out to be, it will not obliterate the
distinctive character of such rule-conforming, language-structured human
behavior; any adequate neurophysiology will have to fit this, even if it fills
out, or transposes in certain ways, the distinctions that we ordinarily draw.
And this, so some philosophers argue, is why the rule-conforming commonsense model is the natural and indispensable starting point for an
understanding of human behavior. Only if we start here can we hope to
develop an analysis complex enough to deal with language and language-
mediated behaviors (e.g., perceptual activities that involve the application
of concepts learned through language, etc.). Mathematical formulations involving "forces" and the like tend to assimilate the study of actions to dynamics, and so are in danger of obscuring these differences between the "phenomena" under investigation. But there is no reason why there should be
only one pattern that every empirical inquiry must take. And if we take the
conceptual framework of common sense as our point of departure for
empirical investigations, then we will be forced to recognize the rule-
following, social and cultural dimensions of human behavior, the central
role that language plays in it, and so on. We may then come to develop a
psychology that, instead of modeling itself on physics or physiology, is
framed in terms of categories appropriate to its own subject matter and
problems.

Still, in spite of all these differences, these two approaches may not be
quite as far apart as first seems. For psychologists make it clear that the
forces that appear in their formulation are psychological forces, and so
very different from physical forces. And the sort of conceptions that they
seek to express in terms of mathematical relations between forces, tendencies, and so on are, in some ways, analogous to what one gets when one
articulates what is ordinarily meant by "wants," "motives," and the like.
For the latter are not, as psychologists, for historical reasons, frequently
suppose (see the introductory chapter of this volume) factors present in the
consciousness of the agent. When we ordinarily speak of "wants" and the
like, what we are saying is not tied essentially to occurrent psychological
states, but involves complex, subjunctive-conditional statements; it explains
behavior, not in terms of clockable mental events, but in terms of complex,
time-consuming patterns and constellations of thought and action (see also
Section IV). In this sense, action tendencies, which interact with each
other in complex ways to influence behavior over time, are not foreign to
the conceptual framework of common sense.

On the other side, philosophers who insist on the centrality of our ordi-

nary categories have no intention of minimizing the importance of empirical investigations of human behavior. Even if we know well enough that a
man who wants A, and believes that B will get him A, will do B, other
things being equal, we do not know a priori what will happen if several of
his wants, or tendencies, conflict. So in order to know what a certain
person is likely to do in specific circumstances, we usually need more than
just our conceptual scheme; we also need to know a lot about the person,
and we may need various empirical generalizations (e.g., about the relative
strength of various tendencies, or wants, in this culture, about the way
they vary with different circumstances, about individual differences).
Again, even if motive and action are linked conceptually in our scheme,
whether, for example, the motive to achieve success is connected with pride
in the task, or with doing it better than others, or with getting approval
from others, and how this motive varies with different individuals and in
different cultures, are clearly empirical questions that can only be answered
through psychological experiments. So even if our ordinary concepts and
distinctions are central, common sense tells us very little about the origins
of tendencies, traits, attitudes, and the like, or about individual and cultural
differences, and obviously needs to be supplemented by empirical generalizations.

Moreover, the very categories and distinctions drawn by common sense
might well be improved not only through more precise formulation, but
also through the empirical investigations of psychologists. For example,
though common sense recognized that people do not always act in ways
that fit the rational rule-following model, Freudian insights about the persistence of childhood wishes and reactions, which can have various influences in later life, obviously depart from anything that could be understood
by the common sense of the nineteenth century. For such unconscious
(repressed) wishes differ from the sort of preconscious phenomena that we
recognize when we say, for example, that a man might really want something even though, at the time, he is not aware of wanting it. But the
question is how such Freudian discoveries are to be conceptualized. Are
the energy models Freud invented, or other quasi-physiological structures
(e.g., "resonators"), essential for expressing these insights? Or is the point
something like this: to understand some human behaviors we need to pay
attention to certain key incidents in the past, which the person himself is
unable to recall (the "reintegrative dimension"); for these surprising behaviors, which seem unintelligible when only the contemporaneous situation is taken into account, become intelligible when they are connected
with those past incidents. If the latter, then what is involved could be
regarded as a form of reclassification; for example, the surprising anger

shown in the present situation becomes intelligible when seen as outrage against unjust authority, manifested by the person's father in the past and brought back by some similarity in the present situation. This would certainly be a highly important extension of our ordinary ways of thinking about human behavior, but one that can be absorbed into common sense without making rubbish of its concepts and distinctions. Even writers who insist on the centrality of our ordinary concepts clearly recognize the need for such extensions and developments of our ordinary conceptual scheme.

Finally, but perhaps most important, a full and clear recognition of the purposive, rule-following character of human actions seems perfectly compatible with an empirical search for generalizations concerning the acquisition and comparative strength of tendencies to follow various rules and to pursue various ends. Rule-following behavior does, after all, involve the going together of various episodes. Of course, it is important to distinguish between laws and rules, and between laws about behavior that is, and behavior that is not, rule following. But, provided we do not freeze the concept of "law" in a Newtonian physical model, it is perfectly appropriate to look for laws concerning rule-following behavior. Indeed, the discovery of laws that can describe and explain the acquisition and manifestation of rule-following behavior may well be the central task of human psychology.

IV. Language, Thought, and Action

But what sort of conceptual scheme is appropriate for formulating laws and generalizations concerning rule-following behavior? Children are not born with many of the wants that they later have. How do they learn to want things and to interpret what other people want? Children are not born following rules. How do they learn to follow rules, including the rules of a language, and how does language learning mediate the learning of non-linguistic behaviors? How are children transformed into potentially rational human beings? Investigation of such questions has barely begun, because, until recently, behaviorists tended to rule them out of court and to focus instead on efforts to interpret all learning on the model of conditioning. One of the virtues of the emphasis on rule following is that it reminds us that a simple model of conditioning can only fit a very small fraction of the behaviors human beings learn. Not only the so-called "higher" processes, but even human habits fit into a category different from eyelid blinks, since they are capable of being modified by the person; nor is it clear that all of the things animals are able to learn can be explained in terms of conditioning. This is being pointed out by psychologists themselves, who argue that much of the work that has been done on human conditioning, and perhaps some animal work, could well be reinterpreted as involving concept formation tasks, and many psychologists are now prepared to take consciousness seriously.

If conscious phenomena are to have a place in psychology, how should their role be conceptualized? One might think of wants, intentions, attitudes, ways of viewing things, and the like as "phenomenological" states or processes, to which the person has privileged access, and which may influence his verbal as well as his nonverbal behavior. If the influence of such "covert" processes on behavior is recognized, then the problem may be seen as that of loosening up and sophisticating behaviorism, so that it will be able to admit more than "overt" behaviors as data, while still retaining the critical, scientific spirit. And a reconciliation between behaviorism and phenomenology can be mediated through the recognition that actions, like words, do not speak for themselves but require interpretation; in this special sense, what an observer says about a man's (or, usually, even an animal's) response to a situation is not something he can read off directly from the "overt" behavior, but is a corrigible "hypothesis." Once it is clear that behavioral data are not "hard," it can be suggested that if we treat what people report about their wants, beliefs, and so forth, as well as their behavior, as fallible indicators for their conscious (phenomenal) processes, then we will be able to make corrigible claims about both "covert" and "overt" processes; the road will then be open for connecting the way people tend to view things with the way they tend to behave, in a manner that is corrigible and scientifically responsible. It will be possible to allow not only overt behaviors, but also covert phenomenal states, a place among the data of psychology, without opening the door to irresponsible claims for incorrigible psychological knowledge.

But, so some philosophers insist, it is misleading to use "consciousness" as a general category that can be stretched to cover wants, pains, awareness of one's behavioral dispositions, emotions, dreams, ways of viewing the world, and so on. For this may tempt one to think of "phenomenal experiences" as something to be understood by reference to a special sort of entity for which we get evidence from the things people say and do; we may thus come to construe consciousness in the way the introspectionists did, as a special sort of stuff that helps to explain the behavioristic appearances. But there may well be good reasons for the suspicions early behaviorists had about the existence of any such stuff. For while there is a rationale for distinguishing between "overt" and "covert" phenomena in specific cases, what is covert is very different in different cases, and it may well be a mistake to lump these all together as a homogeneous self-contained domain of "phenomenological" states or processes. In other words, "covert" seems to cover not one kind of process, but many different kinds of processes operating in different ways and at different levels. When a husband tells us how he views his wife, when someone tells us about what he feels or wants, or about his pains, or about what a distant shape looked like to him, there is, in each case, a sense in which we can speak of "covert processes," a sense in which it is for the individual to say what these are, a sense in which what he says about them may not do justice to what they are. But it is far from clear that these senses are the same; what is covert, or phenomenal, in all these different cases does not seem to be the same kind of thing, present in the same sense, and logically characterizable by the same attributes. To lump these all together on the ground that they are "covert" may be misleading, just as it would be misleading to lump together all behaviors involving bodily movements on the ground that they are "overt."

On one level, there may be no issue here. For philosophers who take this line are not denying that, in some sense, there are conscious phenomena (i.e., that we have feelings, desires, attitudes, and so on); nor are they denying that what people say and do reflects (sometimes inadequately) the way they view things; nor are they denying that it is sometimes for the person, and not for anyone else, to say what these covert phenomena are; nor are they claiming infallibility for what the person himself says about them. But what concerns these philosophers is the role that language has in making possible, and allowing the development of, our conscious experience. Should we think of what people tell us about their wants, intentions, and so on as fallible indicators for certain syndromes of thought and action, or should we think of the uses of such psychological words as themselves constituent elements in such syndromes, thus tightening the inner connections between language, thought, and action? To what extent is our covert mental life, as well as our capacity for rational rule-conforming action, something that is only gradually acquired through sequences of linguistically mediated initiations into a common social life? If the development of human thought and conduct is connected in essential ways with the child's acquisition of language, and other signaling systems through which he interacts with others, then the whole overt–covert distinction takes on a different character. For then it is not a precondition of psychological inquiry, connected with the peculiar inaccessibility to others of one's own phenomenological experiences, but is a product of child development; only after a certain stage in the conceptual development of a child will it make sense to distinguish between its "covert" mental processes and its "overt" behaviors. Questions about the relation of thought to action will then be connected with questions about the way language, thought, and action all come to develop together, as the child is transformed into a human adult by coming to participate in a social life.

The acquisition of concepts and language, the ways children learn to follow rules, to have new wants and to interpret the wants of others, what motivates these developments and the ways in which language learning and the learning of other behaviors interact and build on each other, the ways in which covert locutions and behaviors are gradually learned as extensions of overt ones as mental life develops—this whole area of the development of human rationality might well repay joint investigation by psychologists and philosophers. For what is needed is both conceptual analysis and empirical inquiry. The proper distinctions (e.g., between imitation, instruction, drill, training, conditioning, and so on) must be drawn and the relevant empirical generalizations must be discovered. We need to take a close look at what really happens here, but we are not likely to see it unless we approach it with the right conceptual categories and distinctions. One important result that grew out of our discussions was the increasing recognition, on the part of both philosophers and psychologists, that in spite of all the differences of approach and attitude between them, they were dealing with related questions and had a good deal to learn from each other that might be relevant to their own professional problems and preoccupations.*

* Another conference of this sort, focused on psychological and epistemological issues in the development of concepts, is currently being planned.

AUTHOR INDEX

Numbers in italic indicate the pages on which the complete references are listed.

279

SUBJECT INDEX

Abnormal phenomena, 151
Achievement, generalizations about, 140
Achievement motivation, 128-129, 139
  instigating force and, 129-131
  recent work in, 139
Action
  anger and, 218
  appetitive tendencies and, 178-185
  appraisal for, 171
  "driving springs" of, 18
  emotion and, 158, 167-196
  Hobbes' concept of, 6-7
  ideas and, 18
  identifying of, 8
  language and thought in, 274-277
  motive and, 157
  purpose and, 6-7
  will and, 14
  see also Activity
Action circuit, memory and, 181
Activity
  achievement-oriented, 107
  behavioral tendency and, 109-115
  cessation of, 109
  change of, *see* Change of activity
  consummatory stimulus force and, 112-113
  ongoing, 115
  persistence of, 106
  pleasure in, 194-195
  vacuum, 118-119
Affective memory, 173-174, 181
Aggression, anger and, 210, 212-213
Analysis of the Phenomena of the Human Mind (Hartley), 14
Anger, 153, 156-157, 173
  action and, 218
  aggression and, 210, 212-213
  in animals, 214
  authority and, 274

  bodily feelings accompanying, 206-209
  boorishness and, 216
  classical definitions of, 203
  commonsense distinctions in, 271
  conceptual reconstruction of, 210-213
  concomitants of, 204-210
  dictionary definitions of, 219-220
  in dogs, 217
  emotion of, 200-204
  essence of, 213
  fear and, 157-158
  as feeling, 200
  feelings accompanying, 204-205
  free-floating, 202
  irritation and, 206
  jaw position in, 207-208, 210
  "lashing out" in, 161
  as original existent, 201
  pain and, 206-209
  paradigm case lacking in, 219
  pertinence in, 213
  provocations in, 214
  roots of, 213
  slapping and, 217
  as technical term, 264
  words describing, 209-210
Animal
  aggression in, 217
  anger in, 214
  emotions in, 186-187
  human emotions ascribed to, 266
  needs and interests of, 215
  terror in, 214
Animal behavior
  association and, 232
  causations and, 90
  drive in, 269
  vs. human behavior, 265
  learning and, 50-51, 269